Canon® EOS Rebel SL1/100D

FOR

DUMMIES®

A Wiley Brand

by Doug Sahlin

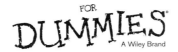

FOR

DUMMIES®

A Wiley Brand

Canon® EOS Rebel SL1/100D For Dummies®

Published by: **John Wiley & Sons, Inc.**, 111 River Street, Hoboken, NJ 07030-5774, www.wiley.com

Copyright © 2013 by John Wiley & Sons, Inc., Hoboken, New Jersey

Published simultaneously in Canada

For general information on our other products and services, please contact our Customer Care Department within the U.S. at 877-762-2974, outside the U.S. at 317-572-3993, or fax 317-572-4002. For technical support, please visit www.wiley.com/techsupport.

Wiley publishes in a variety of print and electronic formats and by print-on-demand. Some material included with standard print versions of this book may not be included in e-books or in print-on-demand. If this book refers to media such as a CD or DVD that is not included in the version you purchased, you may download this material at http://booksupport.wiley.com. For more information about Wiley products, visit www.wiley.com.

Library of Congress Control Number: 2013941602

ISBN 978-1-118-75367-5 (pbk); ISBN 978-1-118-75430-6 (ebk); ISBN 978-1-118-75423-8 (ebk)

Manufactured in the United States of America

10 9 8 7 6 5 4 3 2 1

Contents at a Glance

Table of Contents

Introduction

*Y*our Canon EOS Rebel SL1/100D is the latest and greatest digital camera on the market, sporting a stunning 18-megapixel capture, Live View, high-definition video, and much more. All this technology might be a bit daunting, though, especially if this is your first digital SLR (single lens reflex) camera. If you've used a digital camera before, you're probably accustomed to basic shooting modes like Portrait, Sports, Landscape, and so on. Those are still there for your convenience. But with the SL1/100D, you've also graduated to the big leagues with all the manual settings and shooting tweaks you could ever want. If you're moving to Digital Land from a 35mm film camera background, most of this will be second nature to you.

All you have to do is practice — and have fun in the process — to master the power you hold in your hands. And that's where I come into the picture. I've been using Canon dSLRs since the EOS 10D model debuted, and I've learned a lot about Canon digital cameras since then. In addition to the SL1/100D I'm using to write this book, I also own an EOS 5D MKII and EOS 7D, which have a lot of the features found on your SL1/100D.

My simple goal in this book is to show you how to become one with your camera. I don't get overly technical in this book, even though your camera is very technical. I also do my best to keep it lively. So if you want to master your SL1/100D, you have the right book in your hands.

Note: If you're curious why your camera name isn't "SL1/100D," like shown here, it's because Canon has an international presence. The U.S. name for the camera is the EOS Rebel SL1, and in other parts of the world, it's the EOS 100D. To keep life simple, I just refer to the model as SL1/100D.

About This Book

If you find the buttons and menus on your shiny new SL1/100D a tad intimidating, this book is for you. In the chapters of this book, I take you from novice point-and-shoot photographer, or experienced 35mm camera user, to one who can use all the bells and whistles this dSLR camera offers. You'll find information about virtually every menu and button on your camera, as well as when to use them, and what settings to use for specific picture-taking situations. I also show you how to use the software that ships with your camera.

To make life easier, this book uses several conventions to help you identify pertinent information — in other words, stuff you should know.

- ✓ Terms or words that you might be unfamiliar with in the context of photography, I have *italicized* — and I also define these.

- ✓ Numbered steps that you need to follow and characters you need to type are set in **bold.**

- ✓ Margin art is used to identify camera buttons. When you see one of these icons, it shows you which button to press or tap, or dial to rotate.

- ✓ The SL1/100D menu has pretty little icons for each tab but no text to describe what each tab does. I name the tabs to make things easier for you, dear reader, and for my editor and me. You'll find a table with tab names in Chapter 2.

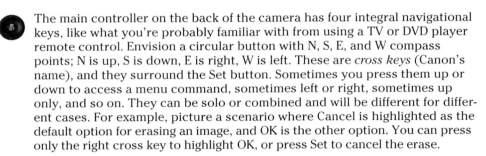 The main controller on the back of the camera has four integral navigational keys, like what you're probably familiar with from using a TV or DVD player remote control. Envision a circular button with N, S, E, and W compass points; N is up, S is down, E is right, W is left. These are *cross keys* (Canon's name), and they surround the Set button. Sometimes you press them up or down to access a menu command, sometimes left or right, sometimes up only, and so on. They can be solo or combined and will be different for different cases. For example, picture a scenario where Cancel is highlighted as the default option for erasing an image, and OK is the other option. You can press only the right cross key to highlight OK, or press Set to cancel the erase.

And if you're more inclined to tap your way through life — say, you're a smartphone devotee — many menu options are available by tapping choices on the camera's LCD monitor. I can't cover every possible way to make menu choices, but you'll get the hang of it and discover which feels right for you.

Foolish Assumptions

Ah, yes. Assume. When broken down to its lowest common denominator. . . . Okay, I won't go there. But as an author, I have to make some assumptions. First and foremost, you should now own, or have on order, an SL1/100D. You should also have a computer to download your images to. A basic knowledge of photography is also helpful but not mandatory. I know, you probably meet all assumptions, but my editor assumes I'll put this section in this part of the book.

Icons and Other Delights

For Dummies books have icons that indicate important bits of information. You can hopscotch from icon to icon and discover a lot. But when in doubt, read the text associated with the icon. In this book, you find the following icons:

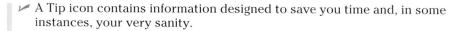 A Tip icon contains information designed to save you time and, in some instances, your very sanity.

 This icon warns you about something you should not do, typically for the safety of your shots or your camera. Perhaps I'm recalling something I did and decided it's not a good thing to do again.

 Consider this icon the equivalent of a virtual piece of string tied around your finger. This is information you want to commit to memory.

 This icon denotes stuff for the geeks in the group who like to know all manner of technical stuff.

You'll also find icons in the margin that show you controls on your camera and menu tabs.

Beyond the Book

You can find book content that exists outside the book itself, including these items:

- **Cheat Sheet:** The Cheat Sheet for this book is located at `www.dummies.com/cheatsheet/canoneosrebelSL1100D`. There you'll find information about some great accessories for use with video and still photography.

- **Dummies.com online articles:** On the Parts pages and elsewhere in the book are references to short online articles that you can find at `www.dummies.com/extras/canon`. There you'll find tips for shooting video and customizing the camera button layout to make it easier to use auto-focus lock.

- **Online Part of Tens chapter:** Also at `www.dummies.com/extras/canon`, you'll find an additional Part of Tens chapter that highlights the top ten cool features of your camera.

Shoot Lots of Pictures and Enjoy!

Your SL1/100D is a great digital camera; use it and use it often. The old adage "practice makes perfect" does apply, though. The only way to become a better photographer and master your equipment is to apply what you know and shoot as many pictures as you can. While you're working your way through this book, keep your camera close at hand. When your significant other pokes his or her head into the room, grab your camera and start practicing your craft. Take one picture, then another, and another, and so on. With practice, you'll know your camera like the back of your hand. You'll also know which rules of photography and composition work for you — and you'll start to develop your own style. For that matter, you'll probably amaze yourself, too.

Part I
Getting Started

getting started
with
Rebel
SL1/100D

web extras

Visit www.dummies.com for great Dummies content online.

In this part . . .

- ✓ Get to know the lay of the land and familiarize you with the controls of your Canon EOS Rebel SL1/D100.

- ✓ Find out how to take great pictures automatically as well as how to specify image size and format.

- ✓ Understand how to get around in the menu.

- ✓ Master your LCD monitor.

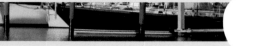

Exploring Your Canon EOS Rebel SL1/100D

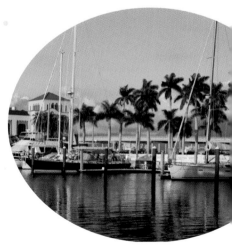

*T*his pint-sized dSLR comes with a shooting mode for every photographer. If you're new to digital photography, or you've graduated from a point-and-shoot digital camera, Canon gives you several modes to create great photographs automatically. Think of these as your training wheels. And if you're a seasoned photographer, Canon also gives you quite a few modes where you can take the reins and create the type of photograph you want. Add Creative Filters, in-camera editing, plus in-camera HDR, and you've got a potent tool for creating cool images.

Getting familiar with all this new technology might seem daunting, even to a seasoned photographer. I was impressed, albeit a tad flummoxed, when I saw the first reviews for this camera. Even though I'm a seasoned Canon dSLR user — my first digital SLR was the EOS 10D — I still had a bit of a learning curve when I first started experimenting with the SL1/100D. But it's my job to get down to brass tacks with new technology and show you how to master it. The fact that you're reading this probably means that you want to know how to use all the bells and whistles Canon has built into the camera. In this chapter, I begin at the beginning: the buttons, knobs, and other controls on the outside of the camera. Getting to know the camera controls like the back of your hand is the first step to taking gorgeous pictures with this new addition to Canon's line of dSLR cameras.

Getting in Touch with the Camera Controls

Think of the SL1/100D like a hybrid car: It has all the features, just not where you find them on your family sedan. Other Canon cameras have a plethora of controls on the outside of the camera. At first glance, it appears as though you've been shortchanged with the SL1/100D, but that's not the case. You do have to go to the menu to access some features typically provided by buttons on a Canon camera body, but access to menu options has never been easier thanks to the Quick Control button, which you push to display shooting settings on the LCD monitor. From this menu, you can specify settings with your finger on the touchscreen, or you can use the cross keys to navigate and specify settings.

The controls for this camera are easy to reach and give you access to many powerful camera features. Try to avoid becoming overwhelmed knowing which button does what. After you use the camera for a while, you'll automatically know which control gives you your desired result and then reach for it instinctively without taking your eye from the viewfinder. But first, you need to know what each control does. I explain the controls you find on the outside of the camera in the upcoming sections.

Exploring the top of the camera

The top of the camera (as shown in Figure 1-1) is where you find the controls you use most when creating images. The top of the camera is where you change settings like ISO (how sensitive the camera sensor is to light), aperture, and shutter speed; choose a shooting mode; and press the shutter button to take a picture. In my humble opinion, the top of the camera is the most important piece of real estate on the camera, except of course for the lens, which is your window to your world as you photograph it.

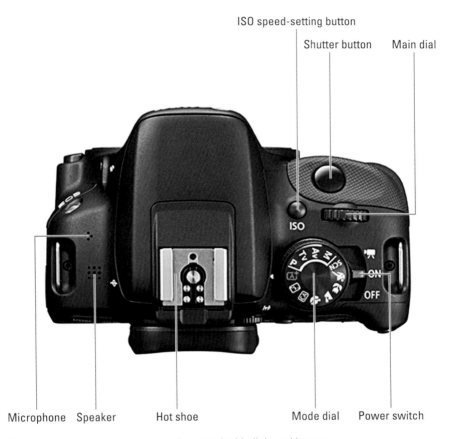

Figure 1-1: On top of your camera, all covered with dials and buttons.

The dial you use to change exposure settings when you use Canon's Creative modes is the Main dial, which I suggest you get to know by feel. The Main dial is just behind the shutter button, so you'll easily be able to find it when you're taking pictures. Here's the lay of the land on the top of the camera:

- **Power switch:** This switch powers the camera on and off. You also use it to capture video.

- **Shutter button:** This button prefocuses the camera and takes a picture. I discuss this button in greater detail in Chapter 2.

- **Main dial:** This dial changes a setting after you press a button. For example, after you press the ISO speed button, you move this dial to change the ISO speed setting. I show you how to use this button as the need arises.

- **ISO speed-setting button:** This button sets the ISO speed setting. (See Chapter 6 for more on the ISO speed setting.) Canon has instituted a nice feature on this button. This is the only button on the top of the camera that's rounded on the top, which makes it easy to find this button by feel. The button is also right next to the Main dial, which makes it easy to find without taking your eye from the viewfinder.

- **Hot shoe:** Slide a compatible flash unit (a Canon flash unit is dubbed a *Speedlite*) into this slot. The contacts in the hot shoe communicate between the camera and the flash unit. (I discuss flash photography in Chapter 6.)

- **Mode dial:** This button determines which shooting mode the camera uses to take the picture. (I show you how to use this dial to choose specific shooting modes in Chapter 6; in Chapter 8, I show you how to choose optimal settings for specific picture-taking situations.)

- **Speaker (monaural):** Playback sound when previewing recorded video.

- **Microphone (monaural):** Record sound when capturing video.

Exploring the back of the camera

The back of the camera is also an important place. Here you find controls to access the camera menu, switch to Live View mode, and much more. The following is what you find on the back of your SL1/100D (see Figure 1-2):

- **Menu:** Press this button to display the last used camera menu on the LCD monitor. (I introduce you to the camera menu in Chapter 2 and refer to the menu throughout this book.)

- **Info button:** Press this button to display shooting information on the LCD monitor. You can choose from many different information screens. (Read about the different screens in Chapter 4.) When you're not in shooting mode, use the Info button to show other information, such as the amount of space remaining on the SD card, the color space, and other camera information.

- **Display Off sensor:** This device is a switch that turns the shooting setting display settings on the LCD monitor off when your eye nears the viewfinder and displays them again when you move your eye away from the viewfinder.

- **Viewfinder/eyepiece:** Use the viewfinder to compose your pictures. Shooting information, battery status, and the amount of shots that can be stored on the memory card are displayed in the viewfinder. The eyepiece cushions your eye when you press it against the viewfinder and creates a seal that prevents ambient light from having an adverse effect on the exposure.

- **Dioptric adjustment knob:** Use this control to fine-tune the viewfinder to your eyesight (see Chapter 2).

- **Live View/Movie Start/Stop button:** Use this switch to engage Live View mode. When you press the Power switch to video shooting mode, this button starts and stops recording a movie (see Chapter 5).

- **AF Point Selection/Magnify button:** Change from multiple autofocus points to a single autofocus point (see Chapter 6). You can also magnify an image when you're reviewing images.

- **AE Lock/FE Lock button/Index/Reduce:** Locks exposure to a specific part of the scene you compose in the viewfinder, or on the LCD monitor (see Chapter 6). When used with a dedicated Canon flash, this button is used to lock flash exposure to a specific part of the scene you compose in the viewfinder. When reviewing images, use this button to display multiple images after you press the preview button and also to reduce magnification of an image you've previously magnified.

- **Aperture/Exposure Compensation button:** This button is also used in conjunction with the Main dial to set the aperture when shooting in Manual (M) mode. You also use this button with the Main dial to increase or decrease the exposure (Exposure Compensation).

- **Cross keys:** These keys are directional (up, down, left and right) and are used to navigate between menu settings. I mention these keys throughout the book as needed in conjunction with specific tasks. Read more about these in the following section.

- **Set/Quick Control button:** Press this button to confirm a task, such as erasing an image or setting a menu option. I show you how to use this button in conjunction with specific tasks throughout this book. When you're in shooting mode, this button is also used to access the Quick Control menu on the LCD monitor. (I show you how to use the Quick Control menu in Chapter 4.) You can also use the Quick Control button in conjunction with the SCN modes, Scene Intelligent Auto, and the CA (Creative Auto) mode.

- **Playback button:** This button displays the last image captured or the last image viewed.

- **Erase button:** Use this to delete a single image or multiple images. (I show you how to delete images in Chapter 4.)

- **Access lamp:** This indicator flashes when the camera writes data to a memory card.

> ✔ **LCD monitor/touchscreen:** Use this to preview images after you take them, display information about the images, access menu settings, and apply menu settings. In addition, the LCD monitor on your camera has a touchscreen, similar to touchscreens on portable devices and smartphones. Here, you can make menu changes, apply shooting settings, and scroll between images as well as magnify them.

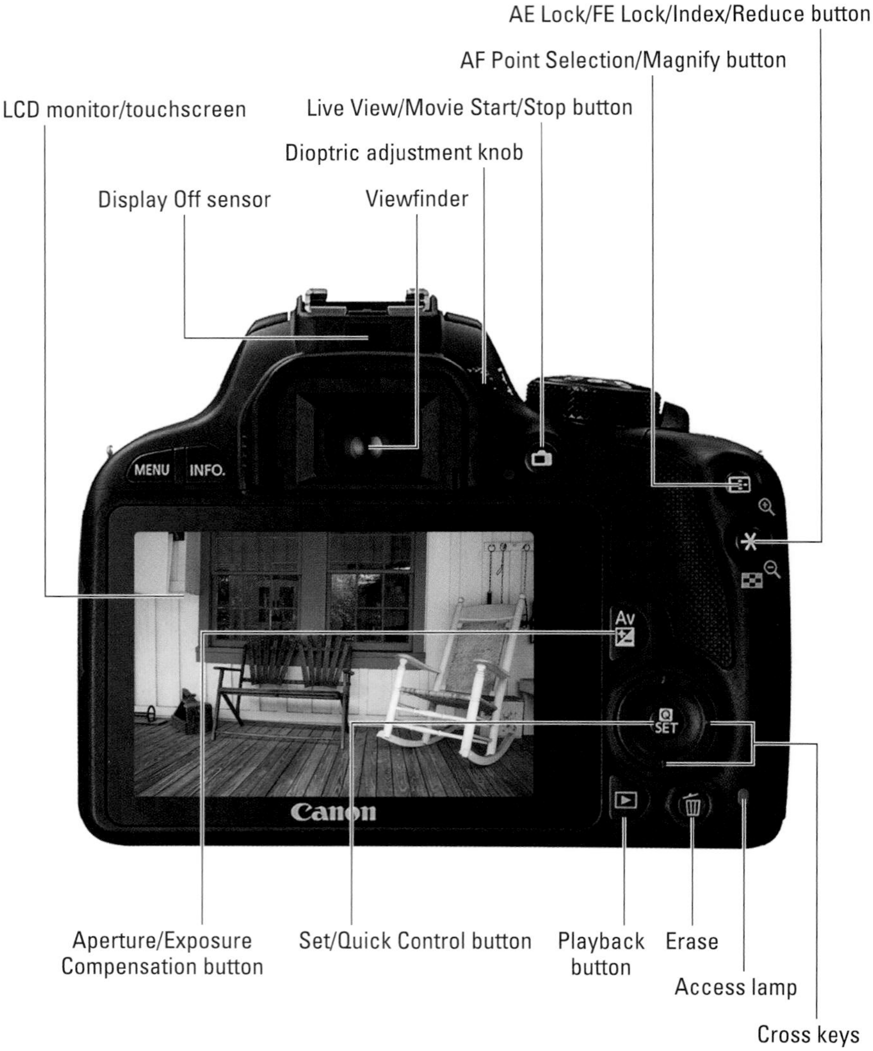

AE Lock/FE Lock/Index/Reduce button

AF Point Selection/Magnify button

LCD monitor/touchscreen   Live View/Movie Start/Stop button

Dioptric adjustment knob

Display Off sensor   Viewfinder

Aperture/Exposure Compensation button   Set/Quick Control button   Playback button   Erase

Access lamp

Cross keys

Figure 1-2: Buttons and dials and switches, oh my.

About the cross keys

Previous versions of Canon cameras have different dials that surround the Set button. Some full-size Canon dSLRs have two dials around the Set button, but the SL1/100D camera has only one dial, and it doesn't rotate. Instead, it sports four directional buttons — cross keys — on one dial. You use these cross keys in conjunction with the Quick Menu and also the menu you access when you press the Menu button.

Similar to a TV remote control or a video game controller, the cross keys are up (north), down (south), left (west), and right (east).

I instruct you to use cross keys when changing menu commands and choosing menu settings. *Note:* Sometimes the key you use depends on the last menu command you used so that, for example, only the up/down cross key will work in order to navigate vertically through a stack of menu commands. Similarly, in some instances, only the left/right cross key will work when you need to navigate horizontally from one menu tab to the next or to choose a setting, and sometimes only the left cross key will work, such as when you need to select OK to finalize a setting.

Exploring the front of the camera

The front of your camera (see Figure 1-3) has controls you can use and other gizmos that the camera uses. Here you'll find a few buttons that you use every time you use the camera as well as some features you'll rarely use.

The following are on the front of your camera:

- **Remote control sensor:** This feature senses the infrared beam from an RC-6 remote controller (sold separately) to actuate the shutter. *Note:* The RC-6 remote is line-of-sight only, meaning that you must point the remote at the front of the camera for it to work.

- **Grip:** Use this indentation to firmly grip the camera when you're shooting handheld. In spite of the small size of the SL1/100D, most adults can use the last three fingers of the right hand to grip the camera and use the forefinger to press the Shutter button.

- **Body cap:** Use the body cap to protect the interior of the camera when the lens isn't attached (not shown in Figure 1-3).

- **EF mount index:** The EF mount is red. Later in this chapter, I show you how to align an EF lens with this mark when attaching it to the camera (see the section, "Attaching a lens"). EF lenses will work on all Canon dSLRs.

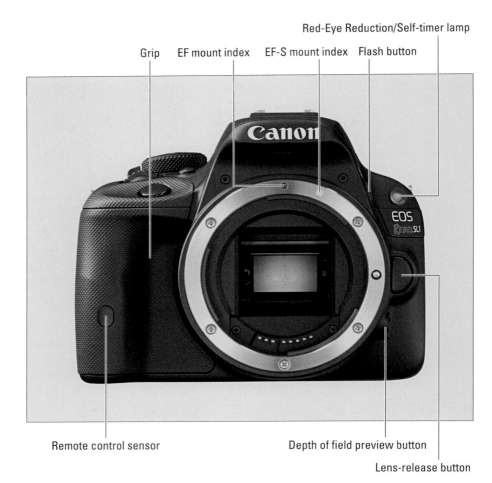

Grip EF mount index EF-S mount index Flash button

Red-Eye Reduction/Self-timer lamp

Remote control sensor   Depth of field preview button

Lens-release button

Figure 1-3: The front of the camera is an ergonomic wonder.

> ✔ **EF-S mount index:** Your camera also accepts Canon EF-S lenses, which are specifically engineered for cameras with a cropped frame sensor (a sensor smaller than the frame of 35mm film). The EF-S mount index is white and is used when aligning EF-S lenses to the camera when mounting them.
>
> ✔ **Flash button:** Use this button to pop the on-camera flash into the upright and locked position. I show you how to flash your subjects in Chapter 7.
>
> ✔ **Red-Eye Reduction/Self-timer lamp:** When you enable the Red-Eye Reduction menu option, this lamp sends out a preflash (before you actually take the picture) to help reduce red-eye, the disease that made

flash photography famous. When not used in conjunction with flash photography, this button flashes when you enable the self-timer. The lamp flashes quicker just before the shutter is released.

- **Lens-release button:** Press this button when releasing a lens from the camera. I show you how to attach and remove lenses in the upcoming sections, "Attaching a Lens" and "Removing a Lens."

- **Depth of Field preview button:** Press this button to preview the *depth of field* (the amount of the image in front of and behind your subject that's in apparent focus) at the current f-stop.

Exploring the bottom of the camera

The underside of your camera (see Figure 1-4) has one door and one female thread socket.

- **Tripod socket:** This socket will accept a 3/8"-headed tripod.

- **Battery/SD card compartment:** A memory card and a battery live in this compartment.

Tripod socket   Battery/SD card compartment

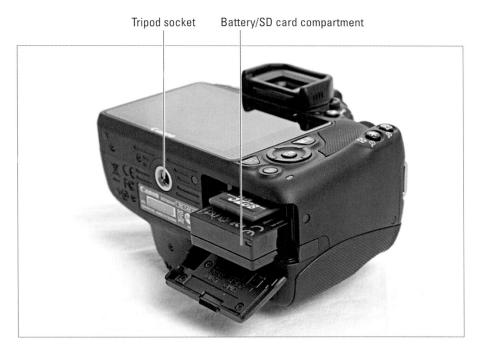

Figure 1-4: The bottom of the camera is not barren.

Peering into the viewfinder

The viewfinder — *Information Central,* as I like to call it — is another place to find a plethora of information. In the viewfinder, you see the image as it will be captured by your camera (see Figure 1-5). Use the viewfinder to compose your pictures and view camera settings while you change them. Figure 1-5 shows many of the icons that can be displayed while taking a picture and also all the autofocus points. You never see this much information displayed while you're taking a picture, though. When you peer into the viewfinder, you find the current shooting settings, ISO speed setting, shots remaining, and much more. Here's the info displayed (from left to right) in your viewfinder:

- ✔ **AE lock/AEB in progress:** You've locked the auto-exposure to a specific point in the frame or autoexposure bracketing is being performed (see Chapter 6).

- ✔ **Flash ready:** The flash has recycled to full power and is ready for use (see Chapter 7).

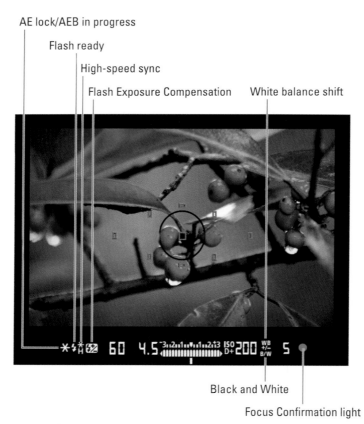

Figure 1-5: Lots of useful information is in the viewfinder.

- **High-speed sync:** You've changed the Flash mode to high speed sync (see Chapter 7).

- **FE (flash exposure) lock/FEB in progress:** You've locked the flash exposure to a specific point in the frame or flash exposure bracketing is being performed (see Chapter 7).

- **Flash Exposure Compensation:** You've employed Flash Exposure Compensation (see Chapter 7).

- **Shutter speed:** This number indicates how long the shutter remains open to take your picture. You can also use this information to manually set the shutter speed when shooting in Shutter Priority mode or Manual mode (see Chapter 6).

- **Aperture:** Displays the f-stop used to take your next picture. You can use this information to manually set the aperture when shooting in Aperture Priority mode or Manual mode (see Chapter 6).

- **Exposure Level indicator:** This tool indicates whether exposure compensation or autoexposure bracketing has been enabled; it's also used to set flash compensation and when you manually set the shutter speed and aperture when shooting in M (Manual) mode. (See Chapter 6 for more on autoexposure bracketing; see Chapter 7 for flash exposure compensation.)

- **Highlight Tone priority:** This icon displays when you enable Highlight Tone priority (see Chapter 6).

- **ISO speed setting:** See your currently selected ISO speed setting (how sensitive the camera sensor is to light). You can also use this information when setting the ISO speed (see Chapter 7).

- **B/W/Monochrome shooting:** This icon is displayed when you enable the B/W/Monochrome option as an Ambience setting. You can change image ambience when shooting in Creative, Portrait, Landscape, Macro, Sports, or any of the SCN modes as I show you in Chapter 2.

- **Max burst:** See the maximum number of shots you can take when shooting in Continuous mode. If fewer shots are remaining on the card than the maximum burst, the shots remaining display.

- **Focus confirmation light:** This indication lights up when you achieve focus.

Introducing the touchscreen

The touchscreen on your camera is very similar to a touchscreen on an iPod or iPad, and similar devices. The touchscreen just gives you another way to navigate between menu commands instead of always using the cross keys.

Just tap a menu command with your finger to see the options, swipe your finger across the screen to change settings, and pinch in (or out) to zoom in (or out) on an image.

- **Tap:** Gently tap or touch your finger on an option or icon to select it. For example, if you press the camera's Menu button, you see the shooting and settings menus denoted by the camera and wrench icons along the top. Switch to another menu by tapping the icon of another menu.

  A gesture you only rarely need to use is the *double-tap,* two taps in quick succession. One instance that calls for the double-tap is when you want to select an image for deletion.

- **Swipe:** Flick your finger quickly to move to a new screen or the next image.

  In some instances, I might also instruct you to *drag* with your finger, a slower gesture that's useful for certain tasks, such as fine-tuning settings.

- **Pinch in/pinch out:** You use both your thumb and your index finger for these gestures. To pinch in, position your thumb and finger in opposite corners of the touchscreen, and then pinch them together. To pinch out, position your thumb and finger close to each other and spread them away from each other.

The touchscreen is available when you're using the Quick Menu mode. Throughout the book, I cover the touchscreen in conjunction with various tasks you perform. Chapter 4 covers the LCD monitor, for example, and there I describe using touchscreen gestures to review images, navigate settings, and more.

Using the touchscreen to adjust menu settings

The touchscreen is extremely versatile if a little small — only three inches wide. To make changes in a menu using the touchscreen, press the Menu button and then let your fingers do the walking. Because of the screen's small size, I can use the touchscreen to navigate the menu and make changes, but sometimes I inadvertently press the wrong menu command. (I don't have the most slender fingers.) So pay attention when you're tapping and swiping to ensure you're choosing the buttons and settings you mean to. The following steps show you generally how to adjust menu settings through the touchscreen:

1. **Press the Menu button.**

2. **Tap the icon of the desired menu tab.**

   Commands for the selected menu appear under the tab you tapped.

3. **Tap the desired menu command.**

This opens the menu and displays the choices. This is the equivalent of pressing the Set button after using the cross keys to select a menu command.

4. **Drag your finger left or right to choose a setting from a scale, such as setting the LCD brightness.**

5. **Tap OK to apply a setting or command.**

If you think using the touchscreen to set menu commands is your cup of tea, I suggest you experiment without a memory card in the camera.

The camera LCD monitor is not pressure sensitive, so don't use sharp instruments (your fingernail or the tip of a ballpoint pen) for touchscreen operations, and don't even press too hard. Use your fingertip. Having said that, *do not* use the touchscreen with wet fingers.

Modifying touch control

Touch control is enabled by default. You can adjust the sensitivity of touch control — or if you don't like the feature, you can disable it. To modify touch control on your camera

1. **Press the Menu button.**

2. **Navigate to the Camera Settings 3 tab, using the cross keys or just tapping its icon.**

3. **Highlight Touch Control (see the left image in Figure 1-6).**

4. **Press the Set button.**

The Touch Control settings are displayed (see the right image in Figure 1-6).

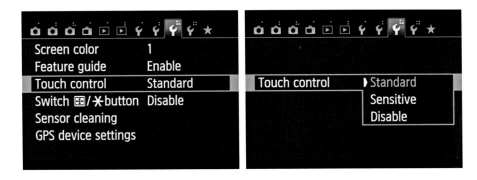

Figure 1-6: Modify Touch Control settings here.

5. **Using the cross keys or by tapping, select one of the following options:**

- *Standard:* This default setting enables touch control.

- *Sensitive:* This setting makes the touchscreen more sensitive. If you find that you like touch control, this option may make more sense for you. Experiment with both settings to see which one suits your needs.

- *Disable:* Choose this option to disable the touch screen.

6. **After highlighting the desired option, press the Set button.**

Exploring Camera Connections

On the left side of the camera (with the viewfinder facing you) is a weather-resistant flap. Under the flap are a plethora of connections, where you connect sundry connectors to your camera, as shown in Figure 1-7.

You have the following connections available on your camera:

- **Microphone:** Connect an external microphone to this port to capture audio with your video. When you connect a microphone to this port, the onboard microphone is disabled. This port will capture stereo sound from a stereo microphone.

- **Remote control:** Connect an RS 60-E3 remote control device to this port, and you can trigger the shutter remotely. The device comes with a 2" cord, which enables you to move away from the camera and view the LCD monitor when shooting in Live View mode.

- **A/V Out and Digital:** Connect an A/V out cord to this port to view video on a TV set that doesn't have an HDMI port. The optional Canon AVC-DC 400ST A/V out cord has three color-coded connectors that plug into color-coded ports on your TV for video plus left and right channel audio. Connect the cord with the Digital plug to a male USB port on a printer, and you can print directly from the camera to your printer. This port can also be used to download images and movies directly from your camera to computer using the EOS Utility software supplied with your camera.

- **HDMI Out:** Connect an HDMI cable from this port to an HDMI port on your TV to watch HD video on your TV that you captured on your camera.

HDMI out   Remote control

A/V Out/Digital   Microphone

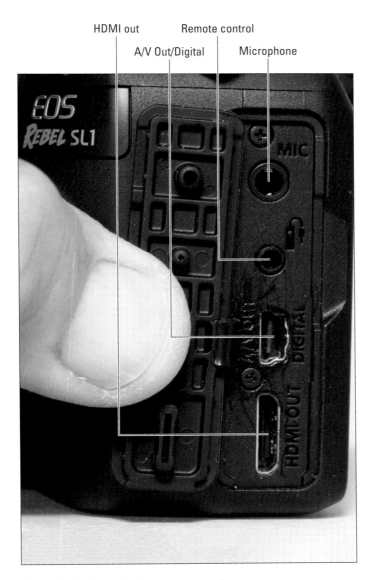

Figure 1-7: Ports just looking to be plugged.

Modifying Basic Camera Settings

Your camera ships with default settings for the country where the camera was purchased. You also have default settings for the amount of time it takes the camera to power off when no picture taking or menu activity has occurred. You can modify these settings to suit your taste, as I show you in the upcoming sections.

Adjusting the date and time

Adjusting your camera to the current date and time is important because your camera records the date and time of every picture you take. The time is based on a 24-hour military clock. You can also consider this to be your baptism by fire on how to use the camera menus, which I discuss in detail in Chapter 2. To set the date and time:

1. **Press the Menu button.**

   The last used menu appears on the LCD monitor.

2. **Navigate to the Camera Settings 2 tab (shown at the left of Figure 1-8).**

   Use the cross keys to navigate to the Camera Settings 2 icon, or tap it. Either way you choose, the menu with the date and time options displays on your LCD monitor.

   The cross keys enable you to navigate left, right, up or down. The key(s) you use depend on the last menu command you used.

3. **Highlight Date/Time/Zone and then press the Set button.**

   The Date/Time/Zone dialog box displays, and the month is selected (shown at the right of Figure 1-8).

4. **Press Set.**

   Up and down arrows appear above the current setting.

5. **Set the month and then press Set.**

   The change is applied, and the up and down arrows disappear.

6. **Navigate to the date setting (use the right cross key) and then repeat Steps 4 and 5 to set the date.**

   Sometimes only one cross key will work. Moving through fields on a setting screen, like Date/Time/Zone, is one of those times. You need to use the right cross key to advance through these fields.

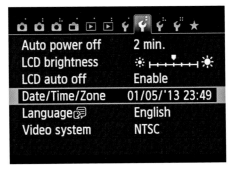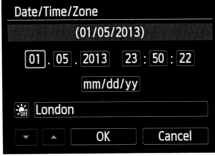

Figure 1-8: Adjusting the date and time.

7. **Set the time: year, hour, minute, and second.**

8. **Set the date format.**

   The default setting is in mm/dd/yy format. If you prefer a different format, press Set to display up and down arrows, and then highlight the method you want. Then press Set to apply the changes.

9. **Navigate to the Daylight Saving option box.**

   Daylight Saving Time changes are disabled by default. If the time zone in which you live observes Daylight Saving Time, press Set to display up and down arrows and then select the Daylight Saving Time option (its icon looks like the sun).

10. **Set the Time Zone.**

    a. Press Set to display an up and down arrow around the Time Zone box.

    b. Select the desired time zone and then press Set.

    The time zones are listed as cities. The default time zone when the camera ships is "London time" (GMT, or Greenwich Mean Time).

11. **Review the settings to make sure you have everything as you want.**

    If you goofed on a setting, use the cross keys to navigate to the setting and change it.

12. **Highlight OK (or tap OK) and then press Set.**

    The Date/Time/Zone changes are applied. Figure 1-9 shows the settings for your friendly author's SL1/100D.

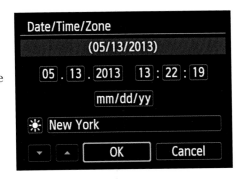

Figure 1-9: Time has come today.

If you photograph events with another photographer, make sure the time and dates are the same on both cameras. That way, when you combine images from the photo shoot and edit them, you'll be able to accurately sort them by time and date.

Modifying the auto–power off time

Your camera powers off automatically after 1 minute of non-operation. You can specify a period of time from 30 seconds to 15 minutes for auto–power off, or you can disable the feature. However, your camera will automatically power off after 15 minutes of non-activity even if you choose to disable this feature. Naturally, choosing a short power-off time helps conserve your battery. After your camera powers off, press the shutter, Info, or Menu button to make the camera power on again. Here's how to change the power-off time:

1. **Press the Menu button.**

   The previously used menu appears on the LCD monitor.

2. **Navigate to the Camera Settings 2 tab (left image, Figure 1-10).**

3. **Highlight Auto Power Off (left image in Figure 1-10) and then press the Set button.**

   The Auto Power Off options display (see the right image in Figure 1-10).

4. **Highlight the desired setting and then press Set.**

   The change is applied.

To restore the camera to its default settings, press the Menu button and then navigate to the Camera Settings 4 tab. Highlight Clear Camera Settings, press Set, highlight Clear All Camera Settings, and then press Set.

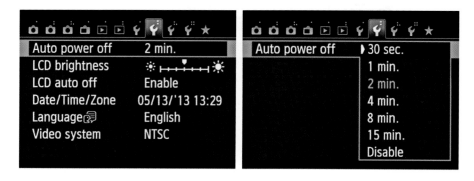

Figure 1-10: Change the power-off time here.

Adjusting the Viewfinder for Maximum Clarity

If you wear glasses or your vision's not perfect, you can adjust the viewfinder clarity, which makes it easier to compose your images and focus manually. After all, if what you see in the viewfinder isn't what you get, you won't be a happy camper. To adjust viewfinder clarity

1. **Attach a lens to the camera and point the camera at a wall.**

    I tell you in the following section how to attach a lens.

    A wall with solid light color and no texture is best. In a pinch, you can point the camera at a concrete sidewalk.

2. **Look into the viewfinder and turn the dioptric adjuster knob (see Figure 1-11) left or right until the autofocus points look sharp and clear.**

Check your viewfinder clarity every time you go on a new photo shoot. It's easy to accidentally turn the dioptric adjuster knob when putting the camera in a case or camera bag.

Dioptic adjuster knob

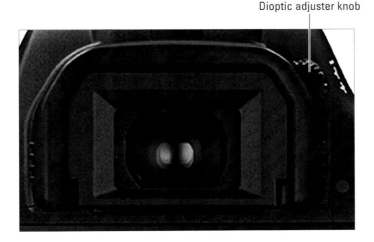

Figure 1-11: I can see clearly now.

Working with Lenses

One of the beautiful things about a dSLR is that you can attach lenses with different focal lengths to achieve different effects. Your SL1/100D accepts a wide range of lenses from super–wide angle lenses to long telephoto lenses that let you fill the frame with far-away objects. If you purchased your SL1/100D as a kit, the included lens is the 18–55mm IS STM lens zoom lens. You can purchase additional Canon or third-party zoom lenses from your favorite camera supplier. Too, you can use Canon EF and EF-S lenses on your camera. In the following sections I show you how to attach and remove lenses.

Attaching a lens

Hey, I bet you're chomping at the bit to attach a lens on your new camera. I show you how in this section. Remember, you can use Canon EF and EF-S lenses on your camera.

To attach a lens to your camera, start by taking off the body cap (the following steps) or the lens that's already attached (see "Removing a lens").

1. **Remove the body cap from the camera.**

   Twist the cap counterclockwise to remove it. Alternatively, you'll remove the lens currently on the camera with the steps I outline in the upcoming "Removing a Lens" section.

2. **Remove the rear cap from the lens you're attaching to the camera.**

   Twist the cap clockwise to remove it.

3. **Align the dot on the lens with the mounting dot on the camera body (see Figure 1-12).**

   - *EF lens:* Align the red dot on your lens with the red dot on the camera body.

   - *EF-S lens:* Align the white square on your lens with the white square on the body.

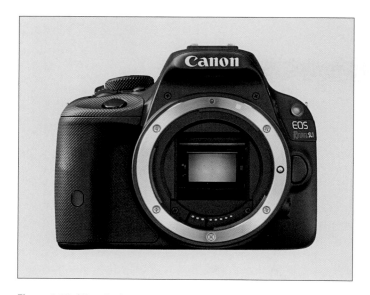

Figure 1-12: Align the lens to attach it.

WARNING!

4. **Twist the lens clockwise until it locks into place.**

Don't force the lens. If the lens doesn't lock into place with a gentle twist, you may not have aligned it properly.

What's my focal length multiplier?

The sensor on your SL1/100D is smaller than the frame size of 35mm film. Therefore, the resulting image is a smaller area than what you'd capture using a 35mm film camera or a dSLR with a sensor that's the same size as a frame of 35mm film (a *full-frame* sensor). When you use a camera with a sensor smaller than the frame size of 35mm film, you can zoom in closer with a telephoto than would be possible with a camera with a full-frame sensor. Photographers who are experienced shooting with 35mm cameras like to know how lenses will behave on a camera without a full-frame sensor. They find out by multiplying their camera's focal length multiplier by the focal length of the lens. The focal length multiplier for the SL1/100D is 1.6. Therefore, a dSLR 50mm lens captures the same field of view as an 80mm (50mm × 1.6) lens does on a 35mm film camera or full-frame digital SLR. When I suggest a focal length, I refer to it as the 35mm equivalent. For example, if I specify a telephoto focal length that's the 35mm equivalent of 80mm, this is a 50mm lens on the SL1/100D.

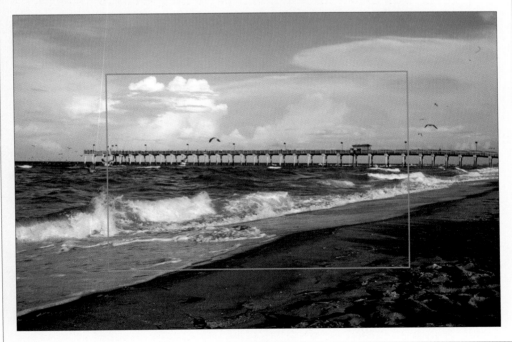

When the lens you have on your camera isn't suited for your subject — say, you have a wide angle lens on but you want to photograph a bird far away — you can quickly change to a lens of a different focal length.

Removing a lens

When you want to use a different lens or store the camera body, you need to remove the lens. Removing a lens and attaching another lens can be a bit of a juggling act. To remove a lens from your camera:

1. **Power off the camera.**

   Never change lenses with the power on because the charge of electricity can turn your sensor into a dust magnet.

2. **Press the lens-release button.**

   This button unlocks the lens from the camera.

3. **Twist the lens counterclockwise until it stops. Then gently pull the lens away from the body.**

4. **Attach another lens to the camera as soon as you can.**

   When you remove a lens, the inside of your camera is exposed to the elements. Dust can adhere to the sensor.

Do not change lenses in a dusty environment because dust may inadvertently blow into your camera. I also recommend pointing the camera body down when changing lenses. Dust on the sensor shows up as little black specks on your images, which is not a good thing.

Never store a camera without a lens or body cap attached because pollutants may accidentally get into the camera, harming the delicate mechanical parts, and possibly fouling the sensor.

Using image stabilization lenses

Many Canon and third-party lenses that fit your camera offer *image stabilization* — a feature that enables you to shoot at a slower shutter speed than you normally are able to use and still get a blur-free image. The actual number of stops you can gain depends on how steady you are when handling the camera. ***Note:*** Image stabilization stabilizes the camera for any motion you transmit to the camera. If you photograph a fast moving object using image stabilization, the subject may be blurred because of the slow shutter speed, even though the camera is stable. To enable image stabilization

1. **Locate the Stabilizer switch on the side of your lens.**

   On Canon lenses, you'll find the switch on the left side of the lens when the camera is pointed toward your subject (see Figure 1-13). If you're using a third-party lens, look for a switch marked IS, or refer to the lens manual.

2. **Push the Stabilizer switch to On to enable image stabilization.**

   Image stabilization uses the camera battery to compensate for operator movement. Therefore, shut off this feature when you need to conserve battery power and don't need image stabilization. Note that some lenses have two image stabilization switches. The second switch changes between stabilizer modes. Mode 1 stabilizes the lens in a horizontal and vertical plane, and Mode 2 and Mode 3 (on super-telephotos) stabilize the lens when you pan to follow a moving object (panning).

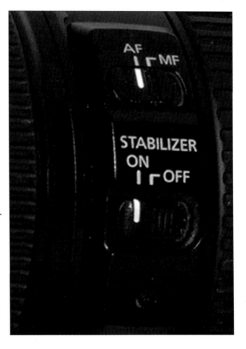

Figure 1-13: Slide the Stabilizer switch to enable image stabilization.

When you take pictures with your camera mounted on a tripod, disable image stabilization. If you don't disable this feature, you may get a less-than-crystal-clear shot because the lens is trying to stabilize motion that is not present (the tripod stabilizes the camera).

Using a zoom lens

Zoom lenses come in two flavors: twist to zoom, or push/pull to zoom in or out, respectively. The lens that comes with the SL1/100D kit is the 18–55mm IS STM lens zoom lens. You twist the lens barrel to zoom in or out. (You can purchase additional Canon or third-party zoom lenses from your favorite camera supplier.)

To use a zoom lens with a barrel that twists to change focal length

1. **Grasp the lens barrel with your fingers.**

2. **Twist the barrel to zoom in or out.**

To use a push/pull zoom lens

1. **Grasp the lens barrel with your fingers.**

2. **Push the barrel away from the camera to zoom in, and pull the barrel toward the camera to zoom out.**

About STM lenses

The Canon STM (Stepper Motor) lens series sport a motor that the camera uses to auto-focus on your subjects. The technology employed in STM lenses allows for silent focusing. When you use an STM lens, you won't hear any mechanical noise from the lens like you would with a non-STM lens. Your camera can auto-focus when you record movies, which is another reason why Canon created this line of lenses. Comparatively, the mechanical noise of a non-STM lens is recorded with the soundtrack of any movie you create.

As of this writing, Canon makes the following models of STM lenses that are compatible with your camera:

- **18–55mm f/3.5–5.6 IS STM:** This is the kit lens for the SL1/100D. It covers a focal length range that enables you to create a wide assortment of images from wide-angle landscapes to up-close-and-personal head-and-shoulders portraits.

- **18–135mm f/3.5–5.6 IS STM:** This lens covers a long focal length range and features image stabilization. The wider focal lengths of this lens are ideal for creating landscape images. The range from 50mm to 80mm is ideal for creating portraits, and the longer focal lengths enable you to zoom in on wildlife, like wading birds.

- **40mm f/2.8 STM:** This lens may be the ideal walkabout lens for your camera. The body and lens combine for a very small footprint, helping make you look relatively innocuous when photographing city and street scenes. The 35mm equivalent focal length for this lens is 64mm, which is close to the area that the human eye can perceive. With a maximum aperture of f/2.8, it's also a *fast* lens, meaning you can more easily create images in dim light without a flash.

Using Digital Film

Okay, so it's not really "film." Instead of those celluloid negatives you've come to know and love (or not), the devices you store your digital images on are memory cards. Memory cards are way better than film because you can reuse them thousands of times before they self-destruct. Well, they don't self-destruct, but like any device, they don't last forever. At least they don't get scratched like film often does. I bring you up to speed on the memory cards your camera uses in the upcoming sections.

Working with SD cards

Your camera uses SD (Secure Digital) cards to store the pictures you take. Note that your camera does not come with a memory card. If your friendly camera salesman did not sell you one, you'll have to purchase a card before using the camera. I recommend starting with a 16 GB card. An *SD Card* is an electrical device similar to a flash drive. You insert a new SD card when you begin shooting and remove the card when it's full.

To insert an SD card

1. **Open the battery/SD card compartment cover on the bottom of the camera. (Refer to Figure 1-4.)**

   To open the cover, push the latch toward the front of the camera. I find it's easier to change cards with the back of the camera facing me.

2. **Insert the card in the slot.**

   As shown in Figure 1-14, the card label should face you, and the end with the contacts should face the front of the camera.

3. **Gently push the card into the slot — and I do mean gently.**

   Never force a card because you could damage the contacts in the camera and the card. The card slides easily into the camera when aligned properly.

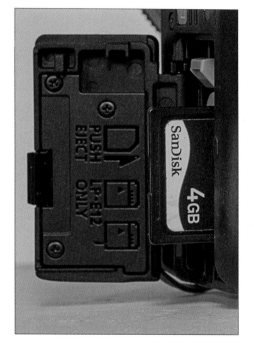

Figure 1-14: Insert a SD card like this.

4. **Close the battery/SD card compartment cover.**

   You're ready to shoot up a storm.

When you see a note in the viewfinder that your SD card is full, remove it from the camera and insert a new one. To remove an SD card

1. **Turn the camera power switch to Off.**

2. **Open the battery/SD card compartment cover by pushing the latch toward the front of the camera.**

3. **Gently push the card in, and then let go to eject it.**

   The SD card pops loose from the card mechanism.

4. **Gently pull the SD card from the slot.**

   You're now ready to insert a new SD card and start shooting.

5. **Pop the full SD card in the protective case from which you removed the blank card.**

You may be tempted to pick up a 32GB or 64GB card, thinking you can store a gazillion images on one card and not worry about running out of room. The truth is, though, that memory cards are simply electrical devices that are subject to failure — and will fail when you least expect it. And if a large card fails, you lose lots of images. The very definition of not good. I carry a couple 16GB SD cards in my camera bag. Although I hate to lose any images, I'd rather lose 16GB worth of images than 32GB or 64GB. I advise you to purchase smaller memory cards.

It bears repeating: A memory card is a mechanical device that can and will fail when you least expect it. If the worst happens and your computer cannot read a card, however, you can purchase a data recovery program to retrieve the data from the card. Data recovery programs also work if you accidentally erase the card before downloading the images to your computer. (Chapter 4 covers deleting images.) A program called CardRecovery, which works with Windows applications, retails for $39.99 (www.cardrecovery.com), or you can purchase CardRescue for the Mac, which retails for $39.99 (www.cardrescue.com). Both applications offer trial versions, which you can use to scan a corrupted card for recoverable data. After you perform a preview scan, you can purchase the applicable application for your operating system to recover the data.

Formatting an SD Card

After you download images to your computer and back them up (see Chapter 9), I strongly recommend formatting your cards before using them again, even if you didn't fill them. Doing this ensures that

- You'll have a full card to work with.
- You won't download duplicate images the next time you download the contents of the card to your computer.

The only way you can restore images from a card that's been formatted is with a data recovery program. Make sure you download all images to your computer before you format a card.

To format an SD card

1. **Insert the card into the camera, as I outline in the preceding section.**
2. **Press the Menu button.**

   The last used camera menu displays on the LCD monitor.
3. **Navigate to the Camera Settings 1 tab.**

   As I discuss earlier in the chapter, you can use the cross keys or tap the icon.
4. **Highlight Format.**

   The Format Card option is selected (see the left image in Figure 1-15).

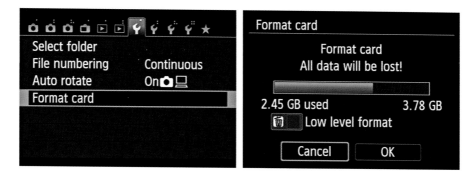

Figure 1-15: Format a card here.

5. **Press the Set button.**

   The menu changes to show the amount of data on the card and displays a warning that all data will be lost (see the right image in Figure 1-15).
6. **Highlight OK and then press Set.**

   Again, use the cross keys to navigate to OK or just tap OK.

   The card is formatted. Now you have a blank card that's ready to capture images from the camera.

The Low-Level format totally erases all data on the card and resets it to its default condition. To enable Low-Level format, follow Steps 1–5 of the previous steps, press the Erase button (the trash can icon) to enable the feature, and then perform Step 6. I recommend doing a Low-Level format every now and again to restore your cards to an almost-new condition.

7. **Press the Shutter button halfway to exit the menu and resume taking pictures.**

About Eye-Fi cards

Another type of memory card you can use is an Eye-Fi SD card. (This doesn't come with your camera.) An Eye-Fi card comes with software that you install on your computer. With an Eye-Fi card, you can download images to your computer wirelessly through a LAN (local area network). Some Eye-Fi card manufacturers have options you can purchase that automatically upload images to a storage *cloud,* which is storage supplied by the card manufacturer, when the card is almost full. Some Eye-Fi cards will also geo-tag images. When an image is geo-tagged, the coordinates are added to the image metadata. You can also use an Eye-Fi card to upload images from your camera to social media sites, such as Facebook. For more information, contact your favorite camera retailer.

Powering Your Camera

Your camera is powered by a sophisticated lithium ion (Li-ion) battery, which enables you to capture hundreds of images before it totally discharges. In addition, Li-ion batteries have a long life. In the upcoming sections, I show you everything you need to know about the battery that powers your camera, and then some.

About your camera battery

The LP-E12 battery in your SL1/100D, a rechargeable Li-ion battery engineered for a long life, enables you to capture about 380 images (with 50 percent flash usage) when you use the camera in warm weather or at room temperature. When you photograph in colder climates, the amount of images you can capture decreases. Here are some recommendations for getting the best performance from your camera battery:

- ✔ **After you charge a battery, replace the cover.** See how to charge the battery in the following section.

- ✔ **Remove the battery from the camera after you finish shooting for the day.** The battery loses a bit of its charge if you store it in the camera.

- ✔ **Keep the camera power-off time to the absolute minimum.** If you choose a longer time than the default 30 seconds, the battery drains quicker. I show you how to set the power-off time in the earlier section, "Modifying the auto–power off time."

- ✔ **Keep the image review time to an absolute minimum.** The default image review time of 2 seconds gives you plenty of time to review an image. If you choose a longer time, your battery will not last as long. I show you how to set the image review time in Chapter 4.

✔ **In cold conditions, place the spare battery in your coat pocket.** Your body heat keeps the battery warm and extends the life of the battery charge.

✔ **Replace the battery immediately when you see the low battery warning.** If you deplete the power completely when your camera is writing data to the memory card, the card may become corrupted.

✔ **Never remove the battery when the data access light is blinking.** This indicates your camera is writing data to the card. Removing the battery prematurely can damage the memory card and cause loss of data.

Charging your camera battery

When you notice the battery status icon is blinking, charge the battery, using the charger supplied with the camera.

When you purchase your camera, the battery is not fully charged. Run your battery through one recharge cycle before using the camera.

To recharge the battery, follow these steps:

1. **Plug the battery charger into a wall outlet.**

   You can use the battery charger in foreign countries as well as the United States. The battery charger works with 110 and 240 volt AC 50/60 Hz power sources.

2. **Insert the battery (see Figure 1-16).**

   After you insert the battery, the charging light glows orange.

3. **Continue charging the battery until the light is green.**

4. **After the battery is fully charged, remove the battery charger from the wall socket and then remove the battery.**

   After removing the battery charger from the wall socket, do not touch the prongs for at least 3 seconds.

5. **Replace the protective cover over the battery.**

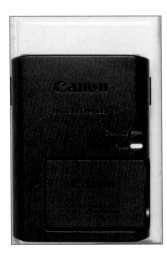

Figure 1-16: Charging the battery.

About Sensor Cleaning

When you power off your SL1/100D, the sensor is automatically cleaned (see Figure 1-17). The camera accomplishes this by jiggling the sensor to dislodge any dust particles. Sometimes, though, stubborn particles of dust don't fall off the sensor with the automatic cleaning. You can, however, manually clean your sensor as outlined in the next section.

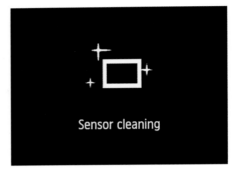

Figure 1-17: Shake it up baby, now. Shake it up, baby. Clean me off.

Cleaning your sensor on command

If you notice black specks in areas of your image that are one solid color (say, in a patch of sky), you have dust on your sensor. Your camera will automatically clean the sensor when you power it off. However, sometimes that's not enough. If you consistently see dust spots in the same area on several images, there's a jiffy menu command you can use to clean your sensor, whenever you feel the need, by following these steps:

1. **Press the camera Menu button.**

   The camera menu is displayed on the LCD monitor.

2. **Navigate to Camera Settings 3 tab (see the left image in Figure 1-18).**

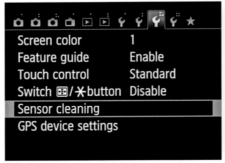 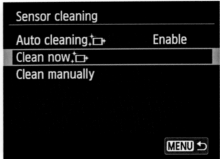

Figure 1-18: Cleaning the camera sensor.

3. **Highlight Sensor Cleaning and then press Set.**

   The Sensor Cleaning options are displayed.

4. **Highlight Clean Now (see the right image in Figure 1-18), and then press Set.**

5. **A dialog box appears, asking you whether you want to clean your sensor now.**

   OK is selected by default.

6. **Press Set.**

   Your camera performs a sensor-cleaning cycle.

After using the Clean Now menu command, put a lens on your camera, manually set the focus to the closest distance at which the lens will focus, and then take a picture of the clear blue sky. Open the image in your image-editing program and zoom in to 100 percent magnification. Sensor dust shows as dark spots. If you have stubborn specks of sensor dust on your camera, run the Clean Now menu command a couple of times.

Keeping your sensor clean

The best way to keep your sensor clean is to never change a lens. However, this defeats the purpose of a dSLR. But if you are meticulous about changing lenses and follow a bit of sage advice, you'll keep your sensor as squeaky-clean as possible. I first learned about sensor dust when I owned my first dSLR, a Canon EOS 10D. I was on a business trip/vacation to California. When I was reviewing some images of the Golden Gate Bridge, I noticed some horrible dust specks on the image. Then I read the manual and learned how to clean the sensor. Since then, I've learned that doing the following minimizes the chances of dust adhering to the sensor:

- **Power off the camera before changing lenses.** If you leave the power on, the sensor maintains a charge that can attract dust.

- **Never change lenses in a dusty environment.** If you're photographing in a dry, dusty environment, find a sheltered area in which to change lenses. When all else fails, the inside of your car is a better place to change lenses than in a dry, dusty area.

- **Never change lenses when it's windy.** In windy conditions, find a sheltered environment in which to change lenses.

- **Point the camera down when changing lenses.** This minimizes the chances of dust blowing into the sensor.

- **Have the other lens ready.** When I change lenses, it's a juggling act. I keep the lens I'm going to put on the camera in one hand with the rear cap off. I point the camera at the ground and grasp the lens I'm going to remove with one hand, and press the lens release button with a finger from the other hand. I then quickly remove one lens and replace it with the other. With practice, you can do this quickly and minimize the chance of dust fouling your sensor.

The sensor chamber of your camera is lubricated, and sometimes that lubricant can get on the sensor and cause a spot to appear on your images. If conventional methods of cleaning the sensor don't work, send the camera to Canon for sensor cleaning, or go to a local camera shop that offers this service.

Accessorizing Your SL1/100D

Your SL1/100D is a mechanical and technological masterpiece. The camera comes with a nice cardboard box — great for shipping the camera but not so great for storing the camera on a day-to-day basis. And the camera ships with this nice strap that tells the world you're shooting with a Canon EOS camera, but the strap is thin. If you're using a long telephoto lens, that strap makes you feel like you're carrying a brick on your neck. So, first and foremost, you need a decent camera case and a good strap. There are lots of other goodies you can invest in that will make using your camera more enjoyable.

I discuss a few useful Canon accessories here and list several third-party camera and video accessories in this book's eCheat Sheet, online at www. dummies.com/cheatsheet/canoneosrebelsl1100d.

Canon sells lots of goodies in its online store that may also be available from other sources such as your local camera retailer or your favorite online camera store. Here are a couple of items you may consider purchasing:

- **Extra LP-E12 battery pack:** Like everything else on this camera, the battery is smaller than you'd find on other dSLR cameras, which means you won't get as many shots on a fully charged battery as you would on a camera with a larger more powerful battery. If you shoot lots of pictures, having an extra fully charged battery in your camera bag can save the day.

- **Remote RC-6 wireless controller:** This accessory enables you to trigger the shutter of your SL1/100D wirelessly.

- **Dedicated Canon flash:** Your SL1/100D has an onboard pop-up flash unit. The camera also has a hot shoe in which you can insert a dedicated, more powerful external flash unit. The beauty of using a dedicated flash is that the camera communicates with the flash unit. The following flash units will work with your SL1/100D: 90EX, 270EX, 320EX, 430EXII, 600EX, and 600EX-RT. Macro Ring light models MR-14EX and MT-24EX are also compatible with your camera. I discuss flash photography with your SL1/100D in Chapter 7.

The Care and Feeding of Your SL1/100D

You've invested a considerable amount of money in your SL1/100D (and accessories, likely). To maintain your investment and keep the camera in top operating condition, you need to take care of your purchase.

As I mention previously, you can clean your lenses with a lens-cleaning fluid and microfiber cloth. However, you should never use a solvent on your camera body. When you want to clean your camera body, wet a soft cloth, and then wring it almost dry. Gently rub the cloth over the camera body to remove any residue from skin oil or airborne pollutants.

Some areas of your camera have ridges that are traps for dirt and debris from your skin. You can clean these areas with a soft toothbrush. It is also recommended that you clean your camera body with a soft, almost-dry cloth whenever you're photographing near the ocean when there's a salty mist in the air. Clean the camera LCD monitor with a microfiber cloth.

2

Creating Great Images on Auto-Pilot

*Y*ou can do some pretty amazing things with your SL1/100D. You have lots of control over the camera to create awesome pictures. And if all that control seems a bit daunting when you're getting to know your new toy, relax. You can let the camera make most of the decisions for you. If you're thinking "point and shoot," yup, that's what you get when you let the camera take the reins. You can definitely create some great pictures with your SL1/100D when you take pictures using one of the automatic modes.

If you're an experienced photographer, breeze through this chapter and you can show someone else how to get great pictures with your high-tech camera — that is, if you can part company with it long enough for someone else to use it. In this chapter, I show you how to get the most out of your camera's auto modes. I also show you how to use the self-timer in case you want to take a self-portrait as well as show you how to use built-in camera flash automatically.

One of the exciting features of the SL1/100D is *Live View mode,* which lets you compose your image with the LCD monitor. In this chapter, though, I deal exclusively with creating pictures through the viewfinder. If you're champing at the bit to find out how to shoot with Live View, fast-forward to Chapter 5.

You can make choices from the menus by using the navigational cross keys or sometimes via the LCD screen, tapping a selection just like on a smart-phone or an iPad. The three-inch screen is a bit small for some folks' fingers, though, so just be patient and precise when you're tapping away, setting preferences and making choices. If you find the screen hard to read in bright sunlight, try to shade the camera a bit with your free hand. You can also use the navigational cross keys (more on those in Chapter 1), but I want you to be able to use the onscreen menu for your ease as well. Some folks like it best.

Ordering from Your Camera Menu

In addition to all the buttons and dials on your camera, some picture-taking tasks require using the camera menu. For example, when you format an SD card, you use the menu. You also use the menu to specify image size and quality as well as to set the parameters for tasks such as automatic exposure bracketing. I give you a brief introduction to the camera menu in Chapter 1 where I show you how to format an SD card and set the date and time. In this section, I give you a brief overview of the menu system. Throughout this book, I show you how to use the menu to perform specific tasks. To access the camera menu

1. **Rotate the Mode dial to P (see Figure 2-1), matching P with the dot.**

2. **Press the Menu button.**

   The last-used menu displays.

   P on the Mode dial stands for *Programmed Auto Exposure mode.* When you access the menu in one of the Creative shooting modes (P, Tv, Av, or M), you have access to all the menu items, and there are 10 menu tabs in all. If you start from a Basic Zone option (A+, CA, SCN) or a scene mode (such as Portrait or Landscape), you have a limited menu: 7 tabs, to be exact. When getting started with this camera, some people like shopping for

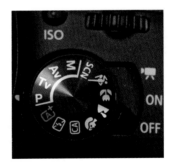

Figure 2-1: Find all menu options from a Creative shooting mode.

options from the smaller amount of selections. For the purpose of getting familiar with the whole menu, though, stick with the P mode.

3. **Use the cross keys to access the left-most tab, the Shooting Settings 1 tab (see the left image in Figure 2-2). Or, you can just tap that first icon.**

   Your camera has four directional buttons — *cross keys* — that you use to navigate menus and settings. See Chapter 1 for more about the cross keys.

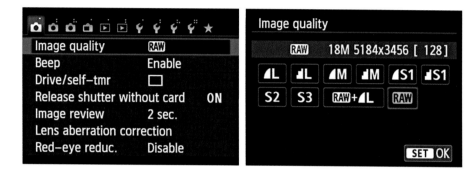

Figure 2-2: This menu has shooting options.

The Shooting Settings 1 menu shows your first set of shooting options. You also have access to these menu options when you shoot in Creative Auto or one of the other Basic Zone modes.

When you access a menu, the last command used is highlighted.

4. **Use the cross keys to highlight Image Quality and then press the Set button.**

   Your menu display changes to reveal the image-quality options (see the right image in Figure 2-2). You use the cross keys to navigate those options. In this menu, the current setting icon is blue, and a red border appears around the currently selected menu item. In menus that sport text instead of numbers or icons, the current setting is still blue, but the currently selected setting has a white left pointing arrow in front of it.

5. **After selecting a menu option, press the Set button.**

   This commits the change and returns you to the previous menu.

6. **Use the cross key to select the second menu tab.**

   This displays the Shooting Settings 2 tab. The amount of tabs you have depends on the mode in which you're shooting. If you followed my instructions in Step 2, you see several menu tabs, plus the My Menus tab which has no commands, but can be customized to house the menu commands and options you use frequently (see Chapter 11). As I mention earlier, when you shoot using one of the Basic Zone modes, you have fewer menu tabs from which to choose. Throughout the rest of the book, I show you how to use options in these tabs to perform various tasks.

7. **Press the Menu button or press the shutter button halfway to exit the menu.**

   Either operation returns you to Shooting mode. I prefer pressing the shutter button halfway.

If this is your first dSLR, you may be slightly overwhelmed that you have so many menu tabs to navigate to find the item you want. Not to worry; Table 2-1 describes the menu tabs and what you can expect to find in each one.

Table 2-1		The Camera Menu Tabs
Icon	**Menu Tab Name**	**Description**
📷	Shooting Settings 1	Used to specify image format, review time, and similar options. Also has options to correct lens aberration and enable red-eye reduction.
📷	Shooting Settings 2	Used to set exposure compensation, Auto Exposure Bracketing, Flash Control, ISO Auto settings, White Balance, and more.
📷	Shooting Settings 3	Used to specify Color Space and picture style, enable AF operation settings, set the metering mode, and so on.
📷	Live View Shooting Settings	Used to enable Live View shooting, display a grid during Live View shooting, and similar options. This becomes Video Settings 1 when you turn the power switch to Movie mode.
▶	Playback Settings 1	Used to protect images, erase images, and similar options. Also holds options to resize images in-camera and use Creative Filters.
▶	Playback Settings 2	Used to crop images, change histogram options, play images as a slide show, and similar options.

Icon	Menu Tab Name	Description
	Video Settings 1	Appears when you turn the power switch to Movie mode; used to change video focus settings, display a grid, and more.
	Video Settings 2	Appears when you turn the power switch to Movie mode; used to change video dimensions, set sound recording levels, and enable video snapshots.
	Camera Settings 1	Used to format cards, specify file numbering, and similar options.
	Camera Settings 2	Used to choose auto power-off option and set LCD brightness, date and time, and similar options.
	Camera Settings 3	Used to specify screen color, enable or disable a feature guide, specify touch control sensitivity, enable sensor cleaning, switch AF point and AE lock buttons, and specify GPS device settings when a GPS device is attached to the camera.
	Camera Settings 4	Used to specify custom functions, add copyright information to images, clear settings, and update firmware and similar options.
	My Menu Settings	Used to create a custom menu with your most frequently used options.

Taking Your First Picture

You can easily get great results with your SL1/100D automatically. For example, in Scene Intelligent Auto mode, all you have to do is compose the picture, achieve focus, and then press the shutter button. The camera literally takes care of everything. You don't have to mess with choosing the shutter speed, aperture, ISO setting, or anything else for that matter. The camera "reads" and controls the amount of light coming to the camera and does all the heavy lifting for you. Can you say, "Point and shoot?"

Depending on the lighting conditions, the camera may have to increase the ISO setting, which makes the camera more sensitive to light. An ISO setting above 800 may result in digital noise in the darker areas of the image. When you shoot in Scene Intelligent Auto mode, the camera also determines the aperture — which, combined with the focal length of the lens you're using, determines how much of the image is in apparent focus from front to back (see the "Understanding Exposure and Focal Length" section of this chapter).

Here's how to take your first shot. You do have to tell the camera how you want to shoot, so to begin with, start in Scene Intelligent Auto mode, where the camera does all the thinking for you. Find the Mode dial on the top-right side of the camera as you look at it from behind — the same position from which you take pictures. See upcoming Figure 2-3. If it's not there already, turn the dial to A+, which is the default setting. Then follow these steps:

1. **Insert a memory card (see how in Chapter 1), attach a lens to the camera (again, see Chapter 1), and power-on the camera.**

2. **If you're using a lens with image stabilization, move the switch to IS.**

   If you bought the camera as a kit with the 18–55mm lens, you'll find this switch on the left side of the lens with the camera in front of you.

3. **Make sure the lens is set to AF (autofocus).**

   If you're using a Canon lens, you'll find a switch labeled AF on the left side of the lens when the camera is pointed toward your subject.

4. **Make sure your Mode dial is set to A+ (Scene Intelligent Auto).**

   Look for the green rectangle (see Figure 2-3).

5. **Look through the viewfinder and compose your scene.**

   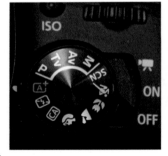

   Figure 2-3: Get your feet wet in an auto mode.

   If you use the kit lens, you can zoom in to compose the picture to include just the objects you want in the photograph. When you look through the viewfinder, you'll see nine black squares — and that's okay. You're supposed to see them. These are *autofocus points* that your camera uses to focus. In Scene Intelligent Auto (or Creative Auto) mode, the focus points are selected automatically, based on the information the camera gathers through the lens. In essence, the camera looks for objects with well-defined edges. You can customize how the autofocus system works to suit your style of photography when shooting in a Creative mode (see Chapter 6).

Make sure your subject is under one of the autofocus squares. If you're photographing a person, don't place the person in the center of the frame. I discuss this composition in the upcoming "Focusing on an Off-Center Subject" section.

6. **Press and hold the shutter button halfway.**

   When your camera achieves focus, a green dot appears on the right side of the viewfinder. If the camera can't achieve focus, the dot flashes. If this occurs, switch to manual focus (see the "Focusing Manually" section later in this chapter). The autofocus points that the camera uses to focus your subject are also momentarily illuminated (see Figure 2-4).

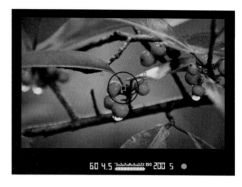

Figure 2-4: Check that your shot is in focus.

7. **Press the shutter button fully.**

   The camera takes the picture.

When the camera records data (your shot) to the memory card, the access light on the right side of the back of the camera illuminates. *Do not turn off your camera while the light is on.* If you do, the image won't record to the memory card. Powering off the camera while the light is illuminated could also damage the memory card, the camera, or both.

That's it! You shot your first picture with your new camera. Your image displays briefly on the LCD monitor. To look at your handiwork again, press the Playback button to review the image on the LCD monitor.

You can view other information regarding the image on your LCD monitor. You can view exposure information, a histogram, and much more. I show you how to display image information on the LCD monitor in Chapter 4.

In most situations, you get a beautifully exposed image with Scene Intelligent Auto mode. This default shooting mode can work for a lot of shooting conditions. If, however, you're photographing a scene with tricky lighting or photographing to create a portrait of a person, try using Creative Auto mode for options to modify the automatic settings to get an image that suits your taste. I show you how to use Creative Auto mode in the "Shooting Pictures in Creative Auto Mode" section later in this chapter. Or maybe now that you've had a taste of the camera's brilliance, you want to get the most out of your camera. If this is the case, fast-forward to Chapters 6 and 7.

Understanding Exposure and Focal Length

Photography literally means "writing with light." Thus, when you take a picture, you have to tell the camera how much light to let in and for how long.

You control that with the aperture and the shutter speed, respectively. When you take a picture in any of the automatic modes, the camera determines the shutter speed and aperture (see Figure 2-5). Handy.

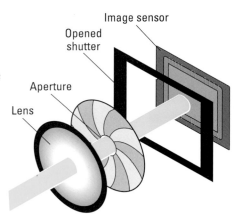

Figure 2-5: The shutter speed and aperture determine the exposure.

The *shutter* is a curtain of sorts that opens and closes, allowing light to come through the aperture in the lens to the camera's sensor. (Think of the sensor as film in a traditional camera.) The *shutter speed* is how long the shutter remains open. This is usually a fraction of a second (although it can be longer) and is even written like a fraction. For example, 1/60 literally means one-sixtieth of a second. When you use a fast shutter speed — photo-lingo, meaning an even shorter fraction of time, like 1/500 — the shutter is open for a shorter amount of time, which helps stop action (captures things in motion in clear focus). A slow shutter speed keeps the shutter open for a longer time, like you don't have a lot of available light.

The *aperture* on the lens you attach to your camera is adjustable, like how the iris of your eye widens in low light and gets smaller in bright light. How large you (or the camera) set the aperture determines how much light enters the camera. Each aperture equates to an f-stop number. A low f-stop number, such as f/2.8, designates a large aperture, which lets a lot of light into the camera. A higher f-stop number, such as f/16, is a small aperture that lets a small amount of light into the camera. Figure 2-6 shows a comparison of apertures and the amount of light they send to the camera.

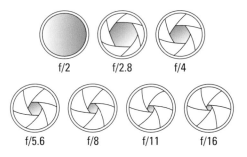

Figure 2-6: The aperture opening determines how much light enters the camera.

The f-stop determines another important factor: namely, depth of field, which is the amount of the image that's in focus in front of and behind your subject. That will become more apparent to you (and important) as you hone your craft.

✔ **Shallow depth of field:** A large aperture (low f-stop number) gives you a shallow depth of field, especially when you're shooting an image with a telephoto lens. A lens with a telephoto focal length has a narrow angle of view, which gets you closer to your subject and results in an even shallower depth of field. Telephoto focal lengths are the 35mm equivalent of 70mm or larger. Large apertures and telephoto lenses are ideal for portrait photography.

✔ **Large depth of field:** Conversely, a higher aperture (large f-stop number) gives you a very large depth of field, especially when you're using a wide-angle lens, which gives you a large angle of view. Wide-angle focal lengths have a range that is the 35mm equivalent from 18mm to 35mm, or if you purchased the camera with the kit lens, the 18mm focal length.

As you can see, what settings you choose determines what your image will look like.

The following list explains what settings the camera chooses when you take pictures in its various modes:

✔ **Basic Zones:** When you photograph using one of the modes from the Basic Zone, the camera makes most of the decisions for you.

  • *Scene Intelligent Auto mode:* A+ on the Mode dial. The camera determines the shutter speed and f-stop based on the lighting conditions and the tonal range from light to dark in the scene that you're photographing.

  • *Creative Auto mode:* CA on the Mode dial. You can apply some settings to blur the background — which, in essence, gives you a more shallow depth of field, brightens the image, and so on.

  • *Scene modes:* You use these modes in conjunction with specific picture-taking tasks. Your modes (and their icons on the Mode dial) are Portrait (a person's profile), Landscape (mountain and a cloud), Close-up (a tulip), and Sports (a running person).

  • *SCN mode:* SCN (short for "scene") on the Mode dial. Use this mode in conjunction with menu commands to choose the scene mode that best suits the type of scene or subject you're photographing. Your choices are Kids, Food, Candlelight, Night Portrait, Handheld Night Scene, and HDR Backlight Control. I show you how to use these picture-taking modes in the "Shooting Pictures in SCN Mode" section later in this chapter.

✔ **Creative modes:** These are P (Programmed Auto Exposure), Av (Aperture Priority), Tv (Shutter Priority), or M (Manual). Choosing a creative mode enables you to take complete control by manually setting aperture and/or shutter speed.

- *Aperture Priority mode:* You set the aperture (f-stop value), and the camera calculates the shutter speed needed for a properly exposed image.

- *Shutter Priority mode:* You set the shutter speed, and the camera provides the aperture (f-stop value) to create a properly exposed image.

- *Manual:* You choose both the shutter speed and aperture. When you shoot in manual, the exposure guide in the viewfinder shows you when you achieve the proper exposure for the current lighting conditions.

- *Bulb:* This mode keeps the shutter open as long as your finger is on the shutter button, or you have an external remote triggered to keep the shutter open. Bulb is not an option on the camera Mode dial. You access Bulb mode through Manual mode (see Chapter 6).

Shutter speed and image sharpness

When you take a picture with the camera cradled in your hands, a certain amount of motion is transmitted to the camera, which is caused by movement made by the camera operator. When you take pictures with a fast shutter speed (like 1/1000), the shutter isn't open long enough for any operator movement to affect the sharpness of the image. However, when you shoot at a slow shutter speed (say, 1/30), the shutter is open long enough for operator movement to be apparent in the image, which shows up as an image that isn't tack-sharp.

Also, due to the narrow angle of view, you'll find that operator movement is very apparent when you take pictures with telephoto lenses. The longer the focal length, the more apparent the operator movement. Takeaway: The clarity of your images depends on how steadily you hold the camera, the shutter speed used to capture the image, and the length of your lens.

The rule of thumb for handheld photography is to shoot with a shutter speed that's at least the reciprocal of lens focal length. For example, if you're using a lens with a focal length that is the 35mm equivalent of 50mm, you should use a shutter speed that is the 35mm equivalent of 1/50 second or faster to get a blur-free image. If the camera chooses a slower shutter speed, you know you need to steady the camera with a tripod. If you use a lens with image stabilization (more on that in Chapter 1), you can shoot at a slower shutter speed than normal. Even without image stabilization, if you hold the camera very steady, you may be able to shoot at a slower shutter speed. Find out how steady you are by experimenting with different shutter speeds on each lens you own.

The decisions the camera makes regarding shutter speed and aperture are determined by lighting conditions. If you're taking pictures in low-light situations or at night, the camera may choose a shutter speed that's too slow to ensure a blur-free picture (see the "Shutter speed and image sharpness" sidebar). If this is the case, you have to mount the camera on a tripod to ensure a blur-free picture. But if you want complete control over the exposure, use one of the Creative modes: P, Av, Tv, or M (or B, via M), which I outline in detail in Chapter 6.

Focusing on an Off-Center Subject

After you get more comfortable with the modes and settings on your camera, it's time to stretch and grow in how you compose your shots. There are lots of rules for composing photographs, but many of them can be broken intentionally. That's part of the fun of photography: doing it your way.

However, I am a fan of one stalwart rule. When you're photographing a person, don't place your subject in the center of the frame. A photograph with your subject to the right or left of center is more interesting.

The trouble is your camera is so helpful that sometimes it's too helpful. Like when you're in an autofocus mode but you want the focus set somewhere other than what the camera thinks you want.

You can easily focus on an off-center subject by following these steps:

1. **Compose your scene through the viewfinder.**

2. **Move the camera until the center autofocus point is positioned in the middle of your subject.**

3. **Press the shutter button halfway.**

   When the camera achieves focus, the green dot on the right side of the viewfinder appears. If the dot is flashing, the camera hasn't focused on your subject.

4. **With the shutter button still held down halfway, move the camera to recompose your picture.**

   By holding down the shutter button halfway, the focus locks on your subject, even as you move the camera.

5. **Press the shutter button fully.**

   The camera records the image.

Focusing Manually

You can have the greatest camera and lens in the world, but if your images aren't in focus, nobody — including you — will care to look at your pictures. As I describe earlier in this chapter, your SL1/100D has a sophisticated 9-point focus system. In Chapter 7, I show you how to modify the autofocus system to suit particular photography situations.

When you shoot images with the lens set to autofocus (AF on Canon lenses) mode, the camera looks for areas of sharp changing contrast (*edges*) or objects that are under autofocus points, and then uses these areas to focus the scene. However, in low light — or when you're taking a picture of a scene with lots of detail in the foreground and background — the camera may not be able to achieve focus. The green focus-indicator light in the viewfinder flashes when the camera cannot achieve focus, and you may also notice the autofocus motor on the lens is quite active as the camera tries to achieve focus. When you can't achieve focus, you have no choice but to manually focus the lens. And Canon lenses and most third-party lenses give you the option of switching to manual focus.

To manually focus the lens, follow these steps:

1. **Move the Focus switch to MF (see Figure 2-7).**

   On most lenses, you'll find this switch on the left side when the camera is facing your subject.

2. **Press the viewfinder to your eye and twist the lens focus ring until your subject is in clear focus.**

   If possible, concentrate on areas with contrast or sharp lines. This makes it easier for you to see when your subject is in focus. Remember to focus on the center of interest in your scene. If you're photographing a person, focus on the eyes. The curve of your subject's eyelid should be in focus in the resulting image; it's also an easy area to focus on.

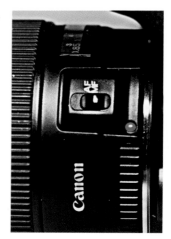

Figure 2-7: Shift to manual focus with this switch.

3. **Take the picture.**

   Switch the lens back to autofocus (AF) when lighting conditions permit the camera to focus automatically. If you switch back to autofocus, and the AF motor still moves, but still can't achieve focus, follow Steps 1 and 2 and get the subject in focus as best you can, and then take the picture.

If you're focusing manually in low light, shine a penlight on the *focal point* of your image: that is, the area that should be in focus. When you're photographing in low light, you should mount the camera on a tripod, which will make it fairly easy to focus on your subject. After you achieve focus, switch off the penlight.

When you mount your camera on a tripod, disable lens image stabilization if the lens is so equipped.

Creating Images with Camera Scene Modes

As I mention earlier, don't get overwhelmed by all the choices available on your dSLR. For example, if you don't know what shutter speed to use to freeze action, or what aperture setting to use when creating a portrait, don't worry. Canon has created several preset modes for popular photography subjects. If you want to create a portrait of your wife or kid, there's a preset for that. If you're going on vacation to the Rocky Mountains in Colorado, there's a preset mode for that as well.

Your camera has Portrait, Landscape, Close-up, and Sports scene modes. In addition, there are several modes (see Figure 2-8) you find when you choose the SCN setting on the Mode dial: Kids, Food, Candlelight, Night Portrait, Handheld Night Scene, and HDR Backlight Control. Each preset mode, with the exception of HDR Backlight Control, is what Canon calls "ambience-based shots."

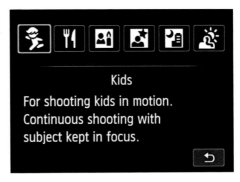

Figure 2-8: Don't make a scene when you use one of these modes.

Many of the modes also give you the option to change the setting for what Canon refers to as "light/scene-based shots," which in essence is setting the lighting so that white objects look white under specific lighting conditions.

Me, I believe in being as green as possible, so instead of destroying a small rain forest somewhere on our lovely planet, I discuss the ambience and lighting choices in the next sections, then I cover each mode in detail, except for ambience and lighting where applicable.

You have access to all image mode and quality settings when shooting in a preset scene mode or SCN mode. However, if you set your camera to shoot RAW images instead of JPEG (default), all color settings won't be applied, and you'll have to do your color tweaking in an image-editing application.

Therefore, I advise you to choose the JPEG Fine quality mode when shooting in one of the preset scene modes or SCN mode.

Setting Ambience in preset scene modes and SCN modes

When you create images using one of the preset scene or SCN modes, you do have a bit of latitude. You can change the way the image looks by changing the Ambience setting. The standard Ambience setting — which oddly enough is called *STD* — is custom tailored for each preset. However, you can change the way the image looks by choosing one of the other Ambience settings:

1. **Rotate the Mode dial and then select one of the presets (Portrait, Landscape, Close-up, or Sports), or select the SCN mode.**

2. **Press the Quick Control button.**

   If you select one of the presets, the Quick Control menu for that mode appears. If you select SCN, the Quick Control menu for the SCN mode appears and displays the icons for each SCN mode (refer to Figure 2-9). After you start shooting with the SCN modes, the last-used mode appears on the Quick Control menu. When this happens, press the Set button to see all SCN mode icons on the LCD monitor. If you select one of the presets, go to Step 4. Otherwise, rock on in numerical order.

3. **Use the cross keys to select the desired mode and then press the Set button.**

   The menu for the selected preset appears. Each scene mode is discussed in detail in the following sections. When you select a mode, the settings are listed. Figure 2-9 shows the menu for the Portrait mode.

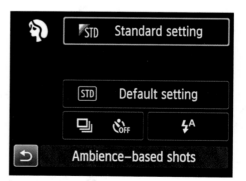

Figure 2-9: Use the Quick menu for each preset mode.

4. **Use the cross keys to highlight the current ambience setting and then press the Set button.**

   The default ambience setting is STD (Standard). You have the following picture ambience options from which to choose (see Figure 2-10). *Note:* You have to scroll down to see all the choices.

- *Standard (STD):* This is the default option for the mode you're shooting in. The settings are designed to render a well-exposed image for the type of image you shoot with this mode.

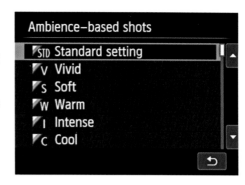

Figure 2-10: Choosing picture ambience.

- *Vivid (V):* This choice enhances colors to give the image some punch. Try Vivid when you're photographing flowers.

- *Soft (S):* This setting creates an image with nice soft muted colors. Try this option when shooting with the Portrait SCN mode.

- *Warm (W):* Try this to warm the colors in the image: for example, photographing on an overcast day to warm up the image. You might also try this setting to warm up a less-than-impressive sunset.

- *Intense (I):* This choice gives you strongly saturated colors. Try this option when photographing architecture and graffiti on the sides of buildings or railroad cars.

- *Cool (C):* This gives colors in the image a bluish tone.

- *Brighter (B):* Make the image brighter than the actual scene you're photographing.

- *Darker (D):* Make the image darker than the actual scene you're photographing.

- *Monochrome (M):* Converts the image to black and white ("grayscale" for you purists).

Some modes don't use each ambience option.

5. **Use the cross key to select the next menu setting.**

This setting determines the level and type of the ambience effect (see Figure 2-11). There is no level setting for Standard. Most ambience settings have three levels. Monochrome has three options: standard black and white, blue tone, and sepia tone. As you select a level

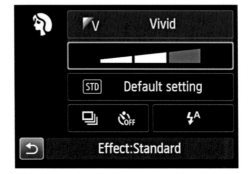

Figure 2-11: Choose the level and type of ambience.

setting, you see a tool tip at the bottom of the menu telling you about the setting.

6. **Use the cross keys to specify the level and type of ambience.**

When you select an option, you see a description of the effect it will have on your image at the bottom of the menu. For example, when you choose Monochrome, your options are Blue, B&W, or Sepia.

Choosing settings for Light/Scene-Based Shots

The other option you can change when using one of the preset or SCN modes is the lighting setting. Think of this as white balance. (Read more about white balance in Chapter 7.) To change the lighting setting

1. **Follow Steps 1–3 in the previous section.**

   In these steps you select the mode that best suits the subject or scene you're photographing.

2. **Use the cross keys to highlight STD Default Setting.**

   This is the default lighting setting.

3. **If you take a picture using the default setting and, when reviewing it on your LCD monitor, notice that the whites have a colorcast, repeat these steps and choose one of the following that may be better suited to the lighting conditions (see Figure 2-12):**

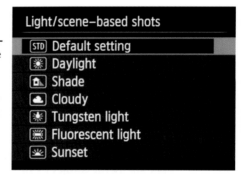

Figure 2-12: Choosing a lighting setting.

   - *Daylight:* Use this option if you're photographing a subject or scene in bright daylight.

   - *Shade:* Use this option if you're photographing a subject or scene in open shade and using one of the Scene modes.

   - *Cloudy:* Use this option when you're photographing a subject or scene on a cloudy overcast day and using one of the Scene modes.

   - *Tungsten Light:* Use this option when you're photographing a subject or scene in a room illuminated by tungsten light bulbs and using one of the Scene modes.

   - *Fluorescent Light:* Use this option when you're photographing a subject or scene in a room illuminated by fluorescent light bulbs and using one of the Scene modes.

- *Sunset:* Use this option when you're photographing a subject or scene in the late afternoon an hour or so before sunset when using one of the Scene modes. I know it seems obvious, but I'll mention it anyway: Make sure the sun is actually out when you use this option. If the sun isn't out and it's close to sunset, switch to Cloudy.

4. **Press the Set button to apply the selected lighting setting.**

   The changes will stay in effect as long as you photograph subjects with that scene mode. The camera will revert to the default settings when you power off the camera or switch to another mode.

Some modes don't use the lighting setting. For example, the Food SCN mode gives you the option to warm or cool the colors.

Creating portraits using the Portrait mode

The Portrait mode is used for creating portraits. If you use the kit lens, back away from your subject, and then zoom in. If you're too close to your subject, you have to zoom out to fit her in the frame. As a rule, you should never create a portrait with a wide angle focal length because it makes the objects closer to the camera look larger than they actually are. When you shoot in Portrait mode, the camera chooses settings to flatter your subject with realistic skin tones.

When you shoot a portrait of a person, I recommend using a telephoto lens with a focal length that is the 35mm equivalent of 80mm or greater. You can, however, create a good portrait using a lens with a focal length that is the 35mm equivalent of 50mm. Don't use a lens with a focal length shorter than the 35mm equivalent of 50mm because to fill the frame with your subject, you have to get very close to get her in the frame. When you do that, a wide-angle focal length makes the object closest to the camera seem larger than it actually is. When you're creating a portrait, the closest object to the camera is usually the subject's nose. I also usually suggest you shoot a person's portrait in portrait orientation. Just rotate the camera 90 degrees, which gives you an image that is taller than it is wide, which matches your subject.

To create a portrait using the Portrait mode

1. **Rotate the Mode dial to Portrait.**

   Look for the icon that looks like the face of a lady with a big floppy hat.

2. **Press the Quick Control button.**

   The Quick Control menu for the Portrait mode appears. This mode uses Standard picture ambience, Default lighting, and Continuous Shooting drive mode with auto-flash enabled (see Figure 2-13). These are the settings Canon has deemed optimum for shooting portraits.

You can, however, deviate from the STD ambience setting by using the down cross key to highlight the first setting and then press Set to see the available options, as outlined in the "Setting Ambience in preset scene modes and SCN modes" section of this chapter. You can also change the setting for lighting as outlined in the "Choosing settings for Light/Scene-Based Shots" section of this chapter. You can also change the drive and flash setting by highlighting the preset, and then pressing the Set button to choose an option.

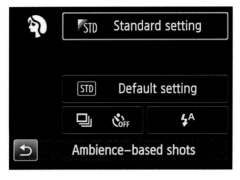

Figure 2-13: Taking pictures in Portrait mode.

3. **Press the shutter button halfway to achieve focus.**

   When you create a portrait of a person, compose the image so that your subject is on one side of the frame. Alternatively, you can have your subject's body pointed away from the camera and the subject looking at the camera. When you create a portrait of a person, make sure the subject's eyes are in focus. The eyes, after all, are the windows to the soul.

4. **Press the shutter button fully.**

   The camera starts capturing images of your subject. For this mode, the default drive mode is Continuous, which means the camera will capture images as long as your finger holds down the shutter button fully. This is a great option, especially when you're photographing someone who is comfortable in front of the camera and is able to express a wide range of emotions over a short period of time. This is also great when you're taking candid portraits.

5. **Release the shutter button to stop taking pictures.**

After you finish taking pictures of your subject, review the images on the Camera LCD monitor to make sure your subject is in focus, the poses are pleasing, and so on. If you didn't capture the essence of your subject, take some more pictures.

Shooting landscapes using the Landscape mode

There are beautiful landscapes all over this grand country of ours. Even if you live in a major metropolitan area, there is undoubtedly a majestic landscape within easy driving distance of your home. When you photograph landscapes, use a wide angle focal length that is the 35mm equivalent from 18mm to 35mm. This focal length range enables you to pack a lot of real estate into an image. When you photograph in Landscape mode, the camera chooses the smallest aperture possible for the lighting conditions and renders blues and greens more vividly.

1. **Rotate the Mode dial to Landscape.**

   The icon bears a reasonable facsimile of a mountain with a teardrop shaped cloud.

2. **Press the Quick Control button.**

   The Quick Control menu for the Landscape mode appears. The picture ambience is Standard, with Default lighting, and the drive mode is single shot (see Figure 2-14). This mode is optimized for a large depth of field. You can change a setting by highlighting it with the down cross key, pressing Set, and then choosing the desired setting.

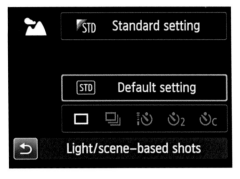

Figure 2-14: Taking pictures in Landscape mode.

3. **Compose the image and then press the shutter button halfway to achieve focus.**

4. **Press the shutter button fully to take the picture.**

   Review the image to make sure the scene is well composed.

When you photograph a vast landscape, make sure you have a large object in the foreground to act as a visual anchor. When you compose the image, place the visual anchor to the left or right of center. The visual anchor is what draws viewers into the image. Without a visual anchor, viewers have no idea where to look or why you were compelled to take the picture.

Shooting images in Close-up mode

If you love nature or have a wonderful garden, you can use the Close-up scene mode to get close-up images of flowers and other objects. To make them appear life size or larger, you'll need to use a macro lens. If you don't own a macro lens, you'll get your best results using a telephoto lens. You should also consider using a tripod when shooting in close-up mode, because any camera movement is amplified due to the extreme magnification. To shoot close-up images

1. **Rotate the Mode dial to Close-up mode.**

   It's the icon that looks like a flower.

2. **Press the Quick Control button.**

The Quick Control menu for the Close-up mode is displayed. This mode uses the Standard picture ambience, Default setting for lighting, in single shot mode, and auto-flash is enabled. See Figure 2-15. You can change a setting by highlighting it with the down cross key, pressing Set, and then choosing the desired setting.

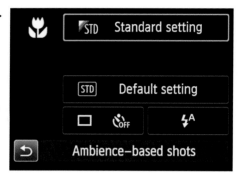

3. **Compose the picture and then press the shutter button halfway to achieve focus.**

When you photograph in Close-up mode, you have a limited depth of field. Make sure your subject is in sharp focus.

Figure 2-15: Photographing using the Close-up mode.

4. **Press the shutter button fully to take the picture.**

When you photograph subjects like flowers, take several pictures and change your vantage point each time. This will give you a variety of images from which you can choose the best one. I also recommend choosing a plain solid color background that contrasts well with the color(s) of the flower you're photographing.

When you photograph flowers and other small subjects, use a telephoto lens with a focal length the is the 35mm equivalent between 80 and 200mm and get as close to your subject as you can and still have it in focus. If you use a zoom telephoto when photographing close-ups, zoom in as close as possible. I cover macro photography in Chapter 8.

Shooting images using Sports mode

If you're photographing a subject such as your son playing soccer or a water-skier, choose Sports mode. When you photograph in this mode, the camera chooses a shutter speed that freezes the action. This mode works well for most action shots. Of course, if you're shooting a racing car coming almost straight at you, the only way to capture the image is to shoot in Shutter Priority mode and pre-focus the camera. I show you how to photograph fast moving objects in Chapter 8. To capture images of moving objects

1. **Rotate the Mode dial to Sports.**

It's the icon that looks like a runner.

2. Press the Quick Control button.

The Quick Control menu for the Sports is displayed. This mode uses the Standard setting for picture ambience, Default setting for lighting, and the drive mode is Continuous, which means you capture a sequence of action images as long as your finger holds down the shutter button. (See Figure 2-16.) You can change a setting by highlighting it with the down cross key, pressing Set, and then choosing the desired setting.

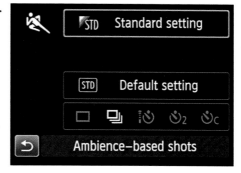

Figure 2-16: Creating images using the Sports mode.

3. Press the shutter button halfway to achieve focus.

Position the center autofocus point over your subject when you press the shutter button halfway. You're also shooting in a mode where the camera updates focus as your subject moves closer to or farther from you. At the risk of being redundant, I'll say it again: Your camera will not be able to keep focus on a very fast-moving object like a jet taking off and flying directly at you.

4. Press the shutter button fully to begin capturing images.

When you shoot in this mode, the camera is in Continuous drive mode, which means the camera will capture images as long as your finger holds down the shutter button. This enables you to capture action sequences of subjects.

5. Release the shutter button to stop taking pictures.

When you photograph moving subjects, switch to a single autofocus point. Make sure the autofocus point is over your subject when you press the shutter button halfway to achieve focus.

Shoot moving objects with a telephoto lens. This enables you to distance yourself from a potentially dangerous subject like a horse running at full gallop. With a telephoto lens, you also end up with a softer background.

Creating images using a SCN mode

When you shoot pictures in one of the preset modes described previously in this chapter, or one of the SCN modes, you choose an option from the Quick Control menu that matches the type of scene you are photographing. In SCN mode, the camera does its best to think like a photographer and choose the proper settings which should result in a good image of the scene you are photographing. For example, if you're photographing your children playing, you choose Kids mode, which uses the continuous drive mode to capture a series of images of your children playing. In continuous drive mode, the camera captures images as long as you fully press the shutter button.

When you choose a preset SCN mode, you can change the settings by highlighting an option with the down cross key and then pressing Set as outlined in the "Setting Ambience in Preset and SCN Modes" section of this chapter. You can also change the setting for lighting as outlined in the "Choosing settings for Light/Scene-Based Shots" section of this chapter. But this defeats the purpose of a SCN preset. Use the SCN presets to get familiar with the camera. When you're familiar with all the controls, then you can branch out and try your hand at some of the Creative Zone modes and choose your own settings.

When you graduate to the Creative Zone modes, you're bound to come home with some bad shots, but that's how you learn. Use your camera often. If you're already familiar with photography, you can graduate from the SCN modes relatively quickly. If you're new to photography, the SCN modes help you get a feel for the camera. Ansel Adams didn't create great landscape pictures overnight. He spent years learning his craft. To me, the sign of a good or great photographer is someone who is a lifelong learner and not afraid to experiment.

Photographing children

Photographing children playing is a daunting task for many beginning and intermediate photographers. However, you can capture wonderful images of your children playing when you use the Kids SCN mode. When you photograph in this mode, I recommend using a telephoto lens so you can distance yourself from the children and let them do their thing, oblivious to the fact that you're photographing them. If you're photographing children at a sporting event, I suggest you switch to Sports mode (see "Shooting images using Sports mode"). To photograph children

1. **Rotate the Mode dial to SCN.**

2. **Press the Quick Control button.**

   The Quick Control menu for the SCN modes is displayed. If you have photographed with a SCN mode before, the last-used mode is displayed on the Quick Control menu. Press Set to display all the SCN mode icons.

3. **Use the cross keys to select the Kids mode and then press Set.**

   The icon for this mode looks like a child. This mode uses the Standard setting for picture ambience, the drive mode is continuous shooting, and flash is set to auto (see Figure 2-17). You can change a setting by using the down cross key to highlight it and then pressing Set.

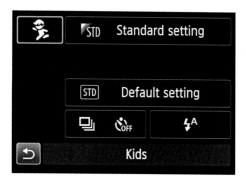

Figure 2-17: Photograph children at play with this mode.

4. **Press the shutter button halfway to achieve focus.**

   Position the center autofocus point over your subject when you press the shutter button halfway.

5. **Press the shutter button fully to begin capturing images.**

   When you shoot in this mode, the camera is in Continuous drive mode, which means the camera will capture images as long as your finger is on the Shutter button. This enables you to capture action sequences of subjects.

6. **Release the shutter button to stop taking pictures.**

Photographing food

If you or your significant other is a gourmet chef, baker, or candy maker, the Food SCN mode is right up your alley. Images created using this mode have vibrant color. The digital images you create with this mode are not edible, but when you use this mode, they look good enough to eat. I'd caution against using this mode to photograph food in a restaurant or supermarket. I've done it and it's always resulted in management stopping by to ask me if everything is OK. If you decide to photograph in a restaurant or supermarket, it's best to get permission first. To photograph food using the Food mode

1. **Rotate the Mode dial to SCN.**

2. **Press the Quick Control button.**

   The Quick Control menu for the SCN modes is displayed. If you have photographed with a SCN mode before, the last-used mode is displayed on the Quick Control menu. Press Set to display all the SCN mode icons.

3. Use the cross keys to select the Food mode and then press Set.

The icon for this mode looks a knife and fork. The ambience setting for this mode is Standard, the drive mode is single shot, and flash is disabled (see Figure 2-18). You can change a setting by highlighting it with the down cross key and then pressing Set. The Food mode also has a color tone option which lets you adjust the color tones in the images you create.

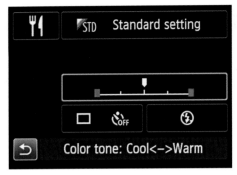

Figure 2-18: With this mode, you can photograph pie à la mode, crème brûlée, and other delights.

4. (Optional) Use the down cross key to highlight the Color Tone setting and press Set.

This setting is optional and enables you to change the color tone of the scene. Use the left cross key to cool the tones in the image or the right cross key to warm the tones in the image.

5. Press the shutter button halfway to achieve focus.

Position the center autofocus point over your subject when you press the shutter button halfway.

6. Press the shutter button fully to take the picture.

Creating portraits by candlelight

Portraits illuminated by candlelight feature a warm glow around your subject. Professional photographers go to a lot of trouble to set up a candlelight portrait. You can achieve almost the same results when you photograph in Candlelight mode. When you create a candlelight portrait, do so at night and extinguish all lights — except, of course, the candles. Three candles should be sufficient to light your subject. Keep the candles below your subject's chin and zoom in on her head and shoulders. The light will probably be dim enough to require a tripod to steady the camera. To create a candlelight portrait

1. Rotate the Mode dial to SCN.

2. Press the Quick Control button.

The Quick Control menu for the SCN modes is displayed. If you have photographed with a SCN mode before, the last-used mode is displayed on the Quick Control menu. Press Set to display all of the SCN mode icons.

3. Use the cross keys to select the Candlelight mode and then press Set.

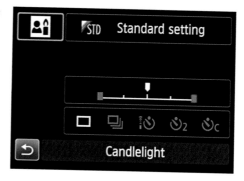

Figure 2-19: Create beautiful portraits with Candlelight mode.

The icon for this mode looks a face and a candle. The ambience setting for this mode is Standard, the drive mode is single shot, and flash is disabled (see Figure 2-19). You can change a setting by highlighting it with the down cross key and then pressing Set. The Candlelight mode also has a color tone option that lets you adjust the color tones.

4. (Optional) Use the down cross key to highlight the Color Tone setting and then press Set.

This setting is optional and enables you to change the color tone of the scene. Use the left cross key to cool the tones in the image or the right cross key to warm the tones.

5. Press the shutter button halfway to achieve focus.

Position the center autofocus point over your subject when you press the shutter button halfway.

6. Press the shutter button fully to take the picture.

Shooting night portraits

When you want to create portraits of subjects at night and use this mode, the shutter stays open long enough to capture detail in the background as well. The flash pops up automatically in this mode, and the shutter stays open long enough to capture detail in the background. To shoot night portraits

1. Rotate the Mode dial to SCN.

2. Press the Quick Control button.

The Quick Control menu for the SCN modes is displayed. If you have photographed with a SCN mode before, the last used mode is displayed on the Quick Control menu. Press Set to display all the SCN mode icons.

3. Use the cross keys to access Night Portrait mode and then press Set.

The icon for this scene mode is a person next to a star. This mode uses the Standard setting for picture ambience, and the drive mode is Single Shot (See Figure 2-20). You can change a setting by highlighting it with the right cross key, pressing Set, and then choosing the desired setting. There is no option to change the lighting setting.

4. **Compose your image and then press the shutter button halfway to achieve focus.**

   When you photograph in this mode, you generally want to show some of the background to give the viewer a sense of the place where the portrait was photographed. Therefore, your subject should be on one side of the frame. Make sure you place the center autofocus point over your subject to achieve focus. Then with the shutter button still pressed halfway, move the camera to achieve the desired composition.

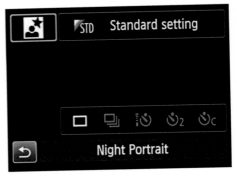

Figure 2-20: Creating images using the Night Portrait mode.

5. **Press the shutter button fully to take the picture.**

 Because the shutter will remain open after the flash fires, ask your subject to remain still so the portrait will not be blurred. I also recommend using a tripod when photographing with this SCN mode. If you don't have a tripod handy, place your camera on a flat surface and then use the 2-Second Countdown Timer (see the section on choosing a Drive mode in Chapter 6). The two-second delay gives the camera time to stabilize from any vibration that may have occurred when you pressed the shutter button.

Shooting night scenes while hand-holding the camera

If you want to take pictures at night, normally you need a tripod. However, if you've got a steady hand and you've left your tripod at home, you can take pictures at night while holding the camera in your hand. When you photograph using the Handheld Night Scene mode, your SL1/100D combines four shots of different exposures to capture the wide tonal range that is prevalent at night. To take a picture of a night scene while holding the camera by hand

1. **Rotate the Mode dial to SCN.**

2. **Press the Quick Control button.**

   The Quick Control menu for the SCN modes appears. If you have photographed with a SCN mode before, the last-used mode is displayed on the Quick Control menu. Press Set to display all the SCN mode icons.

3. Use the cross keys to select the Handheld Night Scene mode and then press Set.

The icon for this scene mode is a sliver of a moon next to a building. This mode uses Standard picture ambience and the Single Shot drive mode. There is no option to change lighting, and flash is disabled. See Figure 2-21. You can change a setting by highlighting it with the right cross key, pressing Set, and then choosing the desired setting.

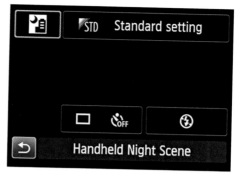

Figure 2-21: Creating images using the Handheld Scene mode.

4. Compose the picture and press the shutter button halfway to achieve focus.

5. Press the shutter button fully.

Your camera takes four pictures, and the internal processor combines them in-camera.

Hold the camera as steady as possible when shooting in this mode. Spread your feet shoulder-width apart and cradle your elbows by your side to be the human equivalent of a tripod. Gently squeeze the shutter button while slowly exhaling. Alternatively, mount your camera on a tripod.

Shooting pictures with the HDR Backlight Control SCN mode

Sometimes you want to photograph a scene with such a wide variance in tonal range that your camera has to compromise, and you end up with an image that has detail in the mid-range but lacks detail in the shadow area. You can rectify this problem by using the HDR Backlight Control SCN mode. When you choose this mode, the camera captures three images with different exposures and merges them into one. To create images using the HDR Backlight mode

1. Rotate the Mode dial to SCN.

2. Press the Quick Control button.

The Quick Control menu for the SCN modes appears. If you have photographed with a SCN mode before, the last used mode is displayed on the Quick Control menu. Press Set to display all the SCN mode icons.

3. **Use the cross keys to select the HDR Backlight Control mode and then press Set.**

   The icon for this mode looks like a person in front of the sun. The settings on this mode are all automatic (see Figure 2-22).

4. **Compose the picture and press the shutter button halfway to achieve focus.**

5. **Press the shutter button fully.**

   Your camera takes three pictures, and the internal processor combines them in-camera.

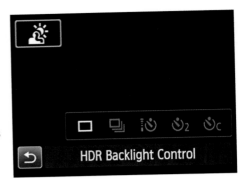

Figure 2-22: Creating images using the HDR Backlight Control SCN mode.

This is another mode where you need to be as still as possible. The best option is to mount your camera on a tripod. Don't photograph a scene with moving objects either because they will appear in different spots on each image the camera merges into the HDR image.

Shooting Pictures in Creative Auto Mode

If you like having control but you're not ready to walk on the wild side and shoot in one of the Creative Modes just yet, Creative Auto mode is right up your alley. When you take pictures in Creative Auto mode, you can control *depth of field* (the amount of the image in front of and behind your subject that's in apparent focus), image brightness, picture style, image format, and shooting mode. When you shoot in Creative Auto mode, all your options display on the camera's LCD monitor. To shoot pictures in Creative Auto mode

1. **Rotate the Mode dial to CA (see Figure 2-23).**

   CA on the Mode dial stands for *Creative Auto mode.* After switching to Creative Auto mode, the camera LCD displays your options.

2. **Press the Quick Control button.**

   This button gives you access to the first set of options: Picture Ambience. The default mode is Standard (see Figure 2-24). However, you can change the mode to suit your taste in the next step.

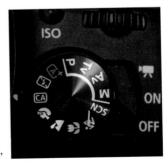

Figure 2-23: Shooting in Creative Auto mode.

3. Press Set and then use the cross keys to choose the desired option.

You can choose any of the following:

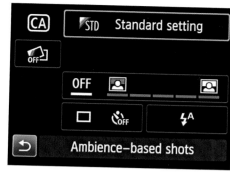

Figure 2-24: A picture's got to have ambience.

- *Standard:* This is the default option and the colors are not altered digitally by the camera. What you see through the lens is what you get.

- *Vivid:* Enhance colors to give the image some punch. Try Vivid when you're photographing flowers.

- *Soft:* Uses settings that render an image with nice soft muted colors. Try this option when shooting portraits in CA mode.

- *Warm:* Warm the colors in the image. Try this option when photographing on an overcast day. You might also try this setting to warm up a less-than-impressive sunset.

- *Intense:* This setting gives you strongly saturated colors. Try this option when photographing architecture and graffiti.

- *Cool:* Give colors in the image a bluish tone.

- *Brighter:* Make the image brighter than the actual scene you're photographing.

- *Darker:* Make the image darker than the actual scene you're photographing.

- *Monochrome:* Convert the image to black and white (grayscale).

For every ambience setting except Standard, another set of options appears in the blank space below the selected ambience setting. Press Set to see the available options. This option, which controls the intensity of the ambience setting, has three settings from which to choose. The settings are self-explanatory and have a tool tip that describes each one. Figure 2-25 shows the options for the Vivid ambience setting.

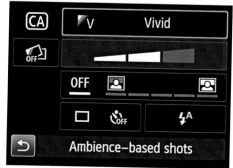

Figure 2-25: Control the intensity of an Ambience setting.

4. **Use the down cross key to highlight the Background section (see Figure 2-26).**

5. **Use the right cross key to determine the amount of background blur.**

   The leftmost setting blurs the background the most, and the rightmost setting provides the sharpest background.

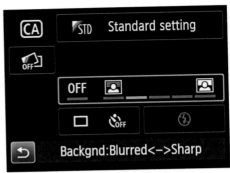

Figure 2-26: Controlling background blur.

6. **Use the down cross key to highlight the Drive section and then press Set.**

   The drive options are displayed (see Figure 2-27).

7. **Use the cross keys to choose one of the following Drive mode options:**

   - *Single Shooting:* Capture a single image each time you press the shutter button.

   - *Continuous Shooting:* Capture images at a maximum rate of 4 frames per second (fps) for as long as you hold down the shutter button.

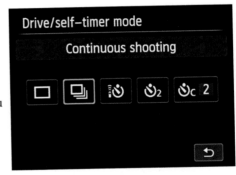

Figure 2-27: Choosing a shooting mode.

   - *10-Second Countdown Timer:* Capture an image 10 seconds after you press the shutter button.

   - *2-Second Countdown Timer:* Captures an image 2 seconds after you press the shutter button.

   - *Self-timer Continuous:* When you choose this option, two arrows appear by the number 2. Use the cross keys to specify a between 2 and 10. This determines how many images the camera captures after the timer counts down.

8. **Press Set.**

   The desired shooting mode is applied and the main CA menu is displayed.

9. **Press the left cross key to select the Two Images option.**

   The default setting is Off.

10. **Press Set.**

    The Two Image options are displayed (see Figure 2-28).

11. **Use the right cross key to enable capturing two images at once, and then rotate the Main dial to choose the effect to be applied to the second image (see Figure 2-29).**

    You can apply any of the ambience effects listed in this section or one of the Creative Filters discussed in Chapter 11. When you choose this option, the camera captures two images at once. After you take the picture, two images are displayed on the screen: the standard image on the left and the image with the effect on the right.

12. **Compose your scene with the viewfinder and then press the shutter button halfway.**

    The green dot on the right side of the viewfinder appears when you achieve focus.

13. **Press the shutter button fully to take the picture.**

    The image appears on your LCD monitor almost instantly.

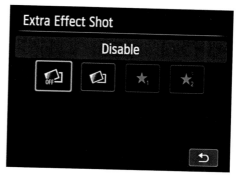

Figure 2-28: Use this setting to capture two images at once.

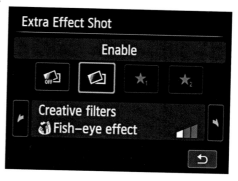

Figure 2-29: Choosing the second effect.

3

Specifying Image Size and Quality

In This Chapter

▶ Determining image size, format, and quality

▶ Comparing image formats and file sizes

▶ Creating folders and a file-numbering method

*T*he EOS Rebel SL1/100D captures images with a resolution of 18 megapixels (MP), which is humongous, ginormous, or any other adjective you prefer to indicate something that's really, really big. The good news: You gain a tremendous amount of flexibility, and you can print images as large as 21.6 x 14.4 inches. Thinking of the possibilities of decorating your house with your photographs? The bad news: The large size takes up lots of room on your memory card and lots of room on the hard drive where you store images. Fortunately, you can specify different sizes by using the camera's menu options if you have memory cards and hard drives with small capacities. But hey, memory cards and hard drives are cheap. Consider investing in a couple of extra memory cards, and perhaps upgrading the hard drive in your computer to a larger size, or purchasing an external hard drive to store the overflow.

In addition to setting the capture image size, you can also choose the file format. Your camera can capture images in the RAW or JPEG format, or capture both formats simultaneously. When you capture images in the RAW format, you must process them. Think digital darkroom in a computer, and you get the idea. The RAW format gives you a tremendous amount of flexibility. After you download RAW images to your computer, you process the images with software included with your camera or with third-party software, such as Adobe Lightroom, Adobe Photoshop Elements, Adobe Photoshop — or, if you're a dyed-in-the-wool Apple user, use Aperture. You can also process images using software that ships with your camera. I show you how to use the Canon software in Chapters 9 and 10.

If you capture images in the JPEG format, the camera does the processing for you. Think of this as the digital equivalent of a Polaroid image. You get instant gratification, and you can crop it and perform minimal image editing. If you capture images in the JPEG format, though, you also have to think about image quality. The setting you choose determines the image quality and the file size.

If you're new to digital photography, these matters of file format, image size, and quality may seem a tad overwhelming. But hey, don't worry — be happy and have a sip of your favorite beverage, or if you're reading this early in the morning, have a cup of coffee and perhaps a croissant. Oh my, I'm getting hungry; I better stop thinking about food and show you how to specify image size and quality, which you need to do before you take a picture.

Understanding Image Size and Quality

Your camera can capture large images. The default option captures images at a size that most photographers — except professionals — won't ever need or use. But before you specify sizes, you need to understand the relationship between the image size and the resolution. The default image size that your camera can capture measures 5184 x 3456 pixels (px). If you do the math:

$$5184 \times 3456 = 17{,}915{,}904 \text{ px}$$

$$17{,}915{,}904 \div 1{,}000{,}000 = 17.92$$

And now round 17.92 up to get 18MP. Oh my, I have to get out the WD-40 to lubricate my abacus after doing all that math.

The default resolution for your camera is 240 pixels per inch (ppi). If you do a little more math, the default image size and resolution equate to an image size of 21.6 x 14.4 inches:

$$5184 \div 240 = 21.6 \text{ inches}$$

$$3456 \div 240 = 14.4 \text{ inches}$$

Don't you just love math?

Another factor to consider is the final destination of the images. If you're going to edit the images with Canon or third-party software and then print them, you need to factor this into the choices you make when specifying image size and quality. You can get high-quality prints with the 240 ppi default resolution. However, some printers prefer 300 ppi. If you're capturing images to display on a website only, you can get by with a much smaller image size and a resolution of 72 or 96 ppi. When you use images on the web, you'll rarely need an image with a dimension that's wider than 640 px. (Chapter 10 has the lowdown on printing.) You can resample images to a different size and resolution with third-party software, such as Elements, Photoshop, or Lightroom. I show you how to resize images with Canon's ImageBrowser EX in Chapter 9.

The default image size is great if you're printing images and have gobs of space on your hard drive and a camera bag full of 16GB memory cards. However, if your storage capacity is at a premium or you're running out of room on your last memory card with no computer readily available to download to, you need to know how to change image size and quality, which I show you how to do in the upcoming sections.

Specifying Image Format, Size, and Quality

Your EOS Rebel SL1/100D has many options that determine the dimensions, image format, quality, and file size. Start by choosing from two image formats — JPEG and RAW. You have five different sizes for the JPEG format; RAW images are captured at full size. If you capture images with the JPEG format, you can also specify image quality. You can capture both formats when you shoot an image, or choose either format.

Your decisions regarding format, image size, and quality determine the crispness of your images, file size, and the amount of flexibility you have when editing your images. To give you an idea of the difference in file sizes, you'll end up with a file size of 0.3MB when you capture an image using the S3 (Small 3) JPEG format with Fine quality compared with a file size of approximately 17.9MB when you capture an image using the RAW format. I explain the differences between the two formats in an upcoming sidebar, "JPEG or RAW? Which is right for you?" I also give you my take on which options you should choose in the upcoming sidebar, "My recommendations."

To specify the image format:

1. **Press the Menu button.**

   This displays the last used menu on your LCD monitor.

2. **Use the cross keys to access the Shooting Settings 1 tab.**

3. **Use the cross keys to highlight Image Quality (the left image in Figure 3-1).**

4. **Press the Set button.**

   Your image format, size, and quality options display (the right image in Figure 3-1).

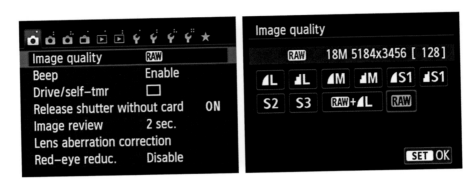

Figure 3-1: Set image format, size, and quality options here.

5. **Use the cross keys to highlight the desired file format and quality.**

   You can capture JPEG images in the following sizes: Large (5184 x 3456 px), Medium (3456 x 2304 px), S1 (2592 x 1728 px), S2 (1920 x 1280 px), S3 (720 x 480 px), RAW + Large (5184 x 3456 px), and RAW (5184 x 3456 px). When you select an option, the file size, image dimensions in pixels, and the number of images that can be captured on your memory card in the camera display on the second line of the Image Quality menu.

   You can capture JPEG images with High quality or Medium quality. High quality gives you the best image quality, but takes up more room on your memory card and hard drive. When you capture images using the Medium quality setting, the camera compresses the image, so some data is lost, and the image isn't as crisp. Medium quality is fine for the web, but if you're going to print your images, I suggest you use the High quality format. If you choose the RAW+Large option, you capture a RAW image and a Large High quality JPEG image simultaneously.

6. **Press Set to apply the change.**

   The selected image information displays next to Quality on the Shooting Settings 1 tab.

JPEG or RAW? Which is right for you?

Choosing between JPEG and RAW depends on how serious you are about your photography. Before you decide, let me point out the differences between the two formats. When you capture an image in the JPEG format, the camera processes the image. The camera also compresses the image based on the quality option you specify in the camera menu. You can store more images on a card when you specify a smaller image size and lower image quality. However, when you opt for the lower quality, you'll notice the difference when you print your images. When you choose the RAW format, you have the ultimate in flexibility. The camera sensor transmits the RAW data to your memory card. Yup. What the sensor captures is what you get. You do have to process RAW images with either the Canon software provided with your camera or with third-party software such as Aperture, Elements, Photoshop, or Lightroom. The software lets you fine-tune virtually everything about the photo, including exposure, contrast, white balance, and much more.

Comparing Image Formats and File Sizes

When you capture images with a higher resolution, the file size is bigger, and the files take up more room on your memory card. The image format also enters into the equation, and if you choose to capture images with the JPEG format, the image quality and size are factors that determine the resulting file size. Photographers also like to know the maximum number of images they can capture when shooting in Continuous (Burst) mode. The number of images depends on the image dimensions and quality, which equates to the file size.

When you capture smaller images in the JPEG format, the file size is smaller; therefore, you can capture more images before the card is filled. Table 3-1 shows you how many images can fit on an 8GB card for each available format and quality option. The information is based on capturing images with an ISO speed setting of 100. This table is only for reference. Your results will differ based on the subjects you photograph and ISO speed setting you select.

Table 3-1	How Many Images Fit on a Card?			
Image Format and Quality	*MP*	*File Size*	*Number of Shots*	*Maximum Burst*
JPEG Large Fine quality	17.9	6.4MB	1,140	28
JPEG Large Normal quality	17.9	3.2MB	2,240	2,240

(continued)

Table 3-1 *(continued)*

Image Format and Quality	MP	File Size	Number of Shots	Maximum Burst
JPEG Medium Fine quality	8.0	3.4MB	2,150	2,150
JPEG Medium Normal quality	8.0	1.7MB	4,200	4,200
JPEG S1 Fine quality	4.5	2.2MB	3,350	3,350
JPEG S1 Normal quality	4.5	1.1MB	6,360	6,360
JPEG S2 Fine quality	2.5	1.3MB	5,570	5,570
JPEG S3	0.35	0.3MB	21,560	21,560
RAW	17.9	23.5MB	290	7
RAW+JPEG Fine quality	17.9	23.5 + 6.4MB	330	4

If you prefer to capture your images in JPEG format, the quality you choose determines what the final image looks like. Compare the Fine quality to the Normal quality, and you'll notice a difference when you print the image at the largest size possible. The Normal quality image won't be as crisp and sharp as the Fine quality image. The image on the left in Figure 3-2 is an enlargement of an image captured with the JPEG Fine quality. The image on the right in Figure 3-2 was captured with the JPEG Normal quality. (The images have been magnified so you can more clearly see the difference in sharpness and detail.)

My recommendations

When I take a photograph, I think of all possible uses. My first option is to post an image I like to my blog. Eventually, I'll make prints of my best images. Some of those prints may be 4 x 6 inches for a small album, or I may have the image printed on a 20 x 16–inch canvas to decorate my home or sell a large image to a client. Therefore, I always capture images with the RAW option. This enables me to do anything I want with the image. Yes, they take up a lot of room, but memory cards and hard drives are fairly inexpensive.

Speaking of memory, my backup system is a Drobo, a case into which you can insert multiple hard drives. The Drobo firmware creates an image of the entire array on each drive. If a drive should ever fail, you simply replace it and the software rebuilds the array from the information on the other drives. I have 7 terabytes (TB) worth of drives in my Drobo. I store my backups and older images on it.

Sometimes I photograph events that require me to produce images quickly, yet I still want to edit them to perfection at some point in time. When I run into a scenario like this, I capture RAW and JPEG images simultaneously. This option enables me to give the client a JPEG image almost immediately and then edit RAW images for other outputs at a later date.

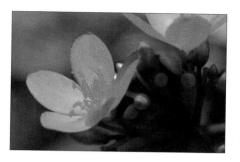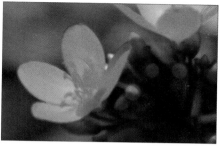

Figure 3-2: Compare the JPEG Fine and Normal quality results.

Managing Image Files

By default, your images are numbered continuously until 9999, and then the file number is reset to 0001. Your images are also stored in a single folder on your memory card. You can, however, create folders to store your images in and then change the file-numbering method, which comes in handy if you don't download each photo shoot to your computer right after you create the images. I show you how in the following sections.

Creating folders

By default, your camera creates the 100Canon folder on your memory card where images are stored. You can, however, create as many folders as you want. A folder can hold a maximum of 9,999 images. When you exceed the maximum allowable images in a folder, a new one with the next available number is created automatically. You can have a maximum of 999 folders on a card. Organizing your work in folders is a good idea if you work with large memory cards and want to store images from multiple shoots in separate folders. Here's how to create a folder:

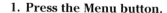

1. **Press the Menu button.**

2. **Use the cross keys to navigate to the Camera Settings 1 tab.**

   Select Folder is highlighted by default unless you've used another menu command.

3. **Use the cross keys to highlight Select Folder (the left image in Figure 3-3).**

4. **Press the Set button.**

   The Select Folder menu appears showing you the current folders on the card and the number of photos in each folder. (See the right image in Figure 3-3.)

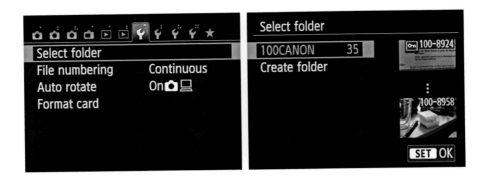

Figure 3-3: Start here to create a folder.

5. **Use the cross keys to highlight Create Folder and then press Set.**

   The menu refreshes, and a command to create a folder appears with the next available folder number (see Figure 3-4).

6. **Use the right cross key to highlight OK and then press Set.**

   The new folder is created. (See the right side of Figure 3-4.)

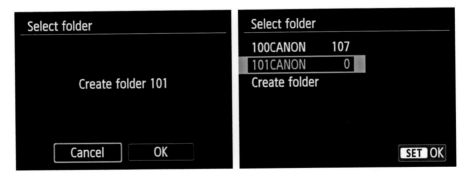

Figure 3-4: Your new folder appears here.

Selecting a folder

Folders are convenient for separating images from different photo shoots. Here's how to select a folder:

  1. **Press the Menu button.**

2. **Use the cross keys to navigate to the Camera Settings 1 tab.**

3. **Use the cross keys to highlight Select Folder and then press the Set button.**

   The folders you've created display.

4. **Use the cross keys to highlight the desired folder and then press Set.**

   The next images you shoot are stored in that folder.

Choosing a file-numbering method

Your camera automatically names and numbers each picture you take. The names aren't all that descriptive, though, and the numbers are consecutive. Some photographers stay with the default numbering system because it helps them keep track of the number of shutter actuations. Here's how to change the file-numbering system:

1. **Press the Menu button.**

   The last used menu command is highlighted.

2. **Use the cross keys to navigate to the Camera Settings 1 tab.**

3. **Use the cross keys to highlight File Numbering (the left side of Figure 3-5) and then press the Set button.**

   A menu appears with your file-numbering options. (See the right side of Figure 3-5.)

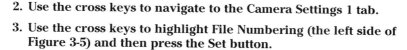

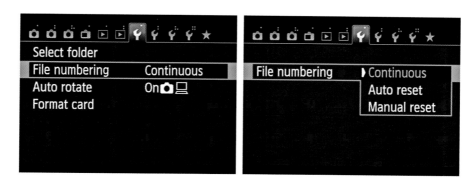

Figure 3-5: Select a file-numbering option.

4. Use the cross keys to highlight one of the following options:

- *Continuous:* Numbers files in sequence, even when you insert a new card or store images in a different folder. Images are numbered to 9999 and then start over at 0001. When you use this option, start with a newly formatted card each time. If you use multiple cards that already have images on them, you may run into problems with duplicate filenames because file numbering may continue from the last image captured on the card. Duplicating filenames isn't a good thing if you're storing all your images in the same folder.

- *Auto Reset:* Numbers the first image with 0001 each time you insert the card in the camera or when images are stored in a new folder. This option works well if you store images from each shoot in their own folder when you download them to your computer, or — as I strongly suggest — rename the images when you download them to your computer.

- *Manual Reset:* Creates a new folder and resets the numbering to 0001 after you press the Set button. After manually resetting file numbering, the numbering system reverts to the last option you specified, whether Continuous or Auto Reset.

5. After highlighting the desired option, press Set to commit the change.

The file-numbering option remains in effect until you change it with this menu command.

4

Using the LCD Monitor

igital photography is all about instant gratification. You snap a picture, and it appears on your LCD monitor almost instantaneously. This gives you a chance to see whether you captured the image you envisioned, or you have an overexposed, out-of-focus dud on your card. And your LCD monitor can do much more than just display your picture. You can get all sorts of useful information, such as the shutter speed, aperture, and other pertinent information about the image. You can even display a spiffy graph known as a *histogram* that shows the distribution of pixels from shadows (the darkest tones) to highlights (the brightest tones).

The information you can display on the camera LCD monitor gives you the opportunity to examine each image and make sure you got it right "in the camera." Photographers should always do their best to get it right in the camera and rely as little as possible on programs like Adobe Photoshop to correct exposure problems and other issues that could have been avoided when taking the picture. After all, Adobe Photoshop is a noun, not a verb. So instead of taking the picture and saying you'll "Photoshop it," rely on the information your camera supplies to determine whether you got the exposure right. Programs like Adobe Photoshop are designed to enhance images, not fix them.

In this chapter, I show you how to use your LCD monitor, including using the touchscreen options, to review images, display image information, and much more. I also show you how to erase, rotate, and protect images.

Displaying Image Information

When you take a picture, you see it almost immediately on your LCD monitor. When you want the big picture, you view the image and nothing else so you can evaluate things like composition and image sharpness to help decide whether the image is worth keeping. However, if you can deal with a smaller image, you can view all sorts of information about the image that can tell you whether you nailed the shot. If you're shooting in one of the Basic Zone automatic modes, examining this information helps you become a better photographer. If you're an astute student, and remember some of the settings the camera uses in the automatic modes, you can venture forth and use one of the Creative modes like Aperture Priority when you want to control depth of field, or Shutter Priority when you want to freeze action.

Getting camera information about an image you're previewing on the camera LCD monitor is easy. All you need to do is press the Info button. Each time you press the button, the display changes to reveal different information. The image size changes depending on the information shown.

 Each time you press the Info button, a different set of information appears, as shown in Figure 4-1. The default display shows the image (upperleft of Figure 4-1). Press the Info button again to add the exposure information as well as the image number of the total number of images recorded on the card to date (upper right of the figure). Press the Info button again to display a histogram with the image, the shooting mode, and other information such as the metering mode, the color profile, and the date and time (lower left). Press the Info button yet again to display a histogram for each color channel and the composite histogram for all channels (lower right).

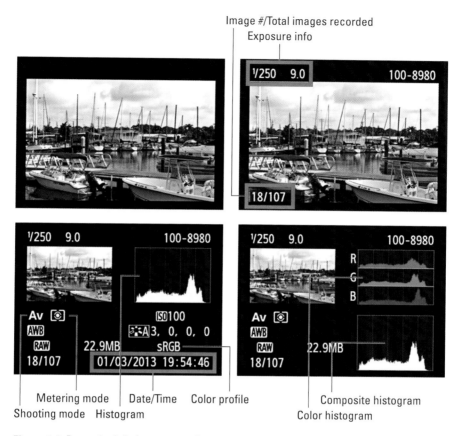

Figure 4-1: Press the Info button to review exposure information.

Using the Histogram

Even though your Canon EOS Rebel SL1/100D is a very capable camera, it can get exposure wrong when you're shooting under difficult lighting conditions. That's why your camera lets you display a histogram (see Figure 4-2) alongside the image on your camera LCD monitor. A *histogram* is a graph — actually, it looks more like a mountain — that shows the distribution of pixels from shadows to highlights. Study the histogram to decide whether the camera — or you, if you used manual settings (M shooting mode) to expose the image — properly exposed the image. The histogram can tell you whether the image was underexposed or overexposed.

Notice the flat area on the right side of Figure 4-2. You might think this would indicate that the image was underexposed. That would have been my conclusion, too, had I relied solely on the histogram. However, the brightness of the image on the LCD monitor matched the scene before me, so I moved on to the next shot instead of fiddling with exposure compensation and taking another picture. Your camera can display a single histogram or display a histogram for the red, green, and blue channels compared with the brightness histogram (see Figure 4-3).

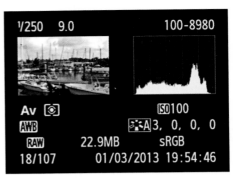

Figure 4-2: Decipher a histogram to gauge exposure settings.

A peak in the histogram shows a lot of pixels for a brightness level. A valley, however, shows fewer pixels at that brightness range. Where the graph hits the floor of the histogram, you have no data for that brightness range.

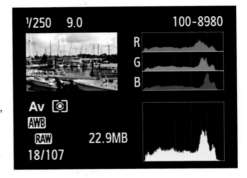

Figure 4-3: Display a histogram for each color channel.

When analyzing a histogram, look for sharp peaks at either end of the scale. If you have a sharp peak on the shadow (or left) side of the histogram, the image is underexposed. Also, if the graph is on the floor of the histogram in the highlight (or right) side, the image is underexposed. However, if a large spike is right up against the highlight (right) side of the histogram, the image is overexposed, and a lot of the details in the image highlights have been "blown out" to pure white. You can correct for overexposure and underexposure to a degree in your image-editing program, but strive to get it right in the camera. If you analyze a histogram and notice that the image is overexposed or underexposed, you can use your camera's exposure compensation feature to rectify the problem. For more information on exposure compensation, see Chapter 6.

The histogram is a tool. Use it wisely. When you're analyzing a scene that doesn't have any bright highlights, you may end up with a histogram that's relatively flat on the right side. When that happens, judge whether the image on the camera LCD monitor looks like the actual scene. If you rely on the histogram when you see a flat area in the highlights and add exposure compensation, you may make the image brighter than the scene actually was.

If the image you're photographing has a wide dynamic range from dark shadows to bright highlights, your camera does its best to deliver a pleasing image. If, however, you notice that there are shadow areas and highlights with no details, it's time to use the HDR (high dynamic range) feature of your camera, which I show you in Chapter 2.

Reviewing Your Images

In addition to displaying information with your images, you can display multiple images on the monitor, zoom in to study the image in greater detail, or zoom out. This flexibility makes it easier for you to select a single image from thumbnails, study the image up close to make sure the camera focused properly, and ensure that you have a blur-free image. And speaking of flexibility, you have the option of using buttons or touchscreen features to review your images. I discuss both ways in this section.

Preview images on the camera LCD monitor by using the buttons on back:

 1. **Click the Playback button to preview an image.**

    The last image photographed or reviewed displays on the monitor (see Figure 4-4). You can change the information displayed with the image or video by pressing the Info button, as I outline in the "Displaying Image Information" section earlier in this chapter.

    A movie is designated by an old-fashioned movie-camera icon with the duration of the movie shown above the icon. For more information on playing movies, see Chapter 5.

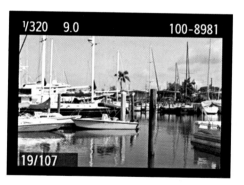

Figure 4-4: Preview a single image with Playback.

 2. **Use the cross keys to navigate from one image to another.**

 3. **Rotate the Main dial to the right to jump ahead 10 images, or to the left to jump back 10 images (see Figure 4-5).**

 4. **Press the AF Point Selection/ Magnify button to zoom in on the image.**

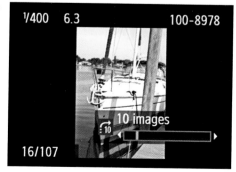

Figure 4-5: Rotate the Main dial to jump ahead 10 images or jump back 10 images.

Each time you press the button, you zoom in on the image (see Figure 4-6). You cannot zoom in on a movie, though.

5. **Use the cross keys to navigate within a magnified image.**

As you navigate within the image, you see a small rectangle in the lower-right corner of the image. Inside the rectangle is a solid square to show you the location in the image that you're exploring.

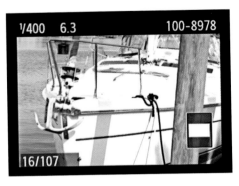

Figure 4-6: Zoom in on the image.

Rotate the Main dial to view another image at the same magnification.

6. **Press the Playback button to return to viewing a single image.**

Alternatively, you can press the FE Lock/Index/Reduce button repeatedly until a single image is displayed.

7. **Press the AE Lock/FE Lock/Index/Reduce button once to display four thumbnails (top-left image in Figure 4-7).**

Press the button twice to view 9 thumbnails (top-right image in Figure 4-7), three times to view 36 thumbnails (lower left), and four times to view 100 thumbnails (lower right). Note that the camera will default to the last mode you specify when you review images again. To see an image full screen, select the thumbnail and press the Set button.

8. **Use the cross keys to navigate between thumbnails.**

When viewing images as thumbnails, rotate the Main dial left to view the previous set of thumbnails, or right to view the next set of thumbnails.

9. **Press the Set button to fill the monitor with the selected image.**

If the image was shot with the camera held vertically, the image doesn't fill the screen unless you enable the menu option to rotate images. (See the upcoming section, "Rotating Images.")

Changing the Jump display

During review, you can change the number of images you jump through when rotating the Main dial. The default number of images you jump through is 10, but you can change it to 1 image, or 100 images; or you can jump through images by date, by folder, display only movies, display only still images, or display by image rating (if indeed you have rated images). Here's how to change the jump display by using the buttons on the camera's back:

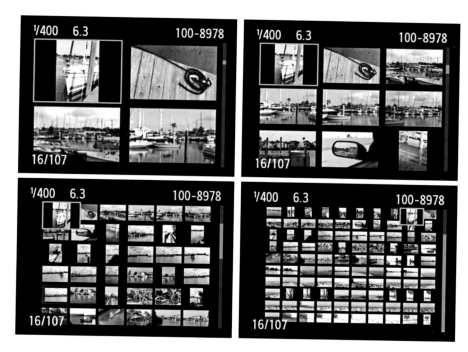

Figure 4-7: View images as thumbnails.

1. Press the Menu button.

The last used menu tab is displayed with the previously used menu option selected.

2. Use the cross keys to navigate to the Playback Settings 2 menu tab.

3. Use the cross keys to highlight the Image Jump With option (the left side of Figure 4-8) and then press Set.

The Image Jump options are displayed with the current option selected.

4. Use the cross keys to navigate between selections.

The option you select has a blue border. If you have rated images and choose the Display by Image Rating option, rotate the Main dial to choose the desired rating by which images will be displayed (see the right side of Figure 4-8).

5. **After selecting the desired option, press Set.**

   The option you select is how images will be displayed, or what type of images will be displayed when you have a single image displayed and rotate the Main dial.

Jump through 1 image   10 images   100 images   By date

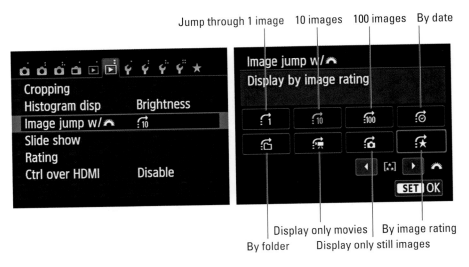

Display only movies | By image rating
By folder   Display only still images

Figure 4-8: Change the jump display option.

You have options to rate images as you review them. Rating images is all well and good, but the place to rate images is in an image-editing program, not when you're out shooting. Use your time wisely to photograph images, and don't get sucked into using technology you don't really need.

Reviewing images with the touchscreen

With the touchscreen, you can review images by tapping, pinching, and swiping with your fingers. You can also zoom in or zoom out on images, view multiple images, and so on. If you have any interest in reviewing images using the features of the touchscreen, I'll reiterate what I've mentioned elsewhere: This is a small screen, and you can easily tap the wrong thing. Pay attention to where you tap. The following steps show you how to review images with your fingertips (see Figure 4-9).

1. **Press the Playback button to display the last image captured or the last image viewed.**

2. **Swipe your finger right to view the next image, or to the left to view the previous image.**

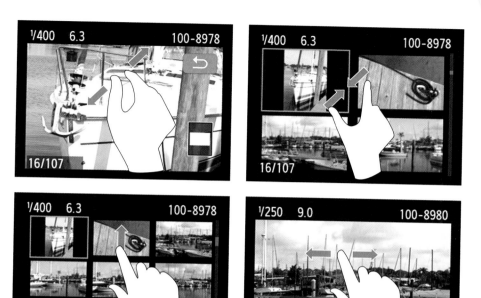

Figure 4-9: Review images with the touchscreen.

3. **Swipe the screen with two fingers to jump through images 10 at a time.**

4. **Pinch your fingers on the screen to display four thumbnail images.**

   Pinch your fingers again to view 9 thumbnails, again to view 36 thumbnails, and once again to view 100 thumbnails.

5. **When viewing multiple thumbnails, swipe a single finger up or down to navigate to the next set of thumbnails.**

   Alternatively, you can swipe your finger on the scrollbar on the right side of the screen to navigate between sets of thumbnails.

6. **Tap a thumbnail to select it.**

   A selected thumbnail has an orange border.

7. **Tap the selected thumbnail again to view it full screen.**

8. **Spread two fingers apart to magnify the image.**

   Use this gesture repeatedly to zoom the higher levels of magnification.

9. **When you're zoomed in on an image, drag one finger across the screen to scroll to different parts of the image.**

   As you scroll, a solid white rectangle appears inside an unfilled rectangle to show you which part of the image you're examining.

10. **Tap the rectangle with a curved arrow to return to single image view.**

Modifying Image Review Time

You can modify the amount of time the image displays on the LCD monitor after the camera writes it to your memory card. You can set the preview time from 2 to 8 seconds or display the image until you turn off the camera. To modify the image review time

1. **Press the Menu button.**

2. **Use the cross keys to navigate to the Shooting Settings 1 tab.**

   Or you can simply tap the desired shooting tab to select it.

3. **Use the cross keys to highlight Image Review (see the left image in Figure 4-10).**

4. **Press the Set button.**

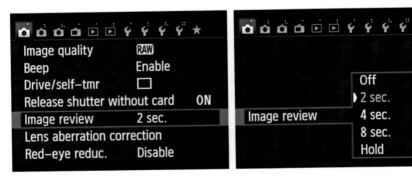

Figure 4-10: Change image review time here.

The Review Time menu appears showing the options for image review (the right image in Figure 4-10). The Hold option displays the image until you press the shutter button halfway, navigate to another image, or power-off the camera.

When you increase image review time, you decrease battery life.

5. **Use the up or down cross keys to highlight the desired option and then press Set.**

    The new review options take effect the next time you take a picture.

Changing Monitor Brightness

Camera LCD monitors have come a long way, baby. The monitor on your SL1/100D offers a brilliant display with lots of pixels (the better to see images with, my dear reader). However, at times the monitor isn't bright enough, like when the setting sun is shining brightly waiting for "Sister Moon" (thank you, Sting). You can get some help by shading the monitor with your hand or the brim of a baseball cap. You can also get some assistance from the camera by changing the monitor brightness. You can increase or decrease the default brightness of your LCD monitor manually.

Here's how to change the brightness of the LCD monitor:

1. **Press the Menu button and then use the cross keys to navigate to the Camera Settings 2 tab (see the left image in Figure 4-11).**

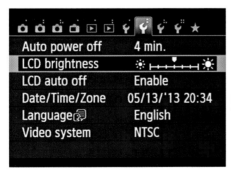
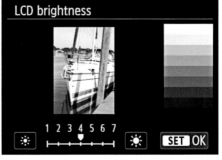

Figure 4-11: Set LCD brightness options here.

2. **Use the cross keys to highlight LCD Brightness and then press the Set button.**

   The LCD Brightness menu displays (the right image in Figure 4-11). In most instances, the default option (setting number 4) is perfect. You can, however, increase or decrease the relative brightness of your monitor to suit your vision and taste.

3. **Use the cross keys to increase or decrease brightness.**

   Use this option if the default brightness of the LCD display is too dark or too bright. As you preview different options, the image thumbnail gets brighter or darker. Note the grayscale tones on the right side of this menu. Use these as reference to what the various tones will look like with different brightness settings.

4. **When the image is the ideal brightness for the current conditions, press Set.**

   Your changes are applied.

Making the monitor brighter saps more juice from your battery, so unless you have a spare battery or two in your camera bag, increase monitor brightness at your discretion.

The LCD monitor on this camera doesn't automatically adjust for brightness. When you change brightness, the setting holds, even when you power off the camera. Reset the brightness to its default level when the ambient light becomes brighter, or when you power off the camera.

Deleting Images

When you review an image, you decide whether it's a keeper. If you don't like the image, you can delete it. However, deleting images needs to be done with extreme caution because *the task can't be undone.* After you delete an image from your card, *it's gone forever. Forever.*

To delete a single image, follow these steps:

1. **Press the Playback button to display the last image reviewed, and then use the cross keys to navigate to and review the images you photographed.**

   Sometimes when you review an image, you'll just know that it's a candidate for the trash can as soon as it appears on the LCD monitor (usually what happens to me). Unless I'm really pressed for time, I examine each image immediately after I shoot it. Sometimes you may find it's necessary to zoom in on an image to get a better look at small details. I always do this when reviewing portraits to make sure the eyes of my subject are in focus.

You can also review the images as thumbnails and delete an image, as I outline previously in this chapter. If you decide this way is faster, I recommend you press the Set button to fill the monitor with the image and review it carefully before you decide to delete it.

2. **After navigating to an image, and deciding it's a dud, press the Erase button.**

   The Erase menu appears at the bottom of your LCD monitor (see Figure 4-12). At the risk of being redundant, *deleting an image can't be undone.* At this stage, you still have the chance to stop this action by highlighting Cancel and then pressing Set.

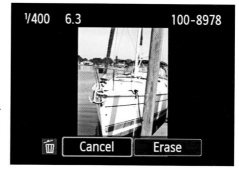

Figure 4-12: Delete images with extreme caution.

3. **Use the right cross key to highlight Erase and then press the Set button.**

   Alternatively, you can swipe to highlight Erase, and then tap Erase.

   The image is deleted.

You can also mark multiple images for deletion, similar to deleting a bunch of images in an image-editing program.

I recommend reviewing images on a computer: You have a bigger screen, and it's easier to examine images in detail. Deleting in the camera should be used only for obvious clunkers, such as out-of-focus images, or when you photographed a moving target like a bird in flight and cut off half its body.

If you find deleting multiple images in-camera useful, however, you can do so with your SL1/100D. To delete multiple images, follow these steps:

1. **Press the Menu button.**

   The last-used camera menu displays on the camera LCD monitor.

2. **Use the cross keys to highlight the Playback Settings 1 tab.**

3. **Use the cross keys to highlight Erase Images (see the left image in Figure 4-13) and then press the Set button.**

   The options for erasing images display on the camera LCD monitor.

4. **Use the cross keys to highlight Select and Erase Images (see the right image in Figure 4-13).**

5. **Press the Set button.**

   A single image displays (the left image in Figure 4-14) on the camera LCD monitor unless you're viewing multiple thumbnails while reviewing. If you're reviewing single images and prefer to view thumbnails while marking images for deletion, press the AE Lock/FE Lock/Index/Reduce button until three thumbnails appear on the LCD monitor.

6. **Press Set again to mark an image for deletion.**

   After you mark an image for deletion, a check mark appears (see the right image in Figure 4-14). If you accidentally select an image for deletion that you don't want to delete, press Set to uncheck the image for deletion.

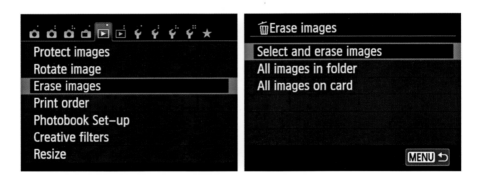

Figure 4-13: Erase images in bulk.

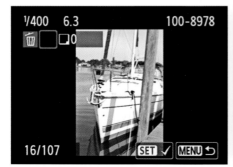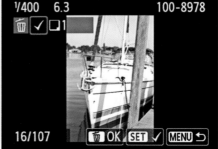

Figure 4-14: Mark images for deletion.

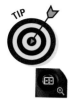

If you're viewing three images as thumbnails, use the cross keys to highlight an image and then press Set to mark it for deletion. After you mark a thumbnail for deletion, a check mark appears above it.

I suggest you view one image at a time when deleting images. The thumbnails are too small to give you enough information to determine whether an image needs to be deleted.

If you're viewing thumbnails and want to see the bigger picture before you mark an image for deletion, press the AF Point Selection/Magnify button to display a single image on the monitor and then press it again to zoom in. You can then use the cross keys to navigate to different parts of the image.

7. Review other images and mark the duds for deletion.

Check marks denote which images are chosen for deletion. The total number of images you've marked for deletion appears to the right of the trash can icon displayed in the upper-left corner of the LCD monitor.

8. Press the Erase button to delete the images.

The Erase Images menu displays (see Figure 4-15). At this stage, you still have the chance to back out if you navigate to the Cancel button and press Set.

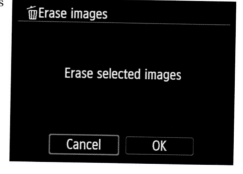

9. Use the right cross key to highlight OK and then press Set.

Faster than a bullet from a gun, the images are toast.

Figure 4-15: Deleting selected images.

Your camera also has menu options to erase all images in a folder or on the card. This type of heavy lifting needs to be done with your computer and not in the camera because erasing images uses battery power. I always review my images after I download them to my computer and do wholesale deletion there. My computer has a bigger monitor in better light and, most important, I'm seated in a comfortable chair. After all the heavy work is done on the computer, format the camera card, and then you're ready to shoot up a storm on your next photo shoot. (For more about card formatting, see Chapter 1.)

If you do a lot of work away from your main computer and need to download cards after a day of shooting, consider investing in a laptop computer. You can install your image-editing software on the laptop computer, download images from a card, and then do some preliminary winnowing and editing.

Rotating Images

Many photographers — me included — rotate the camera 90 degrees when taking a picture in *portrait* orientation: taller than wide. When portrait-style images are displayed on the camera LCD monitor, you must rotate the camera 90 degrees to view them in the correct orientation. Auto-rotation is enabled by default; however, when the camera auto-rotates an image on the LCD monitor, it's very small. Some photographers prefer not to rotate images so they can see the big picture on the camera LCD monitor. You can change the options as follows:

1. **Press the Menu button and then use the right/left cross key to high-light the Camera Settings 1 tab.**

2. **Use the cross keys to highlight Auto Rotate (see the left side of Figure 4-16) and then press the Set button.**

   The Auto Rotate options display (see the right side of Figure 4-16).

3. **Use the cross keys to highlight one of the following options:**

   - *LCD monitor and computer:* The default setting rotates the image automatically on the camera monitor and when downloaded to the computer.

   - *LCD monitor only:* Rotates the image automatically on the computer monitor but not on the camera. Use this option if you prefer to view a bigger image on your camera LCD monitor. Note that you will have to rotate the camera manually to view the image in its proper orientation.

   - *Off:* Images are not rotated.

4. **Press Set.**

   Your desired rotation option is now applied to all images taken from this point forward. If you choose to rotate the image when downloaded to your computer and it doesn't rotate, your software can't automatically rotate images from this command. If the camera is pointed up or down when you take a picture, an image photographed with the camera rotated 90 degrees may not rotate automatically.

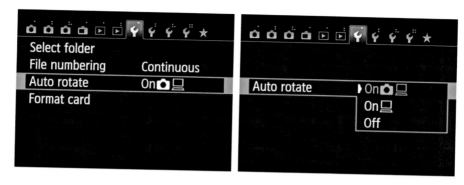

Figure 4-16: Set auto-rotating options here.

The Playback 1 menu also has a menu command to rotate individual images. But face it, folks: If you have time to stop and rotate individual images on a card, you're probably photographing a person, place, or thing that is drop-dead boring. If this is the case, don't muck about in the camera menu; find something, someplace, or someone that gets your photography mojo into high gear. Life is too short to navigate through a million menu commands.

Protecting Images

When you photograph a person, place, or thing, you're freezing a moment in time, a moment that may never happen again. Therefore, you need to be very careful when you delete images from a card because *when deleted, an image is lost forever.* That's why I recommend doing the majority of your *winnowing* (photographer-speak for separating the duds from the keepers) in an image-editing program. However, if you decide to delete lots of your images with camera erase options, you can protect any image to prevent accidental deletion. ***Note:*** This also protects the image in Canon's image-editing software. This option, however, doesn't protect the image when you format the card. To protect an image, follow the bouncing ball:

1. **Press the Menu button and use the left/right cross key to navigate to the Playback Settings 1 tab.**

    Protect Images is the first menu option (see Figure 4-17). If it's not selected, use the cross keys to highlight it.

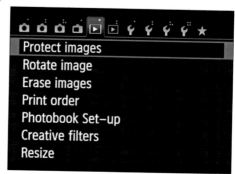

Figure 4-17: The image protection program begins here.

2. Press the Set button.

The Protect Images menu appears (see the left image in Figure 4-18).

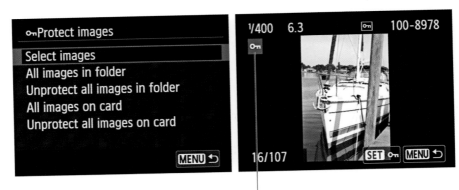

This icon denotes the image is protected.

Figure 4-18: Protected images can't be deleted.

3. Use the cross keys to highlight Select Images and then press the Set button.

When you select images for protection, the blue key icon on the left side of the screen designates that you can protect an image.

4. Use the cross keys to navigate your images, select one that you want to protect, and then press the Set button.

The image is now protected and can't be deleted. A white key icon appears on the screen above the image when it's protected (see the right image in Figure 4-18). Press Set again to unprotect a protected image.

You can also protect images while viewing them as thumbnails. Press the AF Point Selection/Magnify button until you see four thumbnail images. Press the button once more to view nine thumbnail images. Rotate the Main dial to navigate to the next set of thumbnails and then use the Cross Keys to navigate to an individual thumbnail. Press Set to protect the highlighted image.

5. (Optional) Repeat Step 4 to protect additional images.

6. Press the Menu button twice to return to the Playback Settings 1 tab.

The images you marked enter the Pixel Protection Program.

Third-party software is available that can rescue images that were deleted accidentally or were lost when a card became corrupt. In fact, SanDisk includes rescue software with some of its cards. If you do accidentally delete a keeper, immediately remove the card from your camera and insert another to continue taking pictures. If the card with the keeper image you accidentally deleted has a lock, use it to prevent taking more pictures on the card. Unlock the card when you get home and use your recovery software to resurrect the deleted image like a phoenix from the flames.

You can also protect a folder of images, as follows:

1. **Press the Menu button and use the left/right cross key to navigate to the Playback Settings 1 tab.**

   Protect Images is the first menu option. Refer to Figure 4-17.

2. **Use the cross keys to highlight Protect Images and then press Set.**

   The Protect Images menu is displayed. Refer to Figure 4-18.

3. **Use the cross keys to select All Images in Folder and then press Set.**

   All folders on the card are displayed as well as the number of images in each folder (see the left image in Figure 4-19).

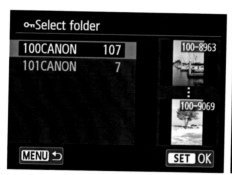 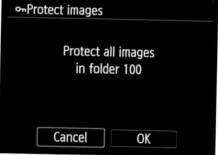

Figure 4-19: Protect images in a folder.

4. **Use the cross keys to highlight the folder you want to protect and then press Set.**

   A dialog box appears, asking you to confirm that you want to protect the folder of images (see the right image in Figure 4-19).

5. Use the right cross key to highlight OK and then press Set.

The images in the folder are protected and cannot be inadvertently deleted. They will be deleted only when you reformat the card.

To unprotect images in a folder, do the following:

1. Press the Menu button and use the cross keys to navigate to the Playback Settings 1 tab.

Protect Images is the first menu option.

2. Use the cross keys to highlight Protect Images and then press Set.

The Protect Images menu is displayed.

3. Use the cross keys to select Unprotect All Images in Folder and then press Set.

All folders on the card are displayed. Image thumbnails are displayed to the right of the selected folder. If the images in that folder are protected, the folder name is blue (see the left image in Figure 4-20).

4. Use the cross keys to navigate to the folder of images you want to unprotect and then press Set.

A dialog box appears, asking you to confirm the fact that you want to unprotect all images in the selected folder (see the right image in Figure 4-20).

5. Use the right cross key to select OK.

If you decide not to unprotect the images, accept the default option of Cancel and press Set.

6. Press Set.

The folder of images is unprotected.

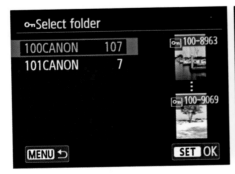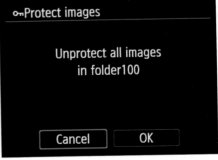

Figure 4-20: A folder of images is about to leave the image protection program.

Here are two more commands on the Protect Images menu:

- **All Images on Card:** Highlight this command and press Set to protect all images on the card.
- **Unprotect All Images on Card:** Highlight this command and press Set to unprotect all images on the card.

Using the Quick Control Menu

Even after you become familiar with what all the dials and buttons on your camera do, sometimes, you might need to make one or more changes quickly — say, change image size, enable the 10-second Self-Timer when shooting in Full Auto mode, or change multiple options quickly when shooting with one of the Creative shooting modes. The Quick Control menu enables you to do these things and more — all in a New York minute. So if you're in a New York state of mind and want to change camera settings in a flash, follow these steps:

1. **Press the Shutter button halfway.**

   This action returns you to shooting mode if you've been reviewing images. If you're in the desired shooting mode, go to Step 3.

2. **Rotate the Mode dial to the desired shooting mode.**

   Now you're cooking with gas.

3. **Press the Quick Control button.**

   The Quick Control menu appears on your LCD monitor. The display varies depending on which mode you selected from the Mode dial.

   Figure 4-21 shows the Quick Control screen when taking pictures in Aperture Priority mode. Note that the shutter speed is not displayed. You can see what shutter speed will be used with the aperture you specify when you press the shutter button halfway.

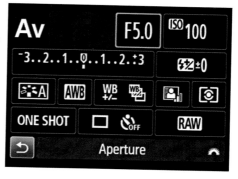

Figure 4-21: Changing shooting options with the Quick Control screen.

4. **Use the cross keys to navigate between shooting options.**

Notice that as you select a shooting option, a dialog box appears underneath to tell you about the option you selected. The left image in Figure 4-22 shows the screen that appears for changing ISO speed with the Quick Control screen. As you rotate the Main dial, the setting changes. I discuss in detail the settings you can change with the Quick Control screen in Chapters 6 and 7. Alternatively, you can press Set to see the complete options for the setting you choose. The right image in Figure 4-22 shows all the settings for ISO. When you display all options, use the cross keys to select the desired option.

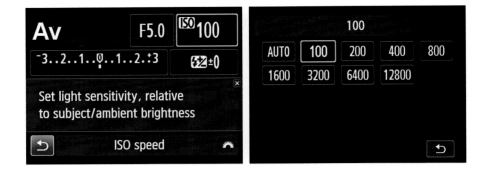

Figure 4-22: Access an option for a setting from the Quick Control screen.

As you move through selections on the Quick Control screen, you notice a text tip appears that tells you about what the setting you're about to change does for the pictures you're about to take. This information is useful. However, when you feel that you're an old hand at photography and the text tip is redundant and annoying, you can navigate to the Camera Setup 3 tab, choose the Feature Guide menu control, and then disable it.

5. **Repeat Step 4 for any other setting you want to modify.**

6. **Press the shutter button halfway to exit the Quick Control menu and begin taking pictures with the new settings.**

Now that was quick and easy, wasn't it?

Using Touch Control with the Quick Control Menu

The Quick Control menu places all the settings you need right on the LCD monitor. You can navigate the Quick Control menu with touchscreen gestures. As outlined in the previous section, you access the Quick Control menu by pressing the Quick Control button. Then, after you display the Quick Control menu, you follow these steps:

1. **Tap a setting to select it.**

   If Feature Guide is enabled, a text tip appears below the setting telling you effect the setting has.

2. **Tap the setting again to see the see the parameters you can change.**

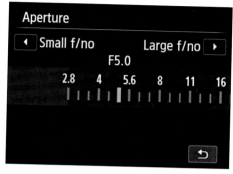

   If you touch the aperture setting, the menu in Figure 4-23 appears. Each menu will be slightly different, but intuitive. For example, to set the aperture, you can either drag your finger across the settings to select the desired

Figure 4-23: Let your fingers do the walking with the touchscreen and the Quick Control menu.

   aperture, or tap the left arrow to select a larger aperture (smaller f-stop value) or tap the right arrow to select a smaller aperture (larger f-stop value).

3. **After choosing the desired setting, tap the rectangle with the curved arrow to return to the Quick Control menu.**

Viewing Images as a Slide Show

If you're the type of photographer who likes to razzle-dazzle yourself and your friends by viewing images you've just shot by putting them on the camera LCD monitor — also known as *chimping* because photographers sometimes make noises like chimpanzees in a zoo when they see a cool image — you'll love viewing images on the camera LCD monitor as a slide show. Here's how to view images as a slide show:

1. **Press the Menu button and use the cross keys to navigate to the Playback Settings 2 tab.**

2. **Use the cross keys to highlight Slide Show (see the left image in Figure 4-24) and then press the Set button.**

   The Slide Show menu appears (see the right image in Figure 4-24). The default slide show displays all images with a 1-second delay, and the show loops until you exit the slide show.

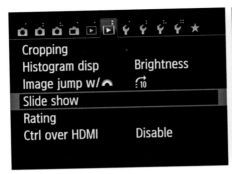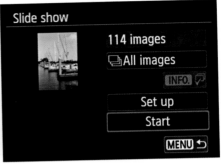

Figure 4-24: Slide show settings — popcorn optional.

3. **To accept the default slide show options, fast-forward to Step 6; otherwise, use the cross keys to highlight All Images and then press Set.**

Two arrows appear indicating that you have options.

4. **Use the cross keys to select the desired option.**

The options vary, depending on what you captured on the card and whether you put images into a different folder. If you have multiple folders, they appear on this menu. If you have movies on the card, you can view movies on the camera monitor. You can also view stills in the slide show only, view images by date, or view images you've rated.

5. **After choosing an option, press Set.**

The images or movies display as a slide show after you set up the slide show.

6. **Use the cross keys to highlight Set Up and then press Set.**

The menu changes to display the playback options (see the left image in Figure 4-25).

7. **Use the cross keys to highlight Display Time and press Set.**

The menu changes to show the options for the duration of each slide (see the right image in Figure 4-25).

8. **Use the cross keys to select a Display Time option and then press Set.**

The setting is applied, and the previous slide show menu displays.

9. **Use the cross keys to highlight Repeat and then press Set.**

The Repeat options display (see the left image in Figure 4-26). The default Enable option repeats the slide show until you press the Shutter button halfway to return to shooting mode or press the Menu button to return to the Slide show menu. The Disable option plays the slide show once. After pressing Set, the previous screen displays.

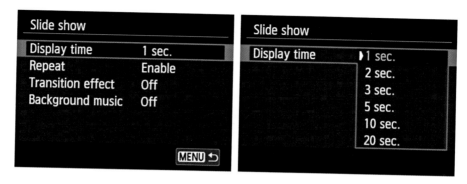

Figure 4-25: Setting playback options for the slide show.

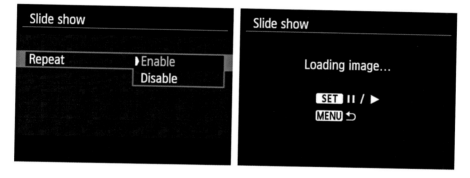

Figure 4-26: Finalizing slide show options.

10. **Use the cross keys to highlight Transition Effect and then press Set.**

    The Transition Effect options are displayed. The transitions can add pizzazz to your slide show when viewed on the LCD monitor or on a TV set. I invite you to investigate these options.

11. **Use the cross keys to highlight the desired Transition Effect and then press Set.**

    The setting is applied, and the previous slide show menu displays.

12. **Use the cross keys to highlight Background Music and then press Set.**

    You can get music files from the EOS Utilities disk, but as a serious photographer, I need to put my two cents' worth in here: Why would you want to take up room on your memory card with music files?

13. **Select the desired music file and press Set.**

Hmm. . . . If you were photographing Bike Week at Daytona Beach, you could have "Born to Be Wild" on your memory card. But I digress and assume you are a serious photographer as well. I'm also quite sure that Steppenwolf has not licensed the song to Canon.

14. Press Menu to return to the main Slide Show menu, use the cross keys to highlight Start, and then press Set.

After you press Set, the images load (see the right image in Figure 4-26), and the slide show begins.

15. Press Set to pause the slide show.

Use this option to examine a single image. *Note:* You can't magnify an image while in slide show mode. When the slide show is paused, you can use the cross keys to view a different image. You can press the Info button to show a different display with the image. Pressing Set also pauses a movie that's part of the slide show.

16. Press Set to continue the slide show.

When you're tired of watching the slide show or your battery starts running low (auto power-off is disabled when you view a slide show), press the Shutter button halfway to return to picture-taking mode. Alternatively, you can press the Menu button to specify different slide-show options or to view images in a different folder.

Viewing Images on a TV Set

You have a digital camera capable of capturing colorful images with an impressive resolution of 18 megapixels (MP). Your television set is a grand device on which to display your images. You can display still images or a slide show on your TV screen. And if you have a high-definition (HD) television set, you can knock your socks off — and for that matter, the socks of your friends and anybody else within viewing distance — by viewing your precious images onscreen. Video also looks awesome on a television set.

To view your images on a regular TV set, follow these steps:

1. Open the AV slot on the side of your camera (see Figure 4-27).

2. Insert the AV cable supplied with your camera into the A/V Out/Digital terminal.

The Canon logo needs to face the back of the camera for proper insertion.

3. Connect the other end of the AV cable to your TV set.

The plugs are color-coded. Connect the red and white plugs to the Audio In ports and the yellow plug to the Video In port on your TV set. Refer to your television manual to choose video as the input source.

4. Press the Playback button.

An image displays on your television set.

5. Use the cross keys to view the next image.

You can also set up a slide show, as I outline in the earlier section, "Viewing Images as a Slide Show."

To view images on an HD television set

1. **Open the AV slot on the side of your camera (see Figure 4-27).**

2. **Connect the HDMI cable HTC-100 (sold separately) to the HDMI Out terminal on your camera.**

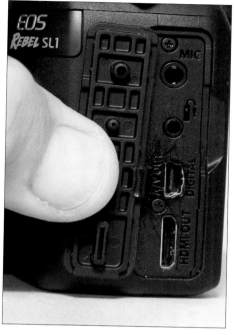

Figure 4-27: Accessing your camera's AV slot.

The HDMI mini logo needs to face the front of the camera for proper insertion.

3. **Connect the HDMI mini cable to your TV set and then press the Playback button.**

An image displays on your television set. Images are adjusted for optimal viewing on an HD television set. If your set can't display the captured images, unplug the HDMI cable from the camera and TV set; then connect the AV cable, as I outline in the preceding steps.

4. **Use the cross keys to view the next image.**

You can also set up a slide show, as I outline in the "Viewing Images as a Slide Show" section earlier in this chapter. In fact, if you're viewing single images and decide you want to view them as a slide show, press the Menu button to display the camera menu on your TV screen and then follow the steps in that section.

Part II
Going beyond Point-and-Shoot Photography

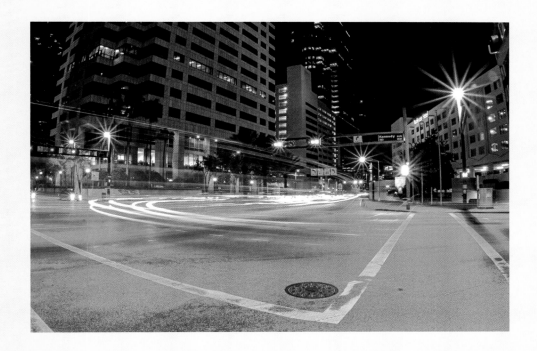

Check out the article "Tips for Movie Shooting" online at www.dummies.com/
extras/canon.

In this part . . .

✔ Find out how to use some of the very cool features of your SL1/
D100. Gain the ability to shoot photographs outside Scene
Intelligent Auto mode and take full advantage of your camera's
high-powered technology.

✔ Get familiar with Live View and compose your images through
the LCD monitor. Discover how to capture movies in Live View
mode as well as how to use Live View features.

✔ Explore how to use the creative shooting modes to photograph
action, wildlife, people, pets, places, and things.

5

Shooting Pictures and Movies in Live View

In This Chapter

▶ Exploring Live View menu options and photography

▶ Shooting and focusing in Live View mode

▶ Using the Quick Control menu

▶ Recording and previewing movies

*P*hotographers who own point-and-shoot cameras use the LCD monitor to compose their pictures, which has some definite advantages. For instance, you can place the camera close to the ground and compose an image through the monitor, or hold the camera over your head to do the same. Digital SLR owners didn't have this option until the Live View mode began popping up on dSLR cameras. And fortunately for you, your SL1/100D has this option. Live View mode has lots of benefits when creating images, including "what you see is what you get." However, Live View mode has a few disadvantages as well. You hold the camera in front of you at arm's length, which, unless you work out at the gym five days a week, can be a bit tiring. Many people use tripods when shooting images and movies using Live View mode.

Your camera has a hybrid autofocus system that you can take advantage of in Live View mode. You can focus by touching the screen. You can also take a picture by touching the screen. How cool is that? In addition to taking great pictures in Live View mode, you can also capture high-definition (HD) movies. You can specify the size of the movie and the frame rate. So if you're ready to go live, read on. In this chapter, I show you how to take pictures, capture movies, and more. (Check out www.dummies.com/cheatsheet/canoneos rebelsl1100d for tips on shooting movies.)

Taking Pictures in Live View

Live View is the bee's knees when it comes to picture taking. You have a much larger view of your subject than you get looking through the viewfinder, and you can compose pictures holding the camera low to the ground — which beats crawling on your belly — or holding the camera high. Figure 5-1 shows the Live View Shooting Settings tab.

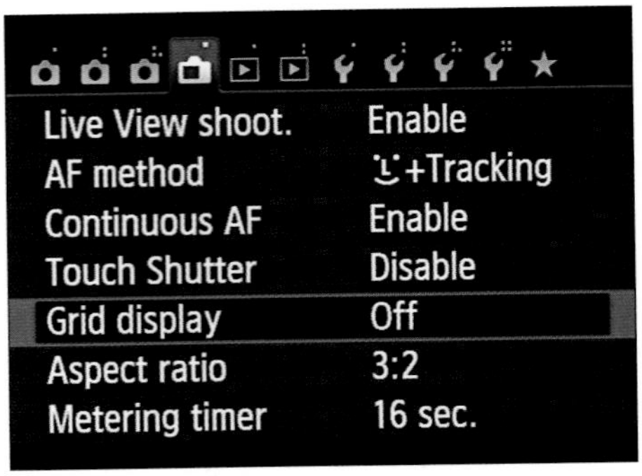

To take pictures in Live View mode

1. **Press the Live View Shooting button.**

   What's in the lens's field of view appears on the camera monitor.

2. **Press the shutter button halfway to focus the scene.**

   When you shoot in Live View, the camera uses the default FlexiZone-Single focusing mode, which gives you a single autofocus point in the center of the LCD monitor. You can use the cross keys to move the AF point when you use the default FlexiZone-Single focusing mode. When the camera achieves focus, the autofocus point turns green (see Figure 5-2).

   The default autofocus mode works great when shooting in Live View mode, but you have other options, as I show you in the "Focusing with Live View" section of this chapter.

3. **Press the shutter button fully to take the picture.**

   The LCD monitor displays the image almost immediately. After the designated image review time, the monitor returns to Live View mode.

4. **Press the Live View Shooting button to exit Live View mode.**

   The camera automatically exits Live View mode after the time designated by auto power-off (see Chapter 1).

Live View shoot.	Enable
AF method	︎+Tracking
Continuous AF	Enable
Touch Shutter	Disable
Grid display	Off
Aspect ratio	3:2
Metering timer	16 sec.

Figure 5-1: Live View at 5:00.

When you shoot in Live View mode, you hold the camera in front of you. That means you can't hold the camera as steadily as you can when shooting through the viewfinder. Using a lens with image stabilization (IS) helps, but if your lens doesn't have that feature, shoot at a higher shutter speed than you normally would. For example, if you're taking pictures in Live View mode with a lens with a focal length with a 35mm equivalent of 85mm, use a shutter speed of 1/200 second or faster. Otherwise, mount the camera on a tripod.

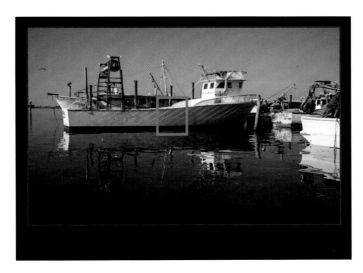

Figure 5-2: Focusing in Live View mode.

Shooting images in Live View mode takes a toll on battery life. You'll get anywhere from 140 to 160 images on a fully charged battery, depending upon the ambient temperature and the amount of images taken with flash.

When you shoot in Live View mode in hot conditions or in direct sunlight, the internal temperature of the camera increases. A white warning icon appears when the internal temperature of the camera is near the danger point, and a red warning light appears when the temperature is at the danger point. When the white warning icon is displayed, image quality will deteriorate if you continue taking pictures. When the red warning icon appears, the camera will probably feel pretty toasty. If you don't disable Live View when the red icon appears, Live View mode will shut down momentarily, and you won't be able to shoot again until the camera cools down. Press the Live View Shooting button to stop Live View as soon as you see the white warning icon and let the camera cool down before taking any more pictures.

When shooting in Live View mode, don't point the camera directly at the sun. Because the mirror is locked up during Live View, exposure to the sun can damage internal components of the camera.

Displaying shooting information

Shooting information is important to many photographers. When you compose a picture in standard shooting mode, you have a lot of information at your disposal in the viewfinder and on the LCD panel. You can also display information when shooting in Live View mode by pressing the Info button. Each time you press the button, the screen changes. The default screen shows the autofocus (AF) points without shooting information. Press the Info button once to display the screen, as shown in Figure 5-3.

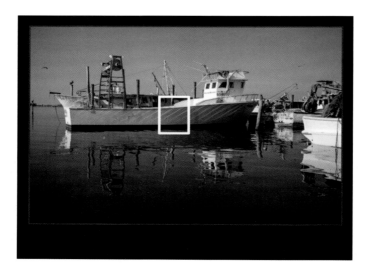

Figure 5-3: Displaying information while shooting in Live View mode.

The information displayed depends on the autofocus mode you choose. The first level of information displays what's in front of the camera as captured by the sensor, a single autofocus point, multiple autofocus points, or a frame depending on which autofocus mode you select. The next level of information displays the number of possible shots, battery status, a button that you touch to access the Quick Control menu, a button you can touch to magnify the view, the ISO setting, the exposure compensation scale, exposure information based on the shooting mode you're using, plus a button you can touch to enable Touch Shutter. If you choose the FlexiZone AF (autofocus) method, a frame is displayed on the LCD monitor.

When you press the shutter button, AF points that are used to achieve focus are highlighted. If you chose the FlexiZone-Single AF point method, an AF point appears on the display, which can be moved to another spot in the frame (use the cross keys). Press the shutter button halfway, and the AF point will turn green when the camera achieves focus and the shutter speed and aperture display. If you choose the Quick autofocus mode, the nine points you normally see when shooting through the viewfinder are displayed. The points that are used to achieve focus are highlighted in green when the resulting image is displayed onscreen. When shooting in Quick autofocus mode, you don't get a preview of which points will be used to achieve focus when you press the shutter button halfway.

To view additional information, press the Info button again. The second level of information (see Figure 5-4) displays all the information from the preceding screen with these additions: shooting mode, drive/self timer, metering mode, image recording quality, Live View AF mode, image format, a button to enable Touch Shutter, Auto Lighting Optimizer mode, picture style, and white balance. You see additional information if you've enabled

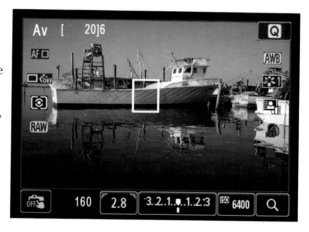

Figure 5-4: Displaying more information.

features, such as flash exposure bracketing, automatic exposure bracketing, and so on. You also see buttons on the screen you can touch for autofocus options, to view the Quick Control menu, and so on.

If you accept the default option of Exposure Simulation, press the Info button again, and a histogram appears (see Figure 5-5). You can use this information to increase or decrease the exposure with exposure compensation.

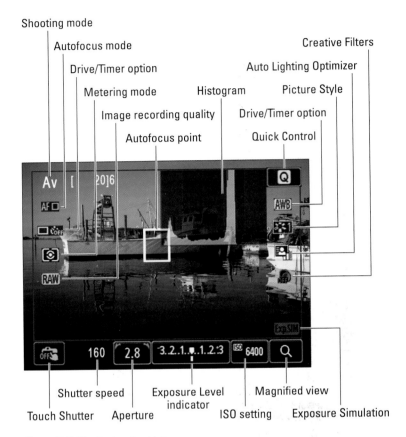

Shooting mode
Autofocus mode
Drive/Timer option
Metering mode
Image recording quality
Autofocus point

Histogram

Creative Filters
Auto Lighting Optimizer
Picture Style
Drive/Timer option
Quick Control

Touch Shutter
Shutter speed
Aperture
Exposure Level indicator
ISO setting
Magnified view
Exposure Simulation

Figure 5-5: Displaying the histogram.

Focusing with Live View

When you shoot in Live View mode, you have four focusing options. Three options are used for taking photographs of landscapes and objects, and the other focusing mode is used to detect faces. To specify the autofocus (AF) mode

1. Press the Menu button.

2. Use the cross keys to navigate to the Live View Shooting Settings tab.

3. Use the cross keys to highlight AF Method (see the left image in Figure 5-6) and then press the Set button.

The Live View AF Method options display on the camera LCD monitor (see the right image in Figure 5-6).

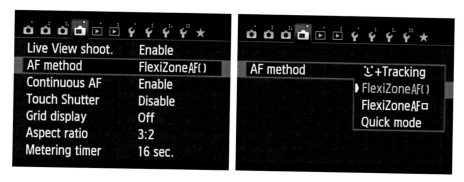

Figure 5-6: Choosing a Live View AF mode.

4. Use cross keys to highlight one of the following options:

- *Face Detection and Tracking:* This is your first menu choice; the face detection is denoted by the smiley face. In essence, this focus mode detects faces (and maybe statues with heads) and tracks the face if your subject moves.

- *FlexiZone-Multiple AF Points:* When you choose this mode, the camera uses the sensor to achieve focus. You can use up to 31 autofocus points with which to achieve focus. If the autofocus point isn't over the part of the scene or subject you're photographing that must be in focus, you can use the cross keys to move the autofocus point to the desired position.

When you use this mode, it may take longer for the camera to achieve focus than when using the Quick mode.

- *FlexiZone-Single AF Point:* The default FlexiZone autofocus method uses a single autofocus point in the center of the monitor to achieve focus. You can use the cross keys to reposition the autofocus point to the part of the image that must be in focus.

- *Quick Mode:* Uses the camera AF sensor to focus the image. As the name implies, this mode is quicker than using the camera sensor. The Live View image momentarily blacks out while the camera achieves focus. You also have all 9 autofocus points to work with.

5. Press the Set button.

The selected focusing mode is used whenever you shoot images with Live View.

After you choose a Live View autofocus mode, it's time to focus on a subject.

To focus on people using the Face Detection and Tracking Live View focusing mode

 1. Press the Live View Shooting/Movie Shooting button to enable Live View shooting.

The Live View image appears on the LCD monitor.

 2. Press the shutter button halfway.

The camera sensor detects faces in front of the lens by placing a rectangular AF frame over them. When the camera achieves focus, the frame turns green, and the camera beeps. If the camera detects multiple faces, an AF frame with a right- and left-pointing arrow appears.

3. Use the cross keys to drag the AF frame over the person who's the center of interest and should be in focus.

4. Press the shutter button fully.

The camera takes the picture.

To focus the camera while using FlexiZone-Multiple AF point Live Mode focusing

 1. Press the Live View Shooting/Movie Shooting button to enable Live View shooting.

The Live View image appears on the camera LCD monitor.

 2. Press the shutter button halfway to achieve focus.

Multiple AF points appear over the subjects the camera uses to achieve focus.

3. Press the shutter button fully to take the picture.

Here's the fix if the camera doesn't pick up focus on the desired subjects using FlexiZone-Multiple AF points:

 1. Press the Erase button to display an autofocus zone in the center of the image.

 2. Use the cross key to move the autofocus zone over the area of the image that contains the subjects you want to focus on.

3. Press the shutter button halfway to achieve focus.

AF points appear within the AF Zone.

4. Press the shutter button fully to take the picture.

To focus the camera while using FlexiZone-Single AF point Live Mode focusing

1. Press the Live View Shooting/Movie Shooting button to enable Live View shooting.

The Live View image appears on the camera LCD monitor, and a single AF point appears in the center of the frame.

2. If the AF point isn't over the subject you want the camera to focus on, use the cross keys to move the AF point there.

3. Press the shutter button halfway to achieve focus.

The AF point turns green when the camera achieves focus, and the camera beeps.

4. Press the shutter button fully.

The camera takes the picture.

When you focus using Quick Live View focusing mode, the nine autofocus points you use when shooting in normal mode are used to achieve focus. To focus with the Quick Live View focusing mode

1. Press the Live View Shooting/Movie Shooting button to enable Live View shooting.

The AF points for the autofocus point mode you specify for standard shooting appear on the camera LCD monitor. A white frame appears over the AF points. Nine autofocus points appear on the LCD monitor.

2. Press the shutter button halfway to achieve focus.

The point(s) used to achieve focus turns green. Skip to Step 5.

3. If the camera didn't focus over the subject that is to be the focal point of your image, switch to a single AF point (as outlined in Chapter 7), and then use the cross keys to move the AF point over the focal point of your image.

4. Press the shutter button halfway.

The single AF point should turn green, and the camera should beep. If those two things don't happen, you may have to move the AF point again over a different object or focus the camera manually.

5. Press the shutter button fully.

The camera takes the picture.

If the camera has a difficult time achieving focus in Live View mode, switch your lens to manual focus and then press the AF Point Select/Magnify button to display a small frame in the center of the image. You can then use the cross keys to move the frame over the part of the subject or scene that you're photographing that needs to be in sharp focus. Press the AF Point Selection/Magnify button again to magnify the area in the frame five times; press the AF Point Selection/Magnify button one more time to magnify the area 10 times. You can then easily focus manually on the magnified portion of the scene. Alternatively, you can press the magnifying glass in the lower-left corner of the screen instead of the AF Point Selection/Magnify button to magnify the area.

Using the Quick Control menu to shoot pictures in Live View mode

When you shoot in Live View mode, you can quickly change the Auto Lighting Optimizer, focusing mode, the image quality, and more through the Quick Control menu. If you're using the Quick Live View autofocus (AF) mode, you can change the AF points as well. To change Live View Shooting settings with the Quick Control menu

1. Press the Live View Shooting/ Movie Shooting button to enable Live View shooting and then press the Quick Control button.

The Quick Control menu appears on the LCD monitor (see Figure 5-7).

2. Use the cross keys to navigate to and highlight a setting.

The setting icon becomes orange.

3. Use the cross keys or rotate the Main dial to change the setting.

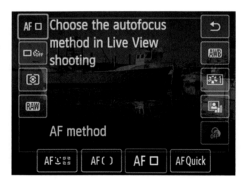

Figure 5-7: Using the Live View Quick Control menu.

You see different icons onscreen. When you select a shooting setting with a cross key, you see text onscreen describing what you can change with the mode, as well as text near the bottom of the screen that describes the shooting setting you are changing. You also see icons at the bottom of the screen for each option for the shooting setting. The icon is selected when you press the left or right cross key or rotate the Main dial and the text for the new option displays.

4. **After changing a shooting setting, use the cross keys to navigate to change other settings as needed and then press the shutter button halfway to return to Live View Shooting mode.**

You're ready to start shooting with your new settings.

Displaying a grid in Live View mode

When shooting in Live View mode, you can display a grid on the LCD monitor. This grid is useful when aligning objects that are supposed to be horizontal or vertical, such as the side of a building. You can also use the grid when composing your images (see Chapter 8). You have two grids from which to choose: a 3 x 3 grid or a 6 x 4 grid. In my opinion, the first grid (with nine squares) is the most useful. This grid is identical to the Rule of Thirds (see Chapter 8) photographers use when composing images.

To display a grid on the camera LCD monitor when shooting in Live View mode

1. **Press the Menu button.**

The previously used menu appears.

2. **Use the cross keys to navigate to the Live View Shooting Settings tab.**

3. **Use the cross keys to highlight Grid Display (see the left image in Figure 5-8) and then press the Set button.**

The Grid Display options display (see the right image in Figure 5-8).

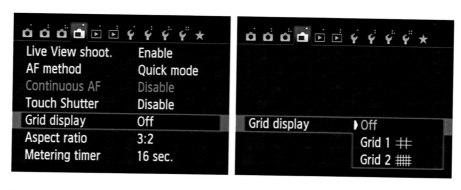

Figure 5-8: Enable the Live View grid here.

4. **Use the cross keys to highlight the desired grid.**

5. **Press Set.**

   The selected grid displays in the monitor when you shoot in Live View mode.

Exploring Other Useful Live View Options

In the previous sections of this chapter, I discuss menu commands that enable Live View shooting, choose a Live View autofocus mode, and display a grid over the LCD monitor while shooting in Live View mode. You may find other Live View menu options and one custom function (that displays a cropping grid) useful.

 To take a look at the other options, press the Menu button and use the cross keys to navigate to the Live View Shooting Settings tab (see Figure 5-9).

Using the cross keys or tapping to select, review the following commands:

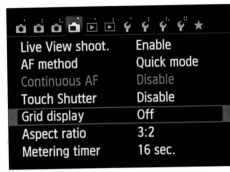

Figure 5-9: Choose Live View options here.

- ✔ **Live View Shooting:** This option is enabled by default. In the event you ever want to disable Live View shooting, select this command and then press Set to display the options. Use the cross keys to highlight Disable and then press the Set button. After doing so, pressing the Live View Shooting/ Movie Shooting button has no effect.

- ✔ **AF Method:** This option determines the autofocus option used to focus scenes or subjects when shooting in Live View mode.

- ✔ **Continuous AF:** This option is available with every autofocus mode except Quick Autofocus. This option is enabled by default and causes the camera to seek focus even when your finger is not pressing the shutter button halfway. This option makes it easier to achieve focus quickly but can drain the battery quicker. In the event you ever want to disable this option, select this command and then press Set to display the options. Use the cross keys to highlight Disable and then press Set.

✒ **Touch Shutter:** This option is disabled by default. If you enable this option, you can focus on a specific part of the scene on your LCD monitor by touching that area, which will simultaneously take a picture at the same time. This enables Touch Shutter any time you switch to Live View shooting. I find this to be a tad quirky, and instead always press the shutter button to take pictures, even in Live View mode. If you want to use Touch Shutter occasionally, you can enable it by touching the icon in the lower-left corner of the LCD monitor. When you enable Touch Shutter by touching the icon, it stays in effect until you touch the icon again.

✒ **Grid Display:** This option determines whether you display a 3 x 3 grid, a 6 x 4 grid, or no grid.

✒ **Aspect Ratio:** With this option, you can change the aspect ratio of the image in camera. This option is available only for images you capture in JPEG format. I don't find this option especially useful. I suggest you stick with the default 3:2 aspect ratio, which is the aspect ratio of the sensor. This enables you to create images with all the pixels the sensor is capable of capturing. You can always crop the image to a different aspect ratio in your favorite image-editing application.

✒ **Metering Timer:** This option enables you to change how long time exposure settings are displayed on the LCD monitor. The default setting of 16 seconds gives you plenty of time to examine the histogram and change exposure compensation, but you can decrease the display time to 4 seconds or increase it to as long as 30 minutes. Note that if you choose a longer duration than the default, your battery will not last as long.

Making Movies with Your Camera

With your SL1/100D, you can create high-definition (HD) video. SD (Standard Definition) video is great for the web or for viewing video on portable devices, such as the iPad, but when you view video on a large screen monitor, HD gives you more clarity than SD. Your camera records video in Apple's QuickTime MOV format. You can specify the size of the movies you capture and the frame rate. In the following sections, I show you how to capture video and other movie-shooting tasks with your camera.

When you capture video, the Live View Shooting Settings tab becomes a Video Settings tab, and a second additional Video Settings tab appears (see Figure 5-10). The first Video Settings tab is identical to the Live View Shooting Settings tab I discuss earlier.

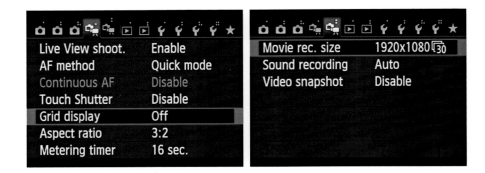

Figure 5-10: Menus for video settings.

Recording movies

Recording movies on your SL1/100D is easy. Just flip a switch and push a button and you're recording. And you see the whole movie unfold on the camera LCD monitor. When you've recorded your fill, push the button again to stop recording and then preview the movie on the LCD monitor to decide whether you want to keep it.

When recording movies in a shooting mode other than M (Manual), the camera automatically determines the aperture, shutter speed, and ISO speed based on the current ambient lighting conditions. Monaural (one channel) sound is recorded with your movie unless you disable sound or insert a stereo microphone into the microphone in-port on the side of the camera.

I suggest you use Aperture Priority mode to record video because you can control how much of the scene you're recording is in focus by aperture choice. Choose a small aperture (large f-stop value) when you want a large depth of field. A small aperture with a wide angle lens is the perfect recipe for recording a video of a beautiful landscape like the Grand Canyon. Choose a large aperture (small f-stop value) when you're recording a video of a person. In conjunction with a medium telephoto lens with a focal length of 80 or 105 mm, your subject will be in focus, but the foreground and background will be out of focus.

To record a movie

1. **Move the power switch to video (the icon that looks like a movie camera).**

   The image appears on the LCD monitor.

2. **Rotate the Mode dial to choose the desired shooting mode.**

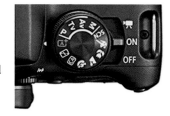

3. Press the shutter button halfway to achieve focus.

When you record movies, you use one of the Live View autofocus modes that I discuss in the "Focusing with Live View" section earlier in this chapter. If you opt for the Continuous AF option discussed previously, the camera should snap into focus fairly quickly. *Note:* The Quick AF method cannot be used for movie shooting.

4. Press the Live View Shooting/Movie Shooting button.

As your movie records, here's what you see on the LCD monitor:

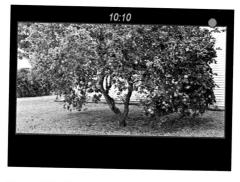

Figure 5-11: Quiet, numbskulls. We're making a movie here.

- A red dot appears in the upper-right corner, as shown in Figure 5-11. The elapsed time appears in the center of the frame near the top.

- A semi-transparent frame appears around the edge of the Live View image.

- The area inside the frame is what the camera records.

Your camera will update exposure and focus as you move the camera. If you move from a dark to a bright area, the camera may take a second or two to meter accurately and focus.

5. Press the Start/Stop button.

Recording stops and the red dot disappears.

Maximum recording time for a 16GB card at the maximum video dimensions is 44 minutes. The maximum amount of time for which you can continuously record video is 29 minutes and 59 seconds. If you record a video that reaches maximum duration, the camera will automatically shut off. Your camera cannot record videos with a file size larger than 4GB. However, if you do reach that magic number, your camera will automatically create a new file so you can record without interruption.

Displaying video shooting information

When recording video, you can display a lot of shooting information, a little information, or no information. You can display the aperture and shutter speed, battery information, exposure compensation scale, autofocus mode, and much more, depending on which information screen you display.

To display information when recording movies, move the power switch to video (the icon that looks like a movie camera) and press the Info button. There are three screens of information. You press the Info button again (and again) to see all the information screens:

- ✔ **1:** The first shooting information screen displays the focus frame. This is perfect for when you're going commando and want to see every subtle nuance of the scene you're recording.

- ✔ **2:** The second shooting screen displays the battery information, aperture, ISO speed rating, and the exposure compensation scale.

- ✔ **3:** The final screen adds the camera mode and any other shooting commands you may be using to capture your video.

Changing video dimensions and frame rate

Your camera can capture HD video with dimensions of up to 1920 x 1080 and a frame rate up to 60 frames per second (fps). You can modify the video dimensions and frame rate to suit your intended destination.

The video dimension and frame rate options are shown in the right image of Figure 5-12. Yikes. I know what you're thinking. It looks all Greek. Well, it looked Greek to me, too, until the great Fredrico Fettuccini spelled it all out with garlic breath and a hint of Chianti. One of the settings you can choose from is 1920 30. The first option is the dimension, and the second is the frame rate measure in frames per second. Here's what all the symbols stand for:

- ✔ **1920 30:** This stands for 1920 x 1080, which is the dimension of the video in pixels. It's full HD — the real deal, Lucille — captured at 30 fps.

- ✔ **1920 24:** This stands for 1920 x 1080, which is the dimension of the video in pixels. It's full HD, captured at 24 fps. This setting is the same frame rate as movie video cameras (can you say, *Steven Spielberg?*) used for the big silver screen. The resulting video has a slightly different look, which is reminiscent of video on the big screen.

- ✔ **1280 60:** This stands for 1280 x 720, which is the dimension of this option in pixels. It's HD video as well captured at 60 fps.

- ✔ **640 30:** This stands for 640 x 480, the dimension of the video in pixels. This is standard-definition video captured at 30 fps.

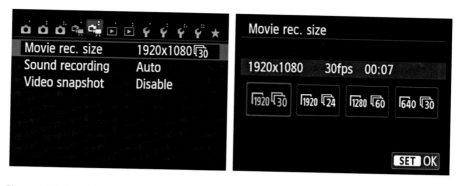

Figure 5-12: Set video dimensions and frame rate here.

To change video dimensions and frame rate

1. **Move the power switch to video (the icon that looks like a movie camera).**

   The image appears on the LCD monitor.

2. **Press the Menu button.**

   The last used menu displays.

3. **Use the cross keys to navigate to the Video Settings 2 tab.**

   Your Live View video recording options display.

4. **Use the cross keys to highlight Movie Rec. Size (refer to the left image in Figure 5-12) and then press the Set button.**

5. **Use the cross keys to select the desired video dimension and frame rate; then press Set.**

6. **Press the Set button.**

   You're ready to record video with the specified dimension and frame rate.

For more information about digital video, check out *Digital SLR Video and Filmmaking For Dummies* by John Carucci.

Changing audio recording options

When you record video with your SL1/100D, you record audio as well. You can change the record level, disable audio, and enable a wind filter and a sound attenuator. And you thought those little holes on top of the camera were just a dinky microphone. To beef up the audio in your movies

1. **Move the power switch to video (the icon that looks like a movie camera).**

   The image appears on the LCD monitor.

2. **Press the Menu button.**

   The last used menu displays.

3. **Use the cross keys to navigate to the Video Settings 2 tab.**

4. **Use the cross keys to navigate to Sound Recording (see the left image in Figure 5-13) and then press Set.**

   The Sound Recording options appear (see the right image in Figure 5-13).

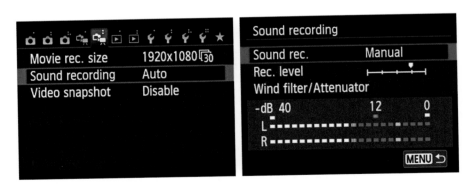

Figure 5-13: Change sound recording options here.

5. **Use the cross keys to highlight Manual and then press Set.**

    The menu to set the sound level (Rec. Level) manually appears (see the left image in Figure 5-14). This menu gives you a right and left meter, which you use to accurately set the recording level. The meters record the highest decibel rating and hold it for three seconds.

6. **While looking at the peak-level meter, rotate the Main dial until the loudest sound recorded is −12 on the scale.**

    If the sound exceeds 0, the sound will be *clipped* (distorted).

7. **After setting the sound level, use the cross keys to highlight Wind Filter/Attenuator and then press Set.**

    The menu to enable or disable these options appears (see the right image in Figure 5-14). The wind filter attempts to reduce wind noise when you capture video in windy conditions, and the attenuator prevents sudden loud noises from distorting.

8. **To enable either option, highlight it with the cross keys, press Set, use the cross keys to highlight Enable, and then press Set.**

9. **Press Menu to apply the changes.**

    The recording level is optimum for the scene you're recording. You'll have to reset the levels when you record a scene in a louder or quieter environment.

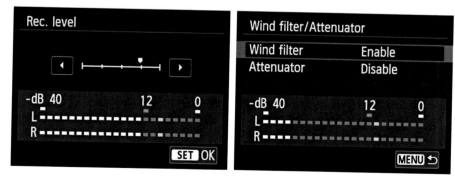

Figure 5-14: Setting sound manually and using the Wind Filter and Attenuator.

Using the Quick Control menu to shoot video in Live View mode

When you shoot video in Live View mode, you can quickly change the movie dimensions, frame rate, and much more through the Quick Control menu. To change Live View Shooting options with the Quick Control menu

1. **Move the power switch to video (the icon that looks like a movie camera).**

   The image appears on the LCD monitor.

2. **Press the Quick Control button.**

   The movie shooting Quick Control menu appears onscreen.

3. **Use the cross keys to select and highlight an option.**

   The option icon becomes orange.

4. **Use the cross keys or rotate the Main dial to change the option setting.**

   As you press the cross keys or rotate the Main dial, you select different settings and text appears onscreen to designate the name of the setting to which you're changing. You also see text that describes what the setting does.

5. **Follow Steps 3 and 4 to change other settings as needed, and then press the shutter button halfway.**

   You're ready to start capturing video with your new settings.

The default focusing mode for video is AF Servo. With this focusing mode, the camera updates focus when your subject moves. When shooting in AF Servo mode, the camera will have a hard time focusing in the following conditions:

- When recording a subject moving rapidly toward or away from the camera
- When recording a subject moving close to the camera

If you use a zoom lens when capturing video in AF Servo mode and you zoom in or out, the camera may temporarily stop focusing.

Taking a still picture while recording a movie

You can take a picture while recording a movie. This option is handy when you're making a recording, and something interesting happens that you want to save as a still picture. The still image uses the exposure information displayed in the Live View Shooting information. The image is the format and quality you specify with the camera menu. To take a still picture while recording a video

1. **Begin recording a movie.**

2. **Press the shutter button fully when you see something you want to record as a still image.**

   The Live View turns black while the camera takes the picture. You may notice a glitch at that point in the video unless you're using a fast SD card.

Previewing Movies on the Camera LCD Monitor

You can preview movies in all their glory on the camera LCD monitor. When you preview a movie, buttons appear that let you play the movie at full speed or in slow motion, pause the movie, preview it frame by frame, and navigate to the first or last frame. You can also edit movies in the camera, which I show you how to do in Chapter 12. To preview a movie on the camera LCD monitor

1. **Press the Playback button to navigate to the desired movie.**

   You can preview images and movies as single images or thumbnails. A movie is designated by an old-fashioned movie camera icon when you view single images or with a filmstrip border when you view them as thumbnails.

2. **Press the Set button.**

   Buttons appear beneath the movie, as shown in Figure 5-15, from left to right:

   - *Play:* Plays the movie at full speed.

   - *Slow Motion:* Plays the movie in slow motion.

   - *First Frame:* Rewinds the movie to the first frame.

   - *Previous Frame:* Rewinds the movie to the previous frame.

   - *Next Frame:* Fast-forwards to the next frame.

   - *Last Frame:* Fast-forwards to the last frame.

   - *Background Music:* Gives you the option to play background music when you preview the video on your camera. You add background music to the card from the EOS Utility disk.

   - *Edit:* Edits the movie.

3. **Use the cross keys or tap to select an option.**

4. **Press the Set button to perform the selected option.**

   If you choose Edit, you can edit the movie in-camera, as I show you in Chapter 12.

5. **Press Menu to exit movie playing mode.**

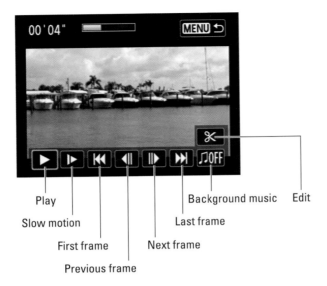

Figure 5-15: Please pass the popcorn.

6

Leaving Auto Mode Behind

Your camera has a plethora of features designed to enable you to capture stunning images. You can shoot images continuously at a rate of 4 frames per second (fps), which is great for action photography. Your camera also has modes that take you way beyond point-and-shoot photography. When you take photographs with either Aperture Priority (Av) or Shutter Priority (Tv) mode, you supply one part of the exposure equation, and your SL1/100D supplies the other part. Plus, you can do all sorts of things to hedge your bet to make sure you get stellar photos from your camera. For example, you can use exposure compensation when you need to tweak the exposure the camera meters. You can also bracket exposure and tweak the white balance.

If you're a geek photographer like me who likes complete control over every aspect of your photography, you'll love the features I show you in this chapter.

Your camera's metering device examines the scene and determines which shutter speed and f-stop combination will yield a properly exposed image. The camera can choose a fast shutter speed and large aperture, or a slow shutter speed and small aperture.

For example, when you take pictures in Scene Intelligent Auto or Creative Auto mode, the camera makes both decisions for you. And that's fine if that's what you want — but you can be just as smart (if not smarter) than the processor inside your camera. You can take creative control of the reins and supply one piece of the puzzle, and the camera will supply the rest. Sweet. And here's why you want to graduate to this level of control: When you're taking certain types of pictures, it makes sense to determine which f-stop will be best for what you're photographing. In other scenarios, it makes more sense to choose the shutter speed and let the camera determine the f-stop. In the upcoming sections, I show you how to use the Creative shooting modes your camera has to offer. In Chapter 8, I show you how to use these modes for specific picture-taking situations.

Using Your Camera's Creative Exposure Modes

With your SL1/100D, you can become a very creative photographer. The SCN, Scene Intelligent Auto, and Creative Auto shooting modes are useful when you're getting used to the camera. After you know where the controls are, though, branch out and use shooting modes where you control how your images are exposed. In the upcoming sections, I show you how to expose images with the Creative shooting modes: P (Programmed Auto Exposure), Av (Aperture Priority), Tv (Shutter Priority), M (Manual), and Bulb.

The following list describes each mode in detail:

- **Programmed Auto Exposure mode (P):** This mode is like stepping out of the kids' pool into the shallow end of the deep pool. The camera still determines what shutter speed and aperture will yield a perfectly exposed image, but you can change the values to suit the type of scene you're photographing.

- **Shutter Priority mode (Tv):** In this mode, you determine the shutter speed, and the camera meter does the math to determine what f-stop value (aperture) is needed to create a pixel-perfect image. The shutter speed determines how long the shutter remains open. A fast shutter speed stops action, and a slow shutter speed will cause fast moving objects to blur, which can be used creatively, as I show you in Chapter 8.

- **Aperture Priority mode (Av):** When you switch to this mode, you supply the f-stop value (aperture; how wide the lens is), and the camera determines what shutter speed will result in a perfectly exposed image.

✔ **Manual mode (M):** When you decide to shoot in this mode, you supply the shutter speed and f-stop, but the camera does give you some help in determining whether the combination you provide will yield a perfectly exposed image.

✔ **Bulb:** When you decide to use this mode, the shutter stays open for as long as you hold the shutter button open. This mode is not on the Mode dial but is accessed from the Manual (M) mode. This mode is used for special effects like star trails, or recording headlight patterns at night. When you shoot in this mode, you mount the camera on a tripod and use a remote to trigger the shutter.

Before you can determine which mode is best for you, you need to understand how exposure works, which is the topic of the next section.

Understanding how exposure works in the camera

Your SL1/100D exposes images pretty much the same way film cameras do. Light enters the camera through the lens and is recorded. On a film camera, the light is captured on treated film. A digital camera uses a sensor instead. The processor (which in essence is a small computer) converts the pixels captured by the sensor into a usable image, which is transferred to the camera's memory (or a memory card). The amount of time the shutter is open and the amount of light entering the camera determines whether the resulting image is too dark, too bright, or properly exposed.

The duration of the exposure is the *shutter speed*. Your camera has a shutter speed range from as long as 30 seconds to as short as 1/4000 second. A fast shutter speed "stops" action, and a slow shutter speed leaves the shutter open for a long time to record images in low-light situations.

The *aperture* is the opening in the lens that lets light into the camera when the shutter opens. You can change the aperture diameter to let a lot, or a small amount, of light into the camera. The *f-stop value* determines the size of the aperture. A low f-stop value (large aperture) lets a lot of light into the camera, and a high f-stop value (small aperture) lets a small amount of light into the camera. Depending on the lens you're using, the f-stop range can be from f/1.2 (sends huge gobs of light into the camera) to f/32 (lets a minuscule splash of light into the camera). The f-stop also determines the depth of field, a concept I explain in the "Controlling depth of field" section later in this chapter.

The duration of the exposure (shutter speed) and aperture (f-stop value) combination determines the exposure. For each lighting scenario you encounter, several different combinations render a perfectly exposed photograph. You use different combinations for different types of photography. The camera's metering device examines the scene and determines which shutter speed and f-stop combination will yield a properly exposed image. The camera can choose a fast shutter speed and large aperture, or a slow shutter speed and small aperture.

Using Programmed Auto Exposure mode

When you take pictures with the Programmed Auto Exposure mode, the camera determines the shutter speed and aperture (f-stop value) that yields a properly exposed image for the lighting conditions. Even though this sounds identical to Scene Intelligent Auto mode, with this mode you can change the AF (autofocus) mode, Drive mode, ISO speed, picture style, and more. You can also change the shutter speed and aperture to suit the scene you're photographing. To take pictures in Programmed Auto Exposure mode

1. **Rotate the Mode dial to P (see Figure 6-1).**

2. **Press the ISO button and then rotate the Main dial to change the ISO speed to the desired setting.**

   You can see the ISO speed change in the viewfinder. Alternatively, if you move your eye away from the viewfinder, the ISO setting menu is displayed on the LCD monitor (see Figure 6-2). You can either tap the desired ISO speed or use the cross keys to select the desired ISO. Higher ISO speeds make the camera sensor more sensitive to light, which is ideal when you're photographing in dim light or at night. For more information on changing ISO speed, see Chapter 7.

3. **Press the shutter button halfway to achieve focus.**

   The green dot on the right side of the viewfinder appears when the camera achieves focus. If the dot is flashing, the camera can't achieve focus, and you must manually focus the camera.

4. **Check the shutter speed and aperture.**

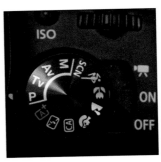

Figure 6-1: Rotate the Mode dial to P.

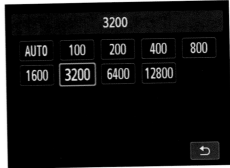

Figure 6-2: Setting the ISO.

When you press the shutter button halfway, the camera meters the scene and determines the shutter speed and aperture needed for a properly exposed image based on the ambient light. You can use the viewfinder or the LCD monitor (see Figure 6-3) to check the shutter speed and aperture. If you notice a shutter speed of 4000 and the minimum aperture for the lens blinking, the image will be overexposed. If you notice a shutter speed of 30 seconds and the maximum aperture for the lens blinking, the image will be underexposed.

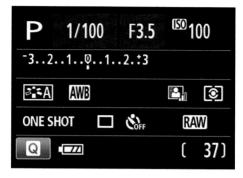

Figure 6-3: Check the shutter speed and aperture.

5. **Press the shutter button fully to take the picture.**

   The image displays almost immediately on your LCD monitor.

You can shift the exposure and choose a different shutter speed and aperture combination. Use this option when you want to shoot with a faster shutter speed to freeze action or a different aperture to control depth of field. Here's how to shift the Programmed Auto Exposure:

1. **Follow Steps 1–3 of the preceding instructions; then press the shutter button halfway.**

   The camera achieves focus.

2. **Rotate the Main dial.**

   As you rotate the dial, you see different shutter speed and aperture combinations in the viewfinder. Alternatively, you can move your eye away from the viewfinder, and see the settings on the LCD monitor (see Figure 6-4). If you notice that the shutter speed is too slow for a blur-free picture, put the camera on a tripod or increase the ISO speed setting.

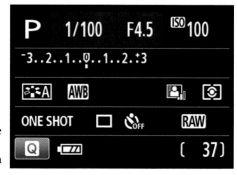

Figure 6-4: You can shift programmed exposure.

3. **When you see the desired combination of shutter speed and aperture, press the shutter button fully to take the picture.**

   The image appears almost immediately on your LCD monitor.

Using Aperture Priority mode

If you like to photograph landscapes or portraits, Aperture Priority mode is right up your alley. When you take pictures with Aperture Priority mode, you choose the desired f-stop, and the camera supplies the proper shutter speed to achieve a properly exposed image. A large aperture (small f-stop value) lets a lot of light into the camera, and a small aperture (large f-stop value) lets a small amount of light into the camera.

The benefit of shooting in Aperture Priority mode is that you have more control over the depth of field. (See the "Controlling depth of field" section later in this chapter.) You also have access to all the other options, such as setting the ISO speed, choosing a picture style, changing the AF mode or Drive mode, and so on. To take pictures with Aperture Priority mode

1. **Rotate the Mode dial to Av (Aperture value) (see Figure 6-5).**

2. **Press the ISO button and then rotate the Main dial to change the ISO speed to the desired setting.**

   When choosing an ISO speed, choose the slowest speed for the available lighting conditions. For more information on changing ISO speed, see Chapter 7.

3. **Rotate the Main dial to select the desired f-stop.**

   As you change the aperture, the camera calculates the proper shutter speed to achieve a properly exposed image. As you rotate the dial, monitor the shutter speed in the viewfinder or on the LCD monitor (if you move your eye away from the viewfinder), as shown in Figure 6-6.

   If you notice that the shutter speed is too slow for a blur-free picture, you have to put the camera on a tripod or increase the ISO speed setting. If you see the slowest shutter speed

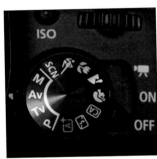

Figure 6-5: Rotate the Mode dial to Aperture Priority.

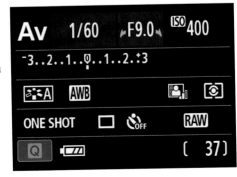

Figure 6-6: Make sure the shutter speed is fast enough for a blur-free picture.

(30 seconds) blinking, the image will be underexposed with the selected f-stop. If you see the fastest shutter speed (1/4000 second) blinking, the image will be overexposed with the selected f-stop.

The scenario in Figure 6-6 would limit the photographer who wants to take a picture hand-holding the camera to a lens with a focal length that is the 35mm equivalent of 50mm.

4. Press the shutter button halfway to achieve focus.

A green dot appears in the viewfinder when the camera achieves focus.

5. Press the shutter button fully to take the picture.

Controlling depth of field

Depth of field determines how much of your image looks sharp and is in apparent focus in front of and behind your subject. When you're taking pictures of landscapes on a bright sunny day, you want a depth of field that produces an image in which you can see the details for miles and miles and miles. Other times, you want to have a very shallow depth of field in which your subject is in sharp focus but the foreground and background are a pleasant out-of-focus blur, like when you're shooting a portrait.

You control the depth of field in an image by selecting the f-stop in Aperture Priority (Av) mode and letting the camera do the math to determine what shutter speed will yield a properly exposed image. You get a limited depth of field when using a small f-stop value (large aperture), which lets a lot of light into the camera. A lens with a large maximum aperture is considered a "fast" lens. The kit lens supplied with your camera is not considered a fast lens because it doesn't have a larger aperture. A fast lens

- Has an f-stop value of 2.8 or smaller
- Gives you the capability to shoot in low-light conditions
- Gives you a wonderfully shallow depth of field

When shooting at a lens's smallest f-stop value, you're letting the most light into the camera — shooting "wide open." The lens you use also determines how large the depth of field will be for a given f-stop. At the same f-stop, a wide angle lens has a greater depth of field than a telephoto lens. When you're photographing a landscape, the ideal recipe is a wide angle lens and a small aperture (large f-stop value). When you're shooting a portrait of someone, you want a shallow depth of field. Therefore, a telephoto lens with a focal length that is the 35mm equivalent of 85mm with a large aperture (small f-stop value) is the ideal solution.

Figure 6-7 shows two pictures of the same subject. The first image was shot with an exposure of 1/640 second at f/1.8, and the second image was shot with an exposure of 1/80 second at f/10. In both cases, I focused on the subject. Notice, though, how much more of the image shot at f/10 is in focus.

The detail of the flowers in the second shot distracts the viewer's attention from the subject. The first image has a shallow depth of field that draws the viewer's attention to the subject.

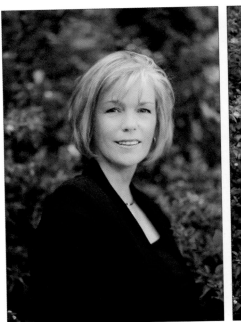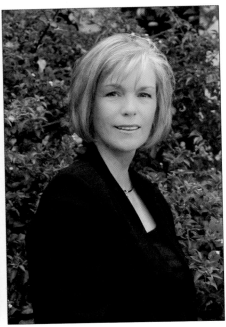

Figure 6-7: The f-stop you choose determines the depth of field.

Using depth of field preview

When you compose a scene through your viewfinder, the camera aperture is wide open, which means you have no idea how much depth of field you'll have in the resulting image. You can, however, preview the depth of field for a selected f-stop by simply pressing a button on your camera. To preview depth of field

1. **Compose the picture and choose the desired f-stop in Aperture Priority (Av) mode.**

   See the section, "Using Aperture Priority mode," earlier in this chapter if you need help.

2. **Press the shutter button halfway to achieve focus.**

   A green dot shines solid on the right side of the viewfinder when the camera focuses on your subject.

3. Press the Depth of Field preview button (see Figure 6-8).

The button is conveniently located on the left side of the camera when your camera is pointed toward your subject. You can easily locate the button by feel. On this camera, I can press the button with the thumb on my left hand. When you press the button, the image in the viewfinder may become dim, especially when you're using a small aperture (large f-stop number) that doesn't let a lot of light into the camera. Don't worry; the camera chooses the proper shutter speed to compensate for the f-stop you select.

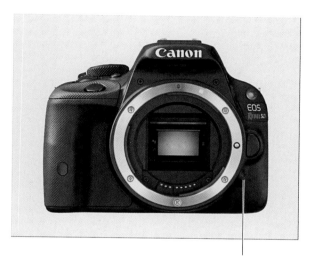

Depth of Field preview button

Figure 6-8: Find the Depth of Field preview button here.

Now check out how much of the image is in apparent focus in front of and behind your subject. To see what the depth of field looks like with different f-stops:

    a. Select what you think is the optimal f-stop for the scene you're photo-graphing.

    b. Press the shutter button halfway to achieve focus, press the Depth of Field Preview button as I outline earlier, and then rotate the Main dial to choose different f-stop values.

    As long as you hold down the Depth of Field Preview button while you're choosing different f-stops, you can see the effect each f-stop has on the depth of field.

Using Shutter Priority mode

When your goal is to accentuate an object's motion, choose Shutter Priority (Tv) mode. Shutter Priority mode is the way to go whenever you need to stop action or show the grace of an athlete in motion. You'd use Shutter Priority mode in lots of scenarios. When you take pictures in Shutter Priority mode, you choose the shutter speed and the camera supplies the proper f-stop value to properly expose the scene. Your camera has a shutter speed range from 30 seconds to 1/4000 second. When you choose a slow shutter speed, the shutter is open for a long time. When you choose a fast shutter speed, the shutter is open for a short duration and you can freeze action. To take pictures in Shutter Priority mode

1. **Rotate the Mode dial to Tv (Time Value), as shown in Figure 6-9.**

2. **Rotate the Main dial to choose the desired shutter speed.**

   As you change the shutter speed, the camera determines the proper f-stop to achieve a properly exposed image. If you photograph in low-light conditions and require a fast shutter speed, the camera will choose a large aperture.

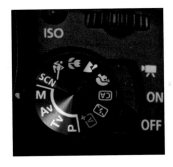

Figure 6-9: Rotate the Mode dial to Shutter Priority.

   If you require a greater depth of field, you'll have to increase ISO speed setting. If you see the minimum aperture (largest f-stop value) for the lens blinking, the image will be underexposed with the selected shutter speed. If you see the maximum aperture (smallest f-stop number) blinking, the image will be overexposed with the selected shutter speed. If you choose a shutter speed that's too slow for a blur-free picture, mount the camera on a tripod or choose a higher ISO speed setting. Note that choosing a higher ISO setting will increase the amount of digital noise in the image.

3. **Press the ISO button and then rotate the Main dial to change the ISO speed to the desired setting.**

   Choose an ISO setting that enables you to achieve the desired shutter speed. For more information on changing ISO speed, see Chapter 7.

4. **Rotate the Main dial to choose the desired shutter speed.**

   As you rotate the dial, the shutter speed value changes in the viewfinder or on the LCD monitor if you move your eye away from the viewfinder.

5. Press the shutter button halfway to achieve focus.

A green dot appears in the right side of the viewfinder. If the dot is flashing, the camera can't achieve focus. If this occurs, switch the lens to manual focus and twist the focusing barrel until your subject snaps into focus. Figure 6-10 shows the viewfinder when working in Shutter Priority mode.

6. Press the shutter button fully to take the picture.

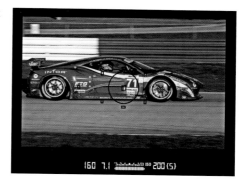

Figure 6-11 shows the effects that you can achieve with dif-

Figure 6-10: Adjusting the shutter speed.

ferent shutter speeds. The image on the left was photographed with a slow shutter speed, and the image on the right was photographed with a fast shutter speed to freeze the action. For more information on using Shutter Priority mode when photographing action, check out Chapter 8.

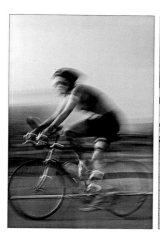
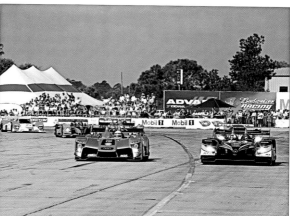

Figure 6-11: A tale of two shutter speeds.

Manually exposing images

You can also manually expose your images. When you choose this option, you supply the f-stop value and the shutter speed. You can choose from several combinations to properly expose the image for the lighting conditions. Your camera meter gives you some assistance to select the right f-stop and shutter speed combination to properly expose the image. If you fast-forwarded to this section and don't understand how your camera determines shutter speed and exposure, check out the "Understanding how exposure works in the camera" section earlier in this chapter. To manually expose your images

1. **Rotate the Mode dial to M (see Figure 6-12) and then rotate the Main dial to set the shutter speed.**

   The shutter speed determines how long the shutter stays open. A slow shutter speed is perfect for a scene with low light, and a fast shutter speed freezes action.

   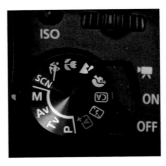

   Figure 6-12: Manually exposing the image.

   As you change the shutter speed, review the exposure indicator on the LCD monitor (see Figure 6-12), or if you have the shutter button pressed halfway, in the viewfinder. When the exposure is correct for the lighting conditions, the exposure level mark aligns with the center of the scale. If the exposure level mark is to the right of center, the image will be overexposed (see Figure 6-13); if to the left of center, the image will be under-exposed. Of course, you're in control. You may want to intentionally overexpose or under-expose for special effects. For example, if you slightly underexpose the image, the colors will be more saturated.

   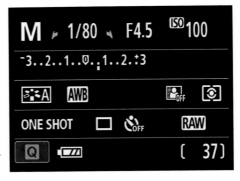

   Figure 6-13: Monitor the exposure on the LCD monitor.

2. **Press and hold the Aperture/ Exposure Compensation button, and use the cross keys to set the f-stop value.**

   The f-stop value determines how much light enters the camera. A small f-stop value, such as f/2.8, lets a lot of light into the camera and also gives a shallow depth of field. A large f-stop value lets a small amount of light into the camera and gives you a large depth of field. Press the shutter button halfway; as you change the f-stop value or shutter speed, review the exposure indicator on the LCD monitor or in the viewfinder. When the exposure is correct for the lighting conditions, the exposure-level mark aligns with the center of the scale, as shown previously in Figure 6-6. If the exposure-level mark is to the right of center, the image will be overexposed; if the mark is to the left of center, the image will be underexposed.

3. **Press the shutter button halfway to achieve focus.**

   A green dot appears in the viewfinder when the camera has achieved focus. If the dot is flashing, the camera can't achieve focus, and you must focus manually.

4. **Press the shutter button fully to take the picture.**

Shooting time exposures

You can shoot time exposures in Manual mode. Here, you can find the B (Bulb) setting, which allows you to make an exposure as long as you want.

B means Bulb mode. Back in the really old days of film cameras, photographers would open the shutter with a bulb-shaped rubber pneumatic device. The shutter opened when the photographer squeezed the device and remained open until the photographer released his grip.

When you shoot a time exposure, the shutter stays open as long as you press the shutter button. If you've ever seen night pictures in which you can actually see trails from stars that follow the curvature of the Earth, you've seen a photograph taken using this technique. The photographer left the shutter open for a long period of time, and the Earth rotated while the photograph was taken. These types of images are known as *time exposures* because the image was exposed over a long period of time. To shoot time exposures

1. **Mount the camera on a tripod.**

   The lens will be open for a long time. The slightest movement will show up as a blur in the final image. Unless you want the image blurred for a creative effect, you need to stabilize the camera on a tripod.

2. **Rotate the Mode dial to M (see Figure 6-14).**

3. **Press and hold the Aperture/Exposure Compensation button, and rotate the Main dial to set the f-stop value.**

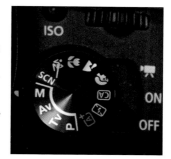

Figure 6-14: Rotate the Mode dial to M to take a time exposure.

The f-stop you choose is determined by the lens you use. The maximum aperture of the 18–55 STM kit lens is f/3.5 at 18mm and f/5.6 at 55mm. A small f-stop value such as f/2.8 (large aperture) lets a lot of light into the camera and gives a shallow depth of field. A large f-stop value (small aperture), such as f/16, lets a small amount of light into the camera and gives a large depth of field. You also need to leave the shutter open longer when using a large f-stop value, which in most instances is desirable. However, a longer exposure can add digital noise to the image. When you have an exposure that leaves the shutter open for several seconds, or perhaps minutes, use an ISO speed setting of 100 to minimize digital noise.

4. **Turn the Main dial to the left until you see Bulb in the viewfinder, or if you move your eye away from the eyepiece, on the LCD monitor (see Figure 6-15).**

5. **(Optional but recommended) Connect a remote switch to the camera.**

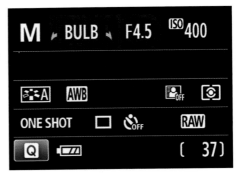

Figure 6-15: Accessing Bulb mode.

You can hold the shutter for the length of the exposure, but if you do, chances are extremely good that you'll transmit vibrations to the camera, which yields a blurry image. I recommend using a remote switch, such as the Canon RS-60E3, to trigger the shutter remotely to prevent vibration being transmitted to the camera. The remote plugs into a port on the side of your camera.

6. **Press the button on the remote switch to open the shutter.**

The shutter remains open as long as you hold the button. The time is noted in the LCD panel.

7. **Release the button on the remote switch to close the shutter.**

8. **Review the image on your LCD monitor.**

I find it useful to take one picture, note the time the lens remained open, and examine the image carefully on the LCD monitor. If I'm not pleased, I take another shot, leaving the lens open longer if the test image is underexposed or for a shorter duration if the test image is overexposed.

Time exposures can be a lot of fun. You can use them to record artistic depictions of headlight patterns on a curved stretch of road (see Figure 6-16) or capture the motion of the ocean at night. The possibilities are limited only by your imagination.

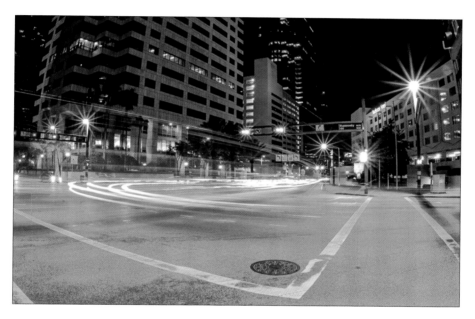

Figure 6-16: Use a time exposure to record headlight trails at night.

Modifying Camera Exposure

Your camera has a built-in metering device that automatically determines the proper shutter speed and aperture to create a perfectly exposed image for most lighting scenarios. However, at times, you need to modify the exposure to suit the current lighting conditions. Modify camera exposure for individual shots, or hedge your bets and create several exposures of each shot. You can also lock focus and exposure to a specific location in the scene you're photographing. I show you how to achieve these tasks in the upcoming sections.

Using exposure compensation

When your camera gets the exposure right, it's a wonderful thing. At times, however, the camera doesn't get it right. When you review an image on the camera LCD monitor and it's not exposed to suit your taste, you can compensate manually by increasing or decreasing exposure. To manually compensate camera exposure

1. **Choose P, Av, or Tv from the Mode dial (see Figure 6-17).**

   Exposure compensation is available only when you take pictures with Programmed Auto Exposure, Aperture Priority, or Shutter Priority mode.

2. **Rotate the Main dial while holding the Aperture/Exposure Compensation button.**

   Rotate the dial left to decrease exposure or right to increase exposure. As you rotate the dial, you see the exposure indicator in the viewfinder move, or if you move your eye away from the viewfinder, you see the indicator on the LCD monitor move, which shows you the amount of exposure compensation you're applying (see Figure 6-18). In this figure, the exposure is decreased by 2/3 of a stop.

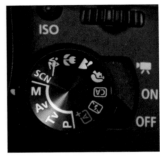

Figure 6-17: Use exposure compensation with these shooting modes.

3. **Press the shutter button fully to take the picture.**

4. **To cancel exposure compensation, press and hold the Aperture/Exposure Compensation button and rotate the Main dial until the exposure indicator is in the center of the exposure-compensation scale.**

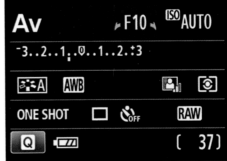

Figure 6-18: Using exposure compensation.

You see the exposure-compensation scale in the viewfinder or on the LCD monitor if you move your eye away from the viewfinder.

Exposure compensation stays in effect even after you power off the camera.

Bracketing exposure

When you're photographing an important event, properly exposed images are a must. Many photographers get lazy and don't feel they need to get it right in the camera when they have programs like Adobe Photoshop or Adobe Photoshop Lightroom. However, you get much better results when you process an image that's been exposed correctly.

Professional photographers "bracket" their exposures when they photograph important events or places they may never visit again. When you bracket an exposure, you take three pictures: one with the exposure as metered by the camera, one with exposure that's been decreased, and one with exposure that's been increased. You can bracket up to plus or minus 3 EV (exposure value) in 1/3 EV increments. To bracket your exposures:

1. **Press the Menu button.**

   The previously used menu displays.

2. **Use the cross keys to navigate to the Shooting Settings 2 tab and then use the cross keys to highlight Expo.Comp./AEB (automatic exposure bracketing).**

   See the left image in Figure 6-19.

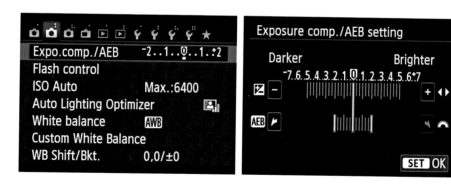

Figure 6-19: Setting automatic exposure bracketing.

3. **Press the Set button.**

   The Exposure Comp./AEB Setting menu appears.

4. Press and hold the Aperture/Exposure Compensation button and rotate the Main dial to set the amount of bracketing.

When you rotate the dial, a new scale appears below the exposure compensation scale and a line appears on each side of the center of the scale (see the right image in Figure 6-19). Each mark indicates 1/3 f-stop correction.

5. Use the cross keys to apply exposure compensation to the settings determined by the camera meter.

This step is optional if you're comfortable with how the camera has been setting exposure. You can use exposure compensation to increase or decrease the exposure metered by the camera. When you add exposure compensation to the mix, the automatic exposure bracketing (AEB) marks move as well. In other words, the exposure will be increased and decreased relative to the compensated exposure.

6. Press Set.

The settings are applied. The Expo.Comp./AEB menu option shows the amount of bracketing and exposure compensation you applied. The AEB icon appears in the viewfinder, and if your eye is pressed to the viewfinder, on the LCD monitor (see Figure 6-20).

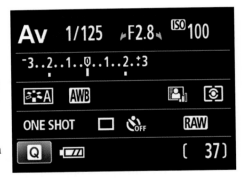

Figure 6-20: The Quick Menu Shooting Settings with AEB applied.

7. Press the Quick Control button and then use the cross keys to highlight the Drive mode option (see the left side of Figure 6-21).

8. Press the Set button and then highlight one of the Continuous Drive modes (see the right side of Figure 6-21).

If you bracket exposure with the camera on a tripod, choose the continuous drive mode with the 2-second countdown. The countdown gives the camera a chance to stabilize the vibration caused by your finger pressing the shutter button.

9. Press the Set button.

The Continuous Drive icon appears on the LCD monitor and in the viewfinder.

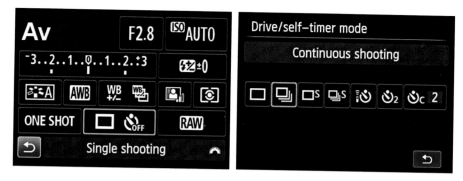

Figure 6-21: Choosing a Continuous Drive mode.

10. **Press the shutter button halfway to achieve focus and then press the shutter button fully.**

   When you press the shutter button, the camera creates three images: one with standard exposure, one with decreased exposure, and one with increased exposure. To cancel AEB, turn off the camera. When you power up the camera again, remember to change the Drive mode to one of the single-shot Drive modes.

Locking exposure

You can also lock exposure on a specific part of the frame, which is handy when you want a specific part of the frame exposed correctly. For example, recently I was photographing a beautiful sunset. The camera meter averaged the exposure for the scene, and the image ended up with blown-out highlights around the sun and clouds that weren't as dark and colorful as I saw them. To compensate for this, I locked exposure on the blue sky, and the picture turned out perfect. To lock exposure

1. **Look through the viewfinder and move the camera until the center of the viewfinder is over the area to which you want to lock exposure.**

2. **Press the AE Lock/FE Lock/Index/Reduce button.**

   The auto-exposure lock icon appears in the viewfinder (see Figure 6-22).

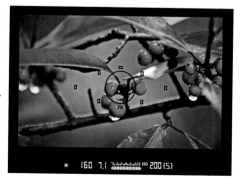

Figure 6-22: This icon notifies you that exposure lock is enabled.

3. **Move the camera to achieve the desired composition.**

   For example, you may want to lock exposure on some clouds, but compose your image so the clouds are near the top of the frame. You do so by locking exposure on the cloud that you want to be perfectly exposed and then moving the camera to frame the scene just the way you want it in the viewfinder.

4. **Press the shutter button halfway to achieve focus.**

   A green dot in the viewfinder tells you that the camera has achieved focus. You also see black rectangles that designate the areas on which the camera has focused.

5. **Press the shutter button fully to take the picture.**

   After you take the picture, Exposure Lock is disabled until the next time you press the Exposure Lock button.

Locking Focus

With the shutter button, you can lock focus on an object that isn't in the center of the frame. This option comes in handy when your center of interest isn't in the center of the frame.

To lock focus with the shutter button

1. **While looking through the viewfinder, move your camera until the center of the viewfinder is over the subject that you want the camera to lock focus on.**

2. **Press the shutter button halfway.**

   Make sure that a black autofocus square appears over your subject. When I'm photographing people not in the center of the frame, I switch to a single autofocus point in the center of the frame and center the single autofocus point over my subject before locking focus. For more information on selecting and modifying autofocus points, see Chapter 7. When the camera achieves focus, a green dot appears in the viewfinder.

3. **While holding the shutter button halfway, recompose your picture.**

4. **Press the shutter button fully to take the picture.**

Choosing a Drive Mode

Your camera can capture multiple images when you press the shutter button. Your camera's Continuous Drive mode can capture images at the rate of 4 fps.

If you're taking pictures at a place where you don't want to be heard, use a Silent Drive mode capturing one shot at a time or continuous images. ***Note:*** The Silent modes aren't completely silent, but they are considerably quieter than the standard Single Shot and Continuous Drive modes. To specify the Drive mode, follow these steps:

1. **Choose desired shooting mode.**

   In many of the automatic modes, the Drive mode is chosen for you, but you can override the Drive mode with the push of a button, or by using the Quick Command menu. However, the Drive mode in most of the SCN modes should not be changed: The default Drive mode was set by Canon engineers and professional photographers as the optimum Drive mode.

2. **Press the Quick Control button.**

   The Quick Control menu appears on the LCD monitor.

3. **Use the cross keys to highlight the Drive Mode option on the LCD monitor (see the left side of Figure 6-23).**

4. **Press the Set button.**

   The drive mode options are displayed.

5. **Use the cross keys to highlight one of the following options (see the right side of Figure 6-23). From right to left, they are**

   - *Single Shot:* You capture one picture each time you press the shutter button.

   - *Continuous Shooting:* You can capture up to 4 fps when you press and hold the shutter button.

   - *Single Shot Silent Shooting:* You capture one image each time you press the shutter button, and the mechanical noise of the shutter is considerably less than the standard single shot mode.

   - *Silent Continuous Shooting:* You can capture up to 4 fps when you press and hold the shutter button, and the mechanical noise of the shutter is considerably less than the standard continuous shooting mode.

   - *10-Second Self-Timer/Remote Control:* Starts the 10-Second Self-Timer when you press the shutter button or trigger the shutter with a remote control unit. A light in front of the camera beeps and blinks while counting down. At the 2-second mark, the light stays on, and the beeping is faster.

   - *2-Second Self-Timer/Remote Control:* Starts the 2-Second Self-Timer when you press the shutter button or trigger the shutter with a remote control unit.

- *Self-Timer Continuous:* Starts the self timer and captures the specified number of images. When you choose this option, an up and
down arrow pair appears around the default number of images (2)
captured with this option. Use the cross keys to choose a value
from 2 to 10.

6. **Take some pictures.**

The Drive mode you select stays in effect until you change it. If you
power off the camera, the Drive mode still stays in effect. Switch back
to Single Shot mode when you no longer need to capture images
continuously.

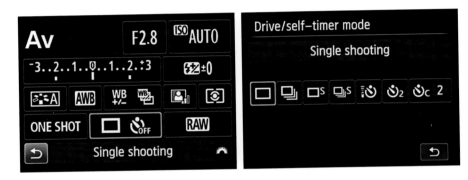

Figure 6-23: Single Shot and Continuous Drive modes.

The 2-Second Self-Timer is ideal when you're photographing with the camera
mounted to a tripod. The 2-second delay gives the camera a chance to stabilize from any vibration that occurred when you pressed the Shutter button.

The Continuous Drive mode's capture rate will be slower than 4 fps when the
battery is near the end of its life or when you choose a shutter speed slower
than 1/1500 second.

Exploring Useful Image Menu Commands

There are lots of menu commands — more than you'll ever use — but the
Canon engineers wanted to cover just about every possible scenario for photographers who own an SL1/100D. In the following sections, I show you some
menu commands that may be useful in specific picture taking scenarios.

Enabling Long Exposure Noise Reduction

If you shoot long time exposures at night in secluded places, you'll capture some wonderful images of the stars in the sky. If you live in a very remote area, or capture your images in an area with little or no ambient light, you'll see galaxies like the Milky Way in your images. However, when you use the Bulb mode (discussed earlier in this chapter) to leave the shutter open for several minutes (or in some cases, several hours), your images will have digital noise, especially in dark areas of solid color. However, you can eliminate some of the noise with Long Exposure Noise Reduction as follows:

1. **Press the Menu button.**

   The previously used menu displays.

2. **Use the cross keys to navigate to the Shooting Settings 3 menu tab.**

3. **Use the cross keys to highlight Long Exp. Noise Reduction (see the left image in Figure 6-24) and then press the Set button.**

   The Long Exp. Noise Reduction options are displayed (see the right image in Figure 6-24).

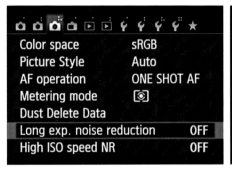
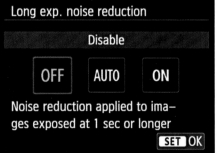

Figure 6-24: Enable Long Exposure Noise Reduction here.

4. **Use the cross keys to highlight one of the following:**

   • *Off:* The default option applies noise reduction to images with an exposure of 1 second or longer.

- *Auto:* This applies long exposure noise reduction with exposures longer than 1 second when typical long exposure noise is detected.

- *On:* This applies long exposure to every image with an exposure longer than 1 second. This option may also reduce noise that the Auto option cannot detect.

5. Press the Set button.

The desired option is applied.

Long exposure noise reduction increases the time it takes for the camera to process each image. If you do occasionally create long time exposures, either choose the Auto option, or choose the On option before the photo shoot, and then change to Off (Disable) when the photo shoot is completed.

Enabling High ISO Speed Noise Reduction

The Canon engineers know that using high ISO settings will increase image noise, which is why they added a feature to your camera that applies noise reduction to all images and is biased to apply more noise reduction to images captured with a high ISO. If you do a lot of shooting in low light with high ISO settings, you can modify the amount of noise reduction applied to images captured at high ISO settings as follows:

1. Press the Menu button.

The previously used menu displays.

2. Use the cross keys to navigate to the Shooting Settings 3 tab.

3. Use the cross keys to highlight High ISO Speed NR (see the left image in Figure 6-25).

4. Press the Set button.

The High ISO Speed NR options are displayed (see the right image in Figure 6-25).

5. Use the cross keys to choose one of the following options:

- *Off:* Noise reduction is not applied to any image.

- *Low:* A low amount of noise reduction is applied to all images.

- *Standard:* The default option applies noise reduction to all images.

- *High:* Applies a stronger amount of noise reduction to all images.

- *Multi-shot Noise Reduction:* This option captures four images and combines them in camera to create a noise free image. This option is not available if you choose the RAW or RAW+L image format.

6. Press the Set button to apply the change.

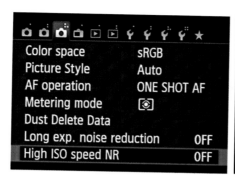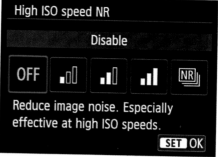

Figure 6-25: Enable High ISO Speed Noise Reduction here.

I haven't performed extensive tests on these options. Change this setting at your discretion and with however many grains of salt you choose.

 If you choose Multi-shot Noise Reduction, your camera will capture four images every time you press the shutter button, regardless of the ISO setting you use, and the combined image will be in JPEG format. I advise you to use this setting only if you're photographing in extreme low light at an ISO higher than 1600. And because the camera is combining multiple images, I suggest you use a tripod to get the sharpest image when using this option.

Changing screen color

Your camera also has the chameleon ability to change Quick Menu shooting screen colors. No, it won't change screen colors to match a background, or if you're a card-holding member of the paparazzi, hide the shooting menu from people you want to photograph, but you can change the screen color to suit your preference. To change the screen color

1. Press the Menu button.

The previously used menu displays.

2. Use the cross keys to navigate to the Camera Settings 3 tab.

3. Use the cross keys to highlight Screen Color (see the left image in Figure 6-26) and then press the Set button.

The Screen Color options are displayed (see the right image in Figure 6-26).

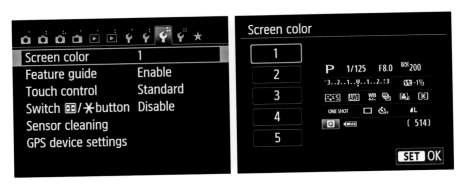

Figure 6-26: Change the background color of the shooting screen here.

4. Use the cross keys to highlight one of the following options:

- *1:* The default option gives you a black background for the shooting screen.

- *2:* This option gives you a gray background for the shooting screen.

- *3:* This option gives you a lovely brown background for the shooting screen.

- *4:* This option gives you a vibrant blue background for the shooting screen.

- *5:* This option gives you a fire-engine red background for the shooting screen.

5. Press Set.

The background color you select is used the next time you access shooting settings with the Quick Control button. Figure 6-27 shows the number 2 option for the shooting screen.

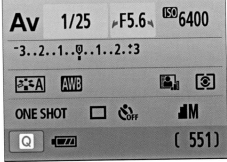

Figure 6-27: Use an optional background color.

Using Custom Functions

Your camera has almost as many custom functions as there are Smiths in the New York City phone book. Well, almost. At any rate, I find some custom functions extremely useful. Unfortunately, I'd have to buy my project editor a year's supply of her favorite hair coloring product if I covered every custom function. In the upcoming sections, I cover the custom functions I think are most important. I leave it to you, dear reader, to explore the other custom functions when the weather's not conducive to photography. But then again, when the weather's bad, you may prefer to try some still-life photography on common household items instead of exploring custom functions.

Enabling a custom function

As I mention previously, there are lots of custom functions. I cover some of these in other chapters of the book, but I can't cover them all. This brief step list will show you how to enable a custom function in case you want to experiment with some that I don't cover. To enable a custom function

1. **Press the Menu button.**

   The previously used menu displays.

2. **Use the cross keys to navigate to the Camera Settings 4 tab (see the left image in Figure 6-28) and then press Set.**

   You can also just tap the Camera Settings 4 tab.

   The Custom Functions are displayed in all their glory (see the right image in Figure 6-28). There are a total of 4 custom function categories: C.Fn I: Exposure ISO Expansion, C.Fn II: Highlight Tone Priority, C.Fn III: Autofocus/Drive, C.Fn IV: Operations/Others.

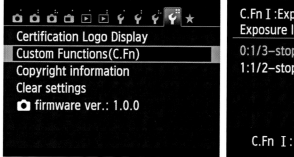
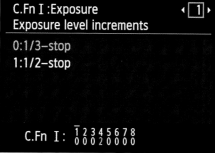

Figure 6-28: Get your red hot custom functions.

3. **Use the cross keys to select a custom function and then press Set.**

The custom function is selected and ready for you to choose an option.

4. **Use the cross keys to select an option for the custom function and then press Set.**

The custom function option is enabled.

5. **Use the cross keys to select another custom function to modify, or press the Menu button to return to the menu.**

Some custom functions may be useful for the type of photography you do, or how you photograph. I invite you to explore the other custom functions to see which ones may be useful to you.

Enable Highlight Tone Priority

If you photograph lots of images in bright light and detail in highlight areas is important to you, consider trying the Highlight Tone Priority menu command. This option ensures that images with a lot of bright highlights will have highlight details. The con for this menu command is that you may find increased noise in shadow areas. When you use this option, the lowest ISO setting available is 200. To use Highlight Tone Priority

1. **Press the Menu button.**

The previously used menu displays.

2. **Use the cross keys to navigate to the Camera Settings 4 tab.**

3. **Use the cross keys to select Custom Functions (see Figure 6-29) and then press Set.**

The Custom Functions options are displayed.

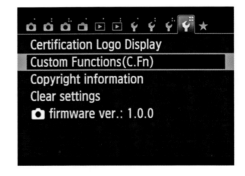

Figure 6-29: Looking for Mrs. Good Custom Function.

4. **Use the cross keys to select C.Fn II: Image Highlight Tone Priority and then press Set.**

C.Fn II is selected and ready for you to modify.

5. **Use the cross keys to highlight Enable and then press Set.**

You've got Highlight Tone Priority (see the left image in Figure 6-30). When you shoot with Highlight Tone Priority, D+ is prominently displayed in the viewfinder and on the LCD monitor when you move your eye away from the viewfinder (see the right image in Figure 6-30).

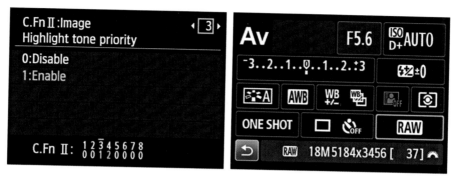

Figure 6-30: You've got Highlight Tone Priority.

Clearing Custom Functions

Enabling custom functions and customizing your camera can be quite useful. However, sometimes you get carried away and go over the top. Other times, you experimented with a bunch of custom functions and decide they no longer suit your style of photography. You can wipe out all the custom functions and any changes you've applied to camera buttons by doing the following:

1. **Press the Menu button.**

   The previously used menu displays.

2. **Use the cross keys to navigate to the Camera Settings 4 tab and then use the cross keys to highlight Clear Settings (see the left image in Figure 6-31).**

3. **Press Set.**

   The Clear Settings menu options appear.

4. **Use the cross keys to highlight Clear All Custom Func. (C.Fn) (see the right image in Figure 6-31) and then press Set.**

    A dialog box appears with the option to Clear All Functions.

5. **Use the right cross key to highlight OK and press the Set button.**

    Any custom functions you've enabled are cleared.

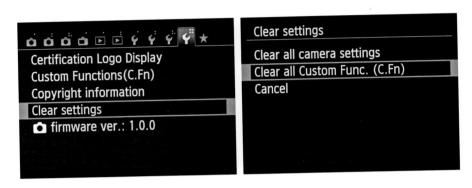

Figure 6-31: Clearing all custom functions.

7

Features That Make Pictures Pop

*Y*our camera has lots of great features that enable you to create great pictures. When you shoot in one of the creative modes, you can modify lots of things. If the light is a bit dim and you don't feel like using flash on your subject, you can increase the ISO speed setting. You can also change how the camera meters the scene, and you have lots of options when using a supported flash unit. In short, the sky's the limit when you employ the advanced features of your camera. This chapter brings you up to speed on those advanced features.

Note: The larger dSLR brethren of the SL1/100D have lots of buttons on the outside of the camera. This camera body is compact, with less available real estate for buttons, so many functions and options assigned to buttons on the bigger cameras are instead menu commands on your camera. Many of these options and settings can also be changed via the Quick Menu. I show you both ways when applicable.

Using the Auto Lighting Optimizer

If you capture images in JPEG format, you can invoke a menu command that gives you better-looking images when you're shooting in dim light. Instead of getting a shot with too much contrast, you end up with a brighter shot. There is a possible downside, though: This option may add *digital noise* to the image. Digital noise comes in two flavors:

✔ **Color:** Shows up as specks of color

✔ **Luminance:** Shows up as random gray clumps

Digital noise is most prevalent in areas of solid color, such as the dark shadow areas in your image. If you shoot images in the RAW format, you can adjust image brightness after you download images to your computer with Canon's Digital Photo Professional, which is one of the software applications that ships with your camera. When you use one of the Basic Zone shooting modes, the Auto Lighting Optimizer option is set to Standard. The Auto Lighting Optimizer enhances images that are dark with low contrast. To enable the Auto Lighting Optimizer

1. **Press the Menu button.**

   The previously used menu displays.

2. **Use the cross keys to navigate to the Shooting Settings 2 tab.**

3. **Use the cross keys to highlight Auto Lighting Optimizer (see the left image in Figure 7-1) and then press the Set button.**

   The Auto Lighting Optimizer menu displays (see the right image in Figure 7-1).

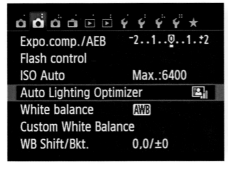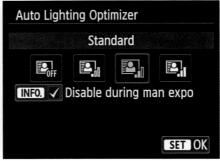

Figure 7-1: Set the Auto Lighting Optimizer here.

4. **Use the cross keys to highlight one of the following options:**

- *Disable:* Brightness and contrast are not corrected when photographing backlit subjects.

- *Low:* Add a minimal amount of brightness to a backlit subject.

- *Standard:* The default option (selected in Figure 7-1) adjusts the lighting to create a picture that brightens backlit subjects.

- *High:* Add a considerable amount of brightness to a backlit subject.

When you photograph using M or B modes, press the Info button to disable this option. When you photograph in M or B modes, you control the exposure and normally won't need to use the Auto Lighting Optimizer.

5. **Press the Set button.**

The change is applied, and you return to the Shooting Settings 2 tab.

6. **Press the shutter button halfway to return to take pictures.**

The Auto Lighting Optimizer setting you choose remains in effect until you select a different option. In some cases, digital noise may be apparent when the Auto Lighting Optimizer is used.

This menu command is disabled when you

✔ Enable the Highlight Tone Priority custom function (see Chapter 6).

✔ Enable HDR shooting. When HDR shooting is cancelled, the Auto Lighting Optimizer returns to the default Standard setting.

Correcting Lens Peripheral Illumination

Some lenses have a problem with *light falloff* (the edges of an image are dark) toward the edge of the frame. The amount of light falloff depends on the lens you're using. You notice these problems with inexpensive lenses, and also notice the problem at either extreme of the focal length range.

Another problem with lenses is *chromatic aberration*, which is color fringing around the edges of subjects. You can, however, go a long way toward correcting both problems with the Lens Aberration Correction command, a feature that's available only for Canon lenses. The peripheral illumination data — that is, the settings that will correct the problem — is stored in the camera's database so this problem can be corrected in-camera instead of using a software application. The Lens Aberration Correction menu command cures the light falloff that makes the corners of images appear darker when using a wide angle focal length, and also removes the color fringing around the edges of objects in your images. To enable lens peripheral illumination

1. **Press the Menu button.**

   The previously used menu displays on the camera LCD monitor.

2. **Use the cross keys to navigate to the Shooting Settings 1 tab.**

3. **Use the cross keys to highlight Lens Aberration Correction (see the left image in Figure 7-2) and then press the Set button.**

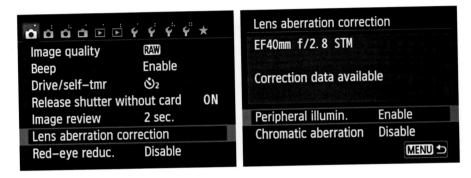

Figure 7-2: Enable Lens Aberration Correction here.

Note that only Peripheral Illumination is corrected by default (see the right image in Figure 7-2). *Don't use this command with a third-party lens* because third-party lenses are not in the camera's database. If you have a Canon lens attached to the camera and data for the lens is in the camera's database, this information is noted in the dialog box. If a third-party lens is attached to the camera, a message appears telling you correction data isn't available.

4. **To correct chromatic aberration, use the cross keys to select the option and then press the Set button.**

   The menu expands, and the options to Enable or Disable (selected by default) are displayed.

5. **Use the cross keys to highlight Enable and then press Set.**

   Chromatic aberration will be corrected.

6. **Press the Menu button to exit.**

Choosing a Metering Mode

When you press the shutter button halfway, your camera meters the scene by evaluating the ambient light and the tones of objects to determine the optimal exposure settings. The default metering mode (Evaluative) works well for most lighting conditions. When you shoot in Scene Intelligent Auto or Creative Auto mode, Evaluative metering mode is used by default. To change the metering mode to suit different lighting and picture-taking situations

1. **Press the Menu button.**

   The last used menu command is displayed on your LCD monitor.

2. **Use the cross keys to navigate to the Shooting Settings 3 tab.**

3. **Use the cross keys to highlight Metering Mode (see the left image in Figure 7-3) and then press the Set button.**

   The metering mode options are displayed on your LCD monitor (see the right side of Figure 7-3).

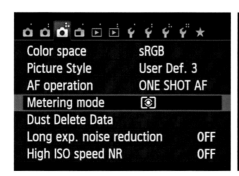
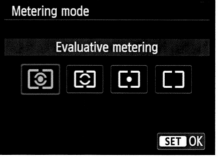

Figure 7-3: Change the metering mode here.

4. Use the cross keys to choose one of the following metering options:

- *Evaluative:* This is the default mode for your camera and is selected in Figure 7-3. You can use this mode for most work, including backlit scenes. The camera divides the scene into several zones and evaluates the brightness of the scene, direct light, and backlighting, factoring these variables to create the correct exposure for your subject.

- *Partial:* This mode meters a small area in the center of the scene. This option is useful when the background is much brighter than your subject. A perfect example of when to use this mode is a beach scene at sunset when you're pointing the camera toward the sun, and your subject is in front of you.

- *Center-Weighted Average:* This metering mode meters the entire scene but gives more importance to the subject in the center. Use this mode when one part of your scene is significantly brighter than the rest — for example, when the sun is in the picture. If your bright light source is near the center of the scene, this mode prevents the image from being overexposed.

- *Spot:* This mode meters a small area in the center of the scene. Use this mode when your subject is in the center and is significantly brighter than the rest of your scene. Your camera also has the option to spot-meter where the autofocus frame is. Simply move the autofocus frame to your subject, and you can accurately spot-meter a subject not in the center of the frame.

5. Press the Set button.

The selected metering mode is in effect.

To change the metering mode using the Quick Menu

1. Press the shutter button halfway to enable shooting mode.

2. Press the Quick Control button.

The Quick Control menu is displayed on your LCD monitor.

3. Use the cross keys to highlight the current metering mode.

The name of the currently selected metering mode displays at the bottom of the LCD monitor (see the left image in Figure 7-4).

4. Rotate the Main dial to select the desired metering mode.

Alternatively, you can press the Set button to display all options (see the right side of Figure 7-4), use the cross keys to select the desired option, and then press Set to enable it.

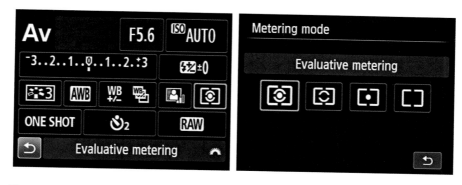

Figure 7-4: Use the Quick Menu to change metering mode.

The metering mode you choose stays in effect after you power off the camera. Change the metering mode back to the default after you finish shooting images that require a different metering mode.

Choosing the Autofocus Mode

Your camera focuses automatically on objects that intersect autofocus points. You have three Autofocus modes on your camera. One is ideally suited for still objects, and another is ideally suited for moving objects. The third Autofocus mode is kind of a chameleon in that you use it for still objects that *might* move. To choose an Autofocus mode

1. **Press the Menu button.**

   The last used menu command is displayed on your LCD monitor.

2. **Use the cross keys to navigate to the Shooting Settings 3 tab.**

3. **Use the cross keys to highlight AF Operation (see the left image of Figure 7-5) and then press the Set button.**

   The AF Operation options are displayed on your LCD monitor (see the right image of Figure 7-5).

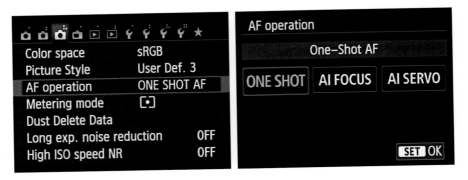

Figure 7-5: Change the AF operation option here.

4. **Use the cross keys to highlight one of the following autofocus modes:**

   - *One Shot:* Use this Autofocus mode for objects that don't move. This Autofocus mode is ideally suited for shooting portraits and landscapes.

   - *AI Focus:* Use this Autofocus mode for objects that are stationary but might move. The camera locks focus using One Shot but switches to AI Servo if the subject starts moving. This option is ideally suited for macro photography of objects, like flowers on a windy day.

   - *AI Servo:* Use this Autofocus mode for objects in motion. After the camera locks focus on the object, the camera updates the focus as the subject moves. This mode is ideally suited for objects that are moving toward or away from you.

5. **Press the Set button.**

   The desired Autofocus mode is in effect until you change the setting.

To change AF Operation using the Quick Control menu

1. **Press the shutter button halfway to return to shooting mode.**

2. **Press the Quick Control button**

   The Quick Control menu for shooting settings is displayed on your LCD monitor.

3. **Use the cross keys to highlight the current Autofocus mode (see the left image of Figure 7-6).**

4. **Rotate the Main dial to select the desired mode.**

   Alternatively, you can press Set to see all options in a single menu (see the right image of Figure 7-6). Use the cross keys to highlight the desired AF mode and then press Set.

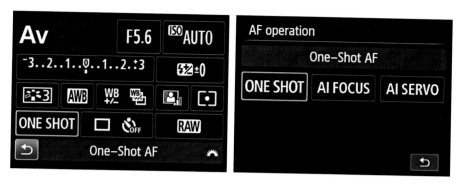

Figure 7-6: Change the AF mode with the Quick Control Menu.

No Autofocus modes are effective on fast-moving objects, such as racecars or airplanes. To capture blur-free shots of objects like these (that move toward or away from you), switch the lens to manual focus and then focus on a spot your subject will cross. Press the shutter button shortly before your subject reaches the point on which you have focused. The amount of time varies, depending on how fast your subject is moving. Find out more about capturing blur-free photos in Chapter 6.

The Autofocus mode you choose stays in effect after you power off the camera. Always change to the default autofocus setting (One Shot; refer to Figure 7-6) after you finish creating images that require a different mode.

Changing the Autofocus Point

By default, your camera displays nine autofocus points. The camera focuses on subjects that intersect autofocus points. The default number of autofocus points works fine for most picture-taking situations. However, at times, it makes sense to switch to a single autofocus point that you align with a single object, such as the edge of a building. This option is useful when you want to focus selectively on a single subject in a scene that has other objects that the camera may lock focus on. To change the autofocus point

1. **Press the shutter button halfway. Then press the AF Point Selection/ Magnify button as you point the camera toward the scene or subject you are photographing.**

2. **While looking at the viewfinder or at the LCD monitor, rotate the Main dial to switch from multiple autofocus points to a single autofocus point.**

This indicates the other possible points on which you can focus. I find it's easier to move my eye away from the viewfinder and use the LCD monitor to select the desired AF point.

3. Rotate the Main dial to select the desired autofocus point.

You can navigate to any of the autofocus targets (the small squares) to designate the point from which the camera will focus. Figure 7-7 shows the LCD monitor as it appears when selecting AF points with one of the side autofocus points selected. The camera focuses on an object under that autofocus point.

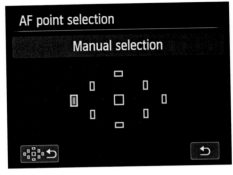

Figure 7-7: Choose an autofocus point.

4. Press the shutter button halfway.

You're ready to take pictures with a single autofocus point. The autofocus point is the default autofocus point until you use the AF Point Selection button to designate another autofocus point.

Choosing a Picture Style

When you photograph a scene or image, your camera sensor captures the colors and subtle nuances of shadow and light to create a faithful rendition of the scene. At times, however, you want a different type of picture. For example, when you're photographing a landscape, you want vivid blues and greens in the image. You can choose from a variety of picture styles and create up to three custom picture styles. When you take pictures in Scene Intelligent Auto mode, this option isn't available. Picture style is not applied to RAW images. However, the camera will render a preview on the LCD monitor that does show the style as it would be applied to a JPEG image. About the only use for this option when shooting RAW is the Monochrome picture style mode, which shows a preview of a black-and-white image on the monitor, which gives you an idea of what the RAW image will look like if you convert it to black and white in an image-editing application. To choose a picture style

1. Press the Menu button.

The last menu command you used is displayed.

2. **Use the cross keys to navigate to the Shooting Settings 3 tab.**

3. **Use the cross keys to highlight Picture Style (see the left image in Figure 7-8) and then press the Set button.**

   The Picture Style options appear on your LCD monitor (see the right image in Figure 7-8). Auto is the default option, which means the camera adjusts the colors based on the scene you're photographing.

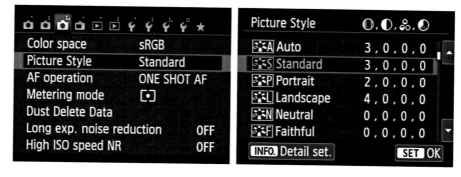

Figure 7-8: Choose a Picture Style option here.

4. **Use the cross keys to choose one of the following styles:**

   - *Auto:* The default style adjusts the color to match the scene you are photographing.

   - *Standard:* This style captures crisp, sharp images and is suitable for most photography situations.

   - *Portrait:* This style renders a soft image with flattering skin tones. This style is ideally suited for portraits of women and children.

   - *Landscape:* This style renders an image with vivid blues and greens. Landscape is ideally suited for — you guessed it — landscapes. I love truth in advertising.

   - *Neutral:* This style renders an image with no in-camera enhancement and is ideally suited for photographers who will be editing and enhancing their images with a computer image-editing application, such as Adobe Photoshop or Adobe Photoshop Lightroom. The resulting image has natural colors.

- *Faithful:* This is another style ideally suited for photographers who like to edit their images with a computer image-editing application. When you photograph a subject in daylight with a color temperature of 5200K, the camera automatically adjusts the image color to match the color of your subject.

- *Monochrome:* This style (not visible in Figure 7-8) creates a black-and-white image. If you use this style and choose JPEG as the file format, you can't convert the image to color with your computer. If you use this style when using the JPEG format, make sure you switch back to one of the other picture styles when you want to capture images with color again.

- *User-Defined Styles:* These slots (not visible in Figure 7-8) are for styles you've created. I show you how to create custom picture styles in Chapter 11.

5. Press Set.

The picture style you select is in effect until you change it.

You can also change the picture style using the Quick Control menu as follows:

1. Press the shutter button halfway to return to shooting mode.

2. Press the Quick Control button.

The Quick Control menu for shooting settings appears on your LCD monitor.

3. Use the cross keys to highlight the current picture style (see the left image in Figure 7-9).

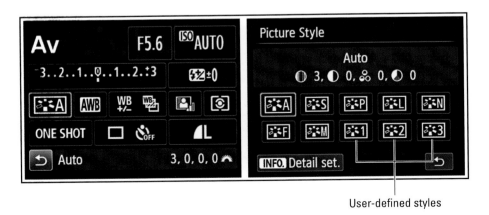

User-defined styles

Figure 7-9: Use the Quick Control shooting settings menu to select a picture style.

4. **Rotate the Main dial to select the desired picture style.**

   Alternatively, press Set to display the Picture Style menu (see the right image in Figure 7-9). Then rotate the Main dial or use the cross keys to select the desired picture style.

Figure 7-10 shows a comparison of the different picture styles.

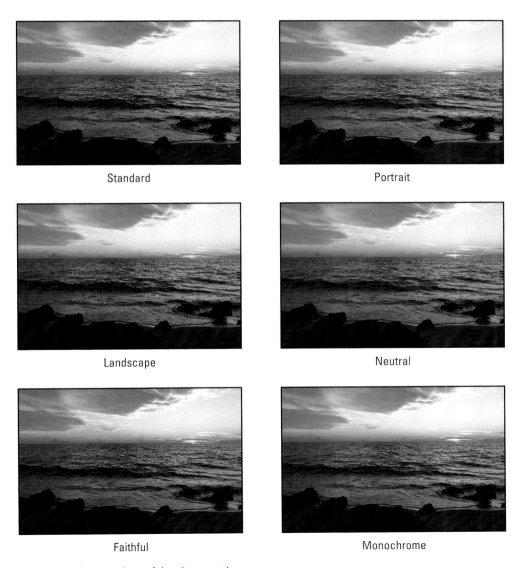

Standard	Portrait
Landscape	Neutral
Faithful	Monochrome

Figure 7-10: A comparison of the picture styles.

Specifying the Color Space

Several color spaces are used in photography and image-editing applications. The *color space* determines the range of colors you have to work with. The default color space (sRGB) in your camera is ideal if you're not editing your images in an application like Adobe Photoshop or Adobe Photoshop Lightroom. However, if you do edit your images in one of those image-editing applications and want the widest range of colors (also known as *gamut*) with which to work, you can specify the Adobe RGB color space. To specify the color space that your camera records images with, follow these steps:

1. **Press the Menu button.**

   The last-used menu displays.

2. **Use the cross keys to navigate to the Shooting Settings 3 tab and then use the cross keys to highlight Color Space (see the left image in Figure 7-11).**

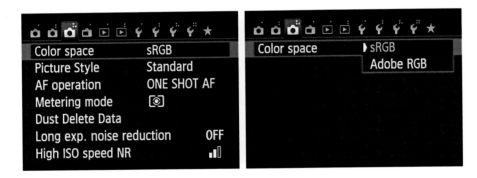

Figure 7-11: Choosing a color space.

3. **Press the Set button.**

   The Color Space menu displays (see the right image in Figure 7-11).

4. **Use cross keys to highlight one of the following and then press Set:**

   - *sRGB:* The default color space is ideal if you don't edit your images or do minimal editing.

   - *Adobe RGB:* Use this color space if you're editing your images in an application, such as Adobe Photoshop or Adobe Photoshop Lightroom.

5. **Press the shutter button halfway.**

   You exit the menu and are ready to shoot pictures with your desired color space.

 After you edit images created with the Adobe RGB color space, you must convert them to sRGB in your image-editing application before printing them or displaying them on the web. For more information, see a *For Dummies* book about the software application you're using to edit your work.

Setting White Balance

The human eye can see the color white without a colorcast no matter what type of light the white object is illuminated with. Your digital camera can't compensate for different lighting scenarios without White Balance. Your camera uses *white balance* in order for white to appear as white in the captured image. Without white balance, images photographed with fluorescent light have a green colorcast, and images photographed with tungsten light sources have a yellow/orange colorcast. Yup, your subject would be "green around the gills," or have some other ghastly colorcast, depending on the light sources used to illuminate the scene.

The default White Balance setting AWB (not to be confused with the old music group "Average White Band") automatically sets the white balance. If, however, you notice that your images have a colorcast when letting the camera automatically set the white balance, you can choose a White Balance setting to suit the light in the scene you're photographing. You can also change white balance when you want to create an image with some special effects.

 If you shoot images in the RAW format and inadvertently choose the wrong White Balance setting or your camera doesn't get it right, you can change the White Balance setting in an application like Adobe Photoshop, Adobe Photoshop Lightroom, or Canon's Digital Photo Professional.

To set white balance

 1. **Press the Menu button.**

   The last used menu displays.

 2. **Use the cross keys to navigate to the Shooting Settings 2 tab.**

3. Use the cross keys to highlight White Balance (see the left image in Figure 7-12) and then press the Set button.

The White Balance menu appears on the LCD monitor (see the right image in Figure 7-12).

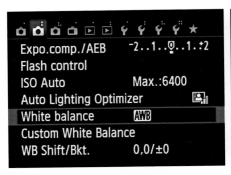 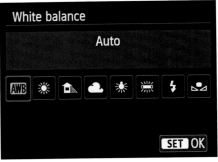

Figure 7-12: Choose a White Balance option here.

4. Use the cross keys to select one of the following White Balance options:

- *Auto White Balance (AWB):* The camera automatically sets the white balance based on the lighting conditions.

- *Daylight:* Use this option when photographing subjects on a bright, sunny day.

- *Shade:* Use this option when photographing subjects in shaded conditions.

- *Cloudy:* Use this option when photographing subjects on a cloudy day.

- *Tungsten:* Use this option when photographing subjects illuminated by tungsten light.

- *White Fluorescent:* Use this option when photographing subjects illuminated by fluorescent lights.

- *Flash:* Use this option when photographing subjects with an auxiliary flash unit.

- *Custom:* Use when creating a custom white balance. See the "Creating a Custom White Balance" section later in this chapter.

5. Press Set.

The White Balance option you choose is used to balance white colors in the scenes you photograph until you choose another setting.

You can also change the White Balance setting using the Quick Control menu. To change the White Balance with the Quick Control shooting settings menu

1. **Press the shutter button halfway to return to shooting mode.**

2. **Press the Quick Control button and then use the cross keys to highlight the current White Balance setting (see the left image in Figure 7-13).**

3. **Rotate the Main dial to choose the desired white balance setting.**

   Alternatively, you can press Set to see the complete menu (see the right image in Figure 7-13), and then rotate the Main dial or use the cross keys to select the desired setting.

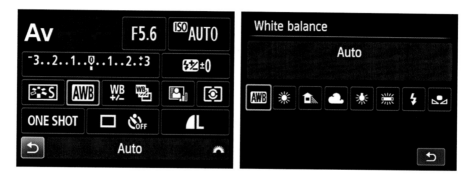

Figure 7-13: Change white balance from the Quick Control shooting settings menu.

Creating a Custom White Balance

When you photograph a scene that's illuminated with several different light sources, your camera may have a hard time figuring out how to set the white balance. And if the camera has a hard time, chances are you can't use one of the presets to accurately set the white balance.

You can, however, set a custom white balance. You'll get better results if you use the Neutral picture style. If you use the Monochrome picture style, you can't obtain a white balance reading. (Read more about Neutral and Monochrome in the earlier section, "Choosing a Picture Style.")

You can purchase an 18% gray card from your favorite camera retailer and use this in place of a white object in Step 1. A card like this gives you extremely accurate results.

Just follow these steps:

1. **Photograph a white object.**

   Photograph the object under the light source that will be used to illuminate your scene. Photograph something that's pure white, such as a sheet of paper without lines. You won't get accurate results if you photograph something that's off-white.

   Note: Some papers contain optical brighteners. If you use one of those to set your white balance, your images may be a little warmer (more reddish-orange in color) than normal.

2. **Press the Menu button.**

   The last used menu command is displayed.

3. **Use the cross keys to navigate to the Shooting Settings 2 tab and then use the cross keys to highlight Custom White Balance (see the left image in Figure 7-14).**

4. **Press the Set button.**

   The image you just photographed (Step 1) displays onscreen (see the right image in Figure 7-14).

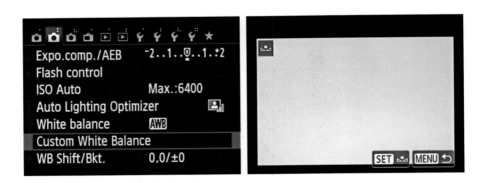

Figure 7-14: Set a custom white balance.

5. **Press Set.**

   A dialog box appears asking you to confirm that you want to use the image to set the white balance (see the left image in Figure 7-15).

6. **Use the right cross key to highlight OK and press Set.**

   The camera calculates the color temperature for the light source. After the camera completes the calculation, a dialog box appears, asking you whether you want to assign the color temperature derived from the calculation to the Custom White Balance setting (see the right image in Figure 7-15).

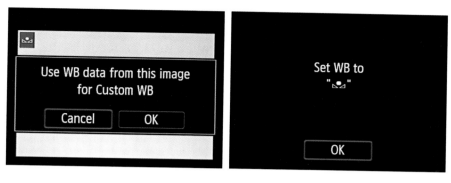

Figure 7-15: Finalizing the custom white balance.

7. **Use the right cross key to select OK and then press Set.**

8. **Use the cross keys to highlight White Balance (see the left image in Figure 7-16) and then press Set.**

   The White Balance options appear.

9. **Use the cross keys to highlight Custom (see the right image in Figure 7-16).**

10. **Press Set.**

   Your custom white balance determines the image's white balance until you select a different White Balance option.

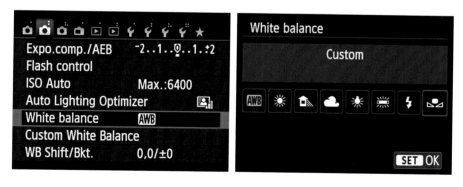

Figure 7-16: Creating a custom white balance.

The custom white balance remains in effect and is used whenever you select the Custom White Balance option. You can register only one custom white balance. When you encounter a different lighting scenario that requires a custom white balance, repeat these steps.

Setting the ISO Speed

The ISO speed determines how sensitive your camera sensor is to light. When you specify a high ISO speed, you can capture images when photographing in dark conditions — however, you also run the risk of adding digital noise to your images. As I mention earlier, noise isn't a good thing. On the plus side, when you specify a higher ISO speed, you also extend the range of the camera flash. To change the ISO speed

1. **Press the shutter button halfway to return to shooting mode.**

2. **Press the ISO button.**

   Look for the domed button in front of the Mode dial on the right side of your camera.

3. **Rotate the Main dial to specify the ISO setting while looking in the viewfinder.**

   The default ISO for the camera is A (Automatic), which means the camera chooses the ISO based on the lighting conditions. As you rotate the Main dial, the settings change. If you move your eye away from the viewfinder, the ISO menu appears on the LCD monitor (see Figure 7-17). With this menu, you can use the Main dial, use the cross keys, or tap a choice to set the ISO.

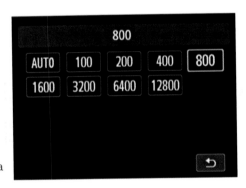

Figure 7-17: Set the ISO here.

Alternatively, you can set the ISO setting from the Quick Control shooting settings menu as follows:

1. **Press the shutter button halfway to return to shooting mode.**

2. **Press the Quick Control button and then use the cross keys to highlight the current ISO setting (see the left image in Figure 7-18).**

3. **Rotate the Main dial to select the desired ISO setting.**

Alternatively, you can press Set to reveal all the ISO options (see the right image in Figure 7-18), and then rotate the Main dial or use the cross keys to set the desired ISO.

4. **Press Set.**

The ISO setting is changed.

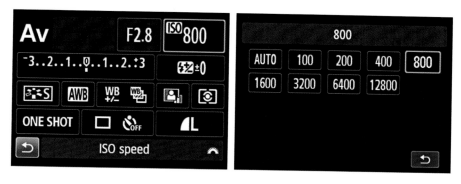

Figure 7-18: Use the Quick Control shooting settings menu to specify the ISO setting.

 When you exceed ISO 1600, you will see digital noise in your image. If you continually shoot at high ISO settings, consider investing in noise reduction software. I use Dfine 2, which is part of the Nik Collection by Google (www. niksoftware.com). I've used it to good effect on images I've photographed at ISO settings as high as 12800.

Expanding the ISO Range

You can extend the ISO range of your camera to give you a range from ISO 100 to ISO 25600. The high end will enable you to photograph fireflies in the dead of night. Kidding. But seriously, the extended ISO range will definitely enable you to capture images in very dim lighting conditions, but there is a payback in the form of some pretty gnarly digital noise. On the low end of the spectrum, you'll be able to shoot at slower shutter speeds, which is a definite bonus when you photograph beautiful flowing waterfalls. To extend the ISO range of your camera

 1. **Press the Menu button.**

The last-used menu command is displayed.

2. **Use the cross keys to navigate to the Camera Settings 4 tab and then use the cross keys to highlight Custom Functions (C.Fn) (see the left image in Figure 7-19).**

3. **Press the Set button.**

   The Custom Functions menu is displayed.

4. **Use the cross keys to highlight C.Fn I: Exposure ISO Expansion (see the right image in Figure 7-19).**

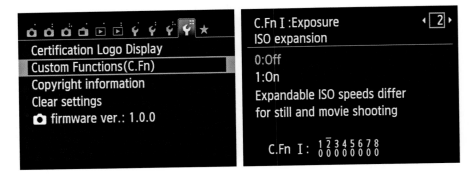

Figure 7-19: Expand ISO settings here.

5. **Press Set and then use the cross keys to highlight Enable.**

6. **Press Set.**

   Your ISO range is now expanded to ISO 25600. Note that when you are creating movies, you are limited to a maximum ISO of 12800.

Using White Balance Compensation

If you find that images photographed with a custom white balance have a colorcast, you can apply compensation to remove that colorcast. This is pretty advanced stuff, so unless you know a lot about color correction, color temperatures, and so on, stick to AWB (Auto White Balance) and do any necessary color correction in your favorite image-editing application. You can only use White Balance Compensation when shooting in the following modes: Programmed Auto, Shutter Priority, Aperture Priority, Manual, and Bulb. With White Balance compensation, you can shift the white balance if your images have a colorcast. You can also bracket white balance, in which case, the camera captures three images with three different white balance settings. So if you're dying to know what it's all about, follow these steps:

1. **Press the Menu button.**

   The previously used menu displays on the camera LCD monitor.

2. **Use the cross keys to navigate to the Shooting Settings 2 tab.**

3. **Use the cross keys to highlight WB Shift/Bkt. (see the left image in Figure 7-20) and then press the Set button.**

   The White Balance Correction window appears (see the right image in Figure 7-20). Notice the four letters: one at the center top (*G* for green), one at the center bottom (*M* for magenta), one at the left center (*B* for blue), and one at the right center (*A* for amber).

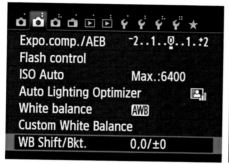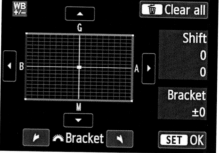

Figure 7-20: Applying a custom white balance.

4. **Move the dot.**

   You can move the dot toward one color and then move it up or down to shift the white balance toward a combination of amber and green. When you're adjusting white balance, you can precisely move the dot to exactly where you want to by using the cross keys or by dragging your finger to place the dot.

   When you move the dot, the color shift is designated in the dialog box (see Figure 7-21). In this case, the white balance is shifted two levels toward amber and two levels toward magenta.

5. **Rotate the Main dial to the left to bracket Green and Magenta, or right to bracket Blue and Amber (see the left image in Figure 7-22) and then press Set.**

Your changes are applied, and the shift is noted next to the WB Shift/Bkt. menu command (see Figure 7-22).

The color shift is designated here.

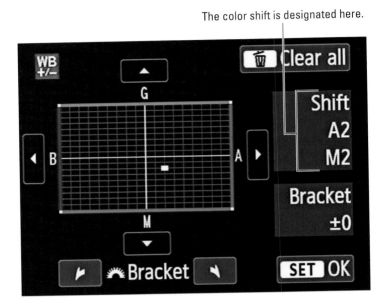

Figure 7-21: Apply a color shift to a custom white balance.

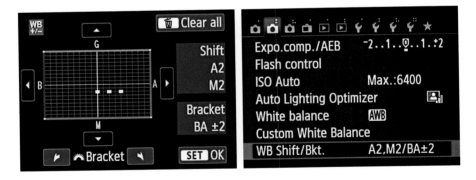

Figure 7-22: Bracketing white balance.

6. **Use the cross keys to highlight White Balance.**

The White Balance options are displayed (see Figure 7-23).

7. **Press Set and then use the cross keys to highlight Custom (the rightmost option).**

8. **If you've enabled White Balance Bracketing in Step 5, press the Quick Control button, use the cross keys to highlight the current drive mode, and then rotate the Main dial to select Continuous Drive (see Figure 7-24).**

9. **Press the shutter button fully to take a picture.**

The color shift is applied to your custom white balance. The colorcast is no more, quoth the raven. If you've enabled White Balance Bracketing, your camera takes three pictures with the bracketing you specify in Step 5.

To remove White Balance Compensation, repeat the preceding Steps 1–3 and then press the Erase button.

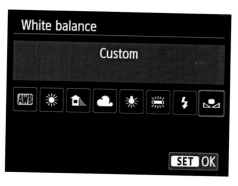

Figure 7-23: Applying the custom white balance.

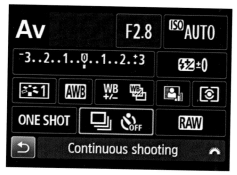

Figure 7-24: Use Continuous Drive when bracketing white balance.

Flash Photography and Your SL1/100D

Your SL1/100D comes equipped with a built-in flash. The pop-up flash isn't very powerful, but it will add some light in a pinch. To up the ante, you can insert a supported flash unit (fits in the camera hot shoe, atop the camera body). When you use a supported flash unit, the camera automatically calculates the amount of flash power needed to illuminate the scene and properly expose the image.

Even though auxiliary flashes are more powerful than the pop-up flash, don't expect to turn night into day when photographing the Grand Canyon with a wide angle lens and a flash unit. However, the flash will come in quite handy when photographing people in dim light.

The following Canon flash units will work with your camera: 90EX, 270EX II, 320EX, 430EX II, 600EX, or 600EX-RT (www.usa.canon.com). Some photographers use a 600EX or 600EX-RT (wireless radio transmission) as *master units* to control multiple flash units. The other units listed function as *slave units,* which receive instructions from the master units, enabling the photographer to set up sophisticated lighting scenarios similar to studio settings. Unfortunately, a tutorial on every lighting scenario you could conceive with your camera is beyond the scope of this book.

In the upcoming sections, I show you how to use auxiliary flash units, and also how to modify the amount of light your flash unit delivers.

Using the pop-up flash

Your camera has a built-in flash that automatically pops up (in certain basic and scene modes) when the metering system determines that additional illumination is needed to properly expose the image. In other modes, you're in total control — you tell the camera when to add additional illumination. You can use the pop-up flash to illuminate a scene or to add additional light to a scene. To enable the pop-up flash

1. **Rotate the Mode dial to select the desired shooting mode.**

   When you choose certain SCN modes, the flash pops up automatically.

2. **Press the Flash button.**

   Pop goes the flash (see Figure 7-25). Now you're ready to start illuminating subjects with the on-camera flash.

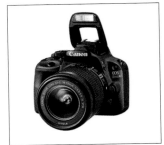

Figure 7-25: Enabling the pop-up flash unit.

Controlling the pop-up flash

Even though the pop-up flash may seem like an itsy-bitsy flash, it's actually quite sophisticated. You can lock flash exposure to a specific part of the frame, increase or decrease the power of the flash, and control the flash with menu settings. I show you how to do all this in the upcoming sections.

Locking flash exposure

When you create an image with camera flash, the exposure is locked to the center autofocus point. You can however, lock flash to a specific part of the scene, person, or object you're photographing, when shooting in Programmed, Aperture Priority, Shutter Priority, or Manual shooting modes. To lock flash exposure

1. **Press the shutter button halfway to return to shooting mode and then press the Flash button.**

   The flash pops to the upright and locked position.

2. **Compose your picture in the viewfinder and then press the shutter button halfway to achieve focus.**

   You cannot lock flash when photographing in Live View mode.

3. **While holding the shutter button halfway, move the center autofocus point over the part of the scene, object, or person you are photographing where you want to lock flash exposure.**

4. **Press the AE Lock/FE Lock/Magnify button.**

   When you press the button, a preflash fires. The camera metering system uses this preflash to determine the proper flash exposure for the area over which you position the center autofocus point.

5. **While still holding the shutter button halfway, move the camera to compose the image.**

6. **Press the shutter button fully to take the picture.**

Enabling Flash Exposure Compensation

When you take a picture with the pop-up flash, sometimes the flash can seem too harsh, or it can seem like the camera dished out more flash than you really needed. At other times, it may seem like not enough flash has been added to the image. When either event occurs, you can enable Flash Exposure Compensation to increase or decrease the amount of light the pop-up flash emits. To enable flash exposure compensation

1. **Press the shutter button halfway to return to shooting mode and then press the Flash button.**

   The flash pops to the upright and locked position.

2. **Compose your image and press the shutter button fully to take a picture.**

   Examine the image on the LCD monitor and determine whether the amount of flash is just right, or you need to increase or decrease the amount of light the unit emits.

3. **Press the Quick Control button.**

   The Quick Control menu appears.

4. **Use the cross keys to highlight the Flash Exposure Compensation setting.**

   Alternatively, you can touch the setting on the screen with your finger.

5. Rotate the Main dial left to decrease flash exposure, or right to increase flash exposure (see Figure 7-26).

If you change flash exposure, the number changes to reflect the number of stops by which you're increasing or decreasing flash exposure, and the orange bar moves left (decreasing flash exposure) or right (increasing flash exposure).

Alternatively, you can press Set to reveal the Flash Exposure Compensation menu (see Figure 7-27), and then rotate the Main dial right to increase flash exposure, or rotate it left. You can also use the cross keys to increase and decrease flash exposure, or drag the slider right and left with your finger.

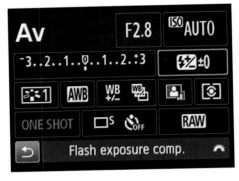

Figure 7-26: Use the Quick Control menu to adjust flash exposure.

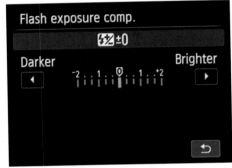

Using built-in flash settings

Your pop-up flash can do lots of cool things in spite of the fact that like the camera, it's diminutive. You can modify when the flash fires and also set exposure compensation with a menu command. To modify the built-in flash settings

Figure 7-27: The Exposure Compensation menu.

1. Press the Menu button.

The last used menu command is displayed.

2. Use the cross keys to navigate to the Shooting Settings 2 tab.

3. Use the cross keys to highlight Flash Control (see the left image in Figure 7-28) and then press the Set button.

The Flash Control menu is displayed (see the right image in Figure 7-28).

4. Use the cross keys to highlight Built-in Flash Settings, which is shown selected on the left image in Figure 7-29; press Set.

The Built-in Flash Settings menu is displayed (see the right image in Figure 7-29).

5. Use the up or down cross key to highlight Shutter Sync. and then press Set.

The Shutter Sync. options are displayed (see the left side of Figure 7-30).

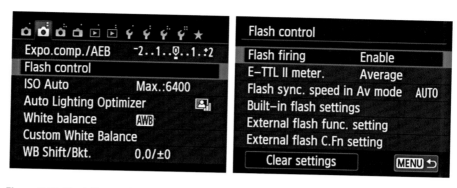

Figure 7-28: Flash Control Central.

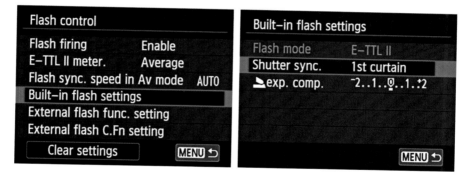

Figure 7-29: Modifying built-in flash settings.

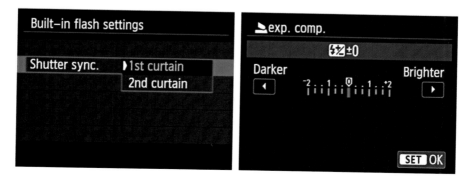

Figure 7-30: Shutter Sync. and Flash Exposure Compensation options.

6. **Use the cross keys to select one of the following options and then press Set:**

   • *1st Curtain:* The default option fires the flash when the shutter opens.

   • *2nd Curtain:* This option fires the flash when the shutter closes. This option is useful when you're photographing moving objects at night with slow shutter speeds.

7. **Use the up or down cross key to highlight Exposure Compensation and then press Set.**

   The Exposure Compensation menu is displayed (see the right image in Figure 7-30). This menu yields the same results shown in the Enabling Flash Exposure Compensation section of this chapter.

8. **Decrease and increase flash exposure by using the cross keys or dragging the slider with your finger; then press Set.**

   Flash exposure has been compensated.

Disabling camera flash

If you photograph in places like museums or aquariums where flash photography is prohibited, there are two ways you can disable the flash. You can either choose a shooting mode or disable flash via the camera menu.

 To disable flash via a shooting mode, rotate the Mode dial to Disabling Flash. When you disable flash, your menu options are limited to two Shooting Settings tabs: the first Shooting Settings tab, and the Live View Shooting Settings tab. In this mode, you are also limited to the first three Camera Settings tabs. If you have a custom menu (see Chapter 11), it's not available when you choose the Disabling Flash shooting mode. Your Quick Control Shooting Settings menu options are limited to choosing Drive Mode (see Figure 7-31).

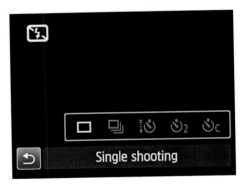

Figure 7-31: The Quick Control Shooting Settings menu in Disabling Flash mode.

In my estimation, the better way to disable flash is with a menu setting. When you use this option, you can still pop up the flash and use it to assist autofocus. To disable camera flash with a menu command

1. Press the Menu button.

The last used menu command is displayed.

2. Use the cross keys to navigate to the Shooting Settings 2 tab.

3. Use the cross keys to highlight Flash Control and then press Set.

The Flash Control menu is displayed.

4. Use the cross keys to highlight Flash Firing (see the left image in Figure 7-32) and then press Set.

The Flash Firing menu is displayed.

5. Use the cross keys to highlight Disable (see the right image in Figure 7-32) and then press Set.

Flash firing is disabled, but you can still press the Flash button to pop up the built-in flash unit and use it to assist autofocus when shooting in dim conditions.

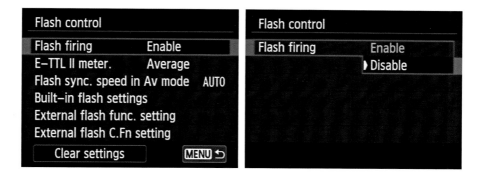

Figure 7-32: Disable flash here.

I know what you're thinking: Why would you disable flash and then shoot in dim lighting conditions? Well, sometimes you want to photograph something or someone at night without blasting the person or scene with flash. In this instance, you'd mount the camera on a tripod. If the camera has a hissy fit trying to focus on your subject, disable flash as outlined in this section, press the Flash button, and the flash will fire a preflash when you press the shutter button halfway, which helps the camera focus on your subject.

Changing the flash-sync speed in Av mode

When you're shooting in Aperture Priority (Av) mode, the camera shutter speed is set by default between 30 seconds and 1/180 second when the flash is enabled. The flash duration is very short and fires when the shutter opens, which gives you a sharp image of your subject. However, if the shutter speed is slow, you see motion trails if your subject moves during the long exposure. This can be very artistic. However, if you want to eliminate the possibility of motion trails, you can use a custom function to change the shutter speed used when a flash unit fires. Choosing one of the options that uses a higher shutter speed prevents motion trails, but the background will be dark. To change the flash-sync speed when shooting in Av mode

1. **Press the Menu button.**

   The last used menu command is displayed.

2. **Use the cross keys to navigate to the Shooting Settings 2 tab.**

3. **Use the cross keys to highlight Flash Control and then press Set.**

   The Flash Control menu is displayed.

4. **Use the cross keys to highlight Flash Sync. Speed in Av Mode (as shown on the left in Figure 7-33) and then press Set.**

   The Flash Sync. Speed in Av Mode options are displayed (see the right image in Figure 7-33).

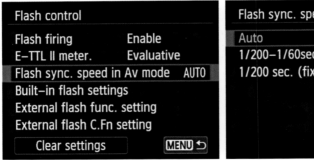
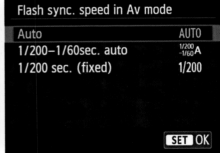

Figure 7-33: Choose a flash-sync speed here.

5. **Use the cross keys to highlight one of the following:**

   - *Auto:* The camera chooses a shutter speed between 30 seconds and 1/200 second when a flash unit is used in Av mode.

- *1/200–1/60Sec. Auto:* The camera automatically chooses a shutter speed between 1/60 and 1/200 second when a flash unit is used in Av mode, which prevents the possibility of a slow shutter speed being selected in low light conditions, which is what would happen with the default Auto mode.

- *1/200Sec. (Fixed):* The camera sets the shutter speed to 1/200 second when a flash is used in Av mode. The fast shutter speed ensures a blur free picture when using a telephoto lens, but the background may be darker than with the second option.

6. **Press Set.**

   Your flash unit is set to the desired flash-sync speed.

Using fill flash

Many photographers think that you use either ambient light or flash to illuminate a scene or subject. However, you can use camera flash to fill in the shadows when you're photographing a subject in the shade or a subject that's backlit. This is "fill flash." When you use fill flash, the camera automatically determines how much power is needed from the flash to augment the ambient light.

 To use fill flash, simply attach a flash unit to the camera as outlined in the previous section, and use one of the Creative Modes to shoot your pictures. I usually choose Aperture Priority mode (Av on the Mode dial), which enables me to control the depth of field when using fill flash.

For example, when photographing flowers in shaded conditions, create your images in Aperture Priority mode using an f-stop of f/6.3 or 7.1. This gives you a limited depth of field and the Fill Flash illuminates your subject perfectly. The light from the flash is also warmer than the shaded light.

 You can use the built-in flash or an auxiliary flash unit for fill flash. I recommend using a diffuser when using any flash. A diffuser diffuses the light making it appear as though it was generated by a larger light source. An overcast day is nature's example of a diffuser; it gives you soft, shadowless light.

Using an auxiliary flash unit

When you need to add some light to a scene or totally illuminate a subject with a supported flash unit, you must seat it in the camera's built-in hot shoe and then power on the flash unit. (Love that whine.) Your camera senses the flash unit and automatically calculates the amount of light needed to illuminate the scene or to fill in the shadows. You can perform flash photography using any shooting mode; however, you'll have the most options when you use the flash with Aperture Priority or Shutter Priority modes. To use an auxiliary flash with your camera

1. **Slide a supported flash unit into the hot shoe.**

   Earlier in this chapter, I list the flash units that your camera supports.

   The flash unit fits in the hot shoe one way and one way only. If in doubt, look at the contacts at the bottom of the flash unit, then look at the contacts on the hot shoe; you'll immediately see the correct orientation.

2. **Lock the flash unit into the hot shoe.**

   The flash unit should have either a thumbscrew that you turn to tighten or a lever that you flip to lock it down securely on the camera. If you cannot lock the flash unit, check to make sure the unit is fully inserted into the hot shoe.

3. **Power on the flash unit.**

   When you power on a supported flash unit, the camera and flash communicate, and you hear a whirring sound and see a solid light appear to let you know the flash is fully charged

4. **Take some pictures.**

   Figure 7-34 shows a Canon 430EX II mounted on the hot shoe of a SL1/100D, ready for action.

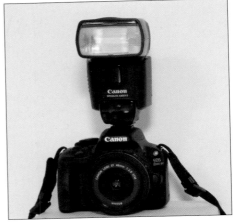

Figure 7-34: Flash photography is fun.

When you use an external Speedlite-type Canon flash, the light source is relatively small in comparison to your subject. If your subject is near a wall or not facing the camera directly, the flash will cast harsh shadows. When you use an external flash unit, always use a diffuser, which softens the light and makes it appear as though it is emanating from a much larger source.

Think about the light you get when photographing in direct sunlight: The light is fairly harsh and casts hard-edged shadows because the sun is a relatively small light source. This is similar to using a flash unit with no diffuser. Now think about the light you get on an overcast day. The clouds diffuse the sunlight (follow me now?) and make it a much larger light source. You get the same thing when you add a diffuser to your camera flash.

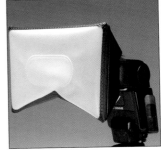

You can purchase a flash diffuser from your favorite camera retailer or purchase one online. I highly recommend the LumiQuest (www.lumiquest.com) line of flash diffusers. They're affordable and easy to attach to your flash (see Figure 7-35).

Figure 7-35: Use a flash diffuser to soften flash light.

Controlling an external Speedlite

When you mount a Canon EX Speedlite in the camera hot shoe, you can control the output with the camera menu and much more. And if you have an EX II Speedlite, you have gobs of control. The following steps show the options you have available with an EX II Speedlite.

The options may be different for your Canon Speedlite. Refer to your Speedlite manual for additional instructions. You can use the discussions from some of the previous sections to control a Canon Speedlite mounted in your camera hot shoe.

To lock flash exposure on a specific part of the frame, refer to the "Locking flash exposure" section of this chapter. You can also change the shutter speed at which the flash synchronizes as outlined in the "Changing the flash sync speed in Av mode" section of this chapter. You can also use a menu command to disable the external Speedlite (although why you'd go to the bother of attaching a Speedlite to the camera and then disabling it is beyond me).

You can also control such external flash functions as flash exposure compensation and the zoom setting for the flash.

To control flash with camera menu commands

1. **Insert a supported Canon Speedlite in the camera hot shoe as outlined in the previous section and then press the Menu button.**

   The last used menu displays.

2. **Use the cross keys to navigate to the Shooting Settings 2 tab.**

3. **Use the cross keys to highlight External Flash Func. Setting (see the left image in Figure 7-36) and then press the Set button.**

   The External Flash Func. Setting menu displays (see the right image in Figure 7-36).

4. **Use the cross keys to highlight ETTL and then press Set.**

   The Flash Mode menu is displayed (see the left image in Figure 7-37). You have two choices:

   - *ETTL:* This is the default, which meters the amount of flash needed "Electronically Through The Lens" — hence, ETTL.

   - *M (Manual):* Choose this option to manually set the flash.

   If you decide to control the flash manually, select the M option and then press Set. Refer to your Speedlite manual for information on controlling the flash manually.

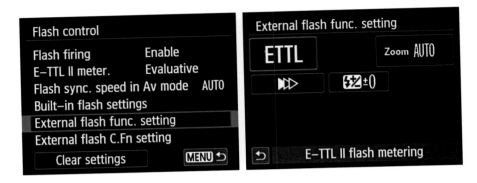

Figure 7-36: I'm in control, Mr. Speedlite.

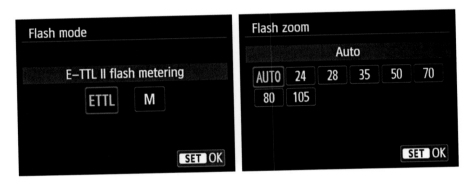

Figure 7-37: Determining flash metering and zoom.

5. **Use the cross keys to highlight Auto (the default flash zoom setting shown in the right image of Figure 7-37), and then press Set.**

   The Flash Zoom options are displayed (see the right image in Figure 7-37). The menu gives you the option to manually set the flash zoom. Normally, the flash zoom matches the lens focal length. However, if you use this option to choose a longer focal length than that to which you've zoomed the lens, the flash sends a narrower beam of light toward your subject. This is useful when you want to highlight part of a subject, such as the center of a flower.

6. **Use the cross keys to highlight the desired setting and then press Set.**

   The flash zoom is set to the desired focal length.

7. **Use the cross keys to highlight the Shutter Synchronization setting (see the left image in Figure 7-38) and then press Set.**

8. **Choose an option from the Shutter Synchronization menu and then press Set.**

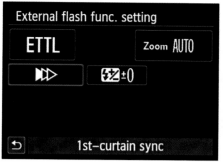 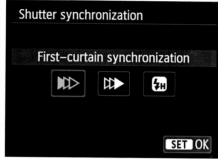

Figure 7-38: Choosing Shutter Synchronization.

Your choices are

- *1st Curtain Synchronization:* The default method, First-Curtain Synchronization, fires the flash when the shutter opens. This is all well and good when you're photographing people or objects that are standing still. However, when you use flash to photograph a moving object, the duration of the flash is much shorter than the shutter speed of the camera, especially when you're photographing in dim conditions or at night. The movement of the object after the flash fires shows up as a blur of motion, but the blur is going away from the object.

- *2nd Curtain Synchronization:* When you enable Second-Curtain Synchronization, the flash fires just before the shutter closes, creating a natural-looking motion trail that goes to the object instead of away from it.

- *High Speed Synchronization:* This option is available if supported by your Speedlite. Refer to the Speedlite manual for additional information.

After you press Set, the option is applied and you're returned to the previous menu.

9. **Use the cross keys to highlight Flash Exposure Compensation (see the left image in Figure 7-39) and then press Set.**

The Flash Exposure Compensation menu is displayed (see the right image in Figure 7-39).

10. **Use the left cross key to decrease flash exposure, or the right cross key to increase flash exposure.**

Each time you press a cross key, you increase or decrease flash exposure by 1/3 EV (Exposure Value).

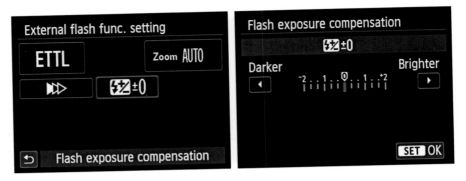

Figure 7-39: Applying Flash Exposure Compensation.

11. Press Set.

Flash Exposure Compensation is applied.

12. Press the shutter button halfway to return to shooting mode.

If you're really into controlling your Canon Speedlite through the camera, check out the External Flash C.Fn (Custom Function) Setting menu. This menu has options for custom functions that you can use to gain further control over your Speedlite. The available functions vary depending on the Speedlite you own. Refer to your Speedlite manual for more information.

Clearing Flash Settings

If you find that you've enabled lots of different flash options and don't want to go through the hassle of going through each and every menu option — or you forget which settings you've enabled — you'll be glad to know about a menu command to clear settings. To clear all flash settings in one fell swoop

1. Press the Menu button.

The last used menu displays.

2. Use the cross keys to navigate to the Shooting Settings 2 tab, and then use the cross keys to highlight Flash Control (see the left image in Figure 7-40). Then press Set.

The Flash Control settings are displayed.

3. Use the cross keys to highlight Clear Settings (see the right image in Figure 7-40).

This command gives you options to clear settings applied to the built-in flash or an external Speedlite.

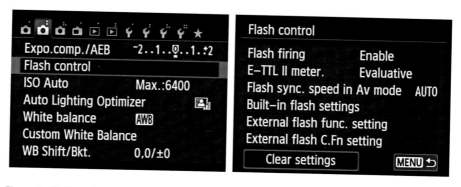

Figure 7-40: Clear flash settings here.

4. **Press Set.**

   The Clear Settings menu appears (see the left image in Figure 7-41).

5. **Use the cross keys to select one of the following options:**
   - *Clear Built-in Flash Set.:* Choose this option when you have applied settings to the built-in flash unit.
   - *Clear External Flash Set.:* Choose this option when you have applied settings to an external Speedlite.
   - *Clear Ext. Flash C.Fn Set.:* Choose this option when you have modified custom function settings of a Speedlite.

6. **Press Set.**

   A dialog box appears confirming that you want to clear all settings. The right image in Figure 7-41 appears when you clear external flash settings. A similar dialog box appears when you clear settings for the built-in flash, or clear custom functions for an attached external Speedlite.

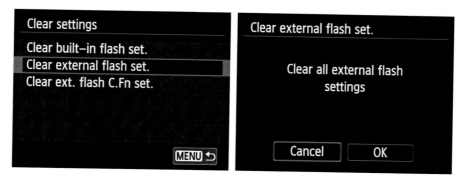

Figure 7-41: The Clear Settings menu and options.

7. **Use the right cross key to highlight OK and then press Set.**

The settings are cleared, and you're returned to the Clear Settings menu. If you're clearing settings for an external Speedlite, you can now clear custom functions. Alternatively, press Menu to return to the menu, or press the shutter button halfway to return to shooting mode.

All flash settings are cleared. Now wasn't that easier than going through each menu?

8

Shooting Frameworthy Photos

In This Chapter

▶ Enhancing your creativity

▶ Composing and visualizing images

▶ Choosing the right settings

▶ Photographing moving objects

▶ Taking photos of landscapes and sunsets

▶ Shooting portraits and wildlife

In earlier chapters, I show you all the bells and whistles on your camera that you can use in your photography. Bells and whistles are cool, but if you don't know when to ring or blow them, they don't do you much good. In this chapter, I cut to the chase and show you how to use these features for specific types of photography. Of course, you may not be interested in all the types of photography I discuss in this chapter, but I like to practice several different photography disciplines.

I find that different disciplines keep me on my toes and keep my work fresh — and they help me get to know my camera better. Try diversifying and shooting different subjects — you might like it. At any rate, in this chapter, I show you what settings to use for specific types of photography. I also sprinkle in some tips that will take your photography to the next level.

Thinking Like a Pro Photographer

Digital photography is a wonderful technology that enables you to take pictures without film. Anybody can learn how to take a picture with a camera, but creating an image is a different story. To create an image, you must embrace the technology, know the camera like the back of your hand, know which settings to use, which lens to use, and so on. If you're thinking about what settings and what lens to use, you're thinking about too many things, and you'll likely miss what's in front of you. To transcend from taking just pictures to creating compelling images, you need the knowledge and time that will allow you to stop and smell the roses and notice the subjects that interest you. The following sections are designed to get you thinking like a pro and creating the most wonderful images.

Enhancing your creativity

Great photographs are made by creative photographers who stretch the envelope. You can enhance your creativity by trying new things. Schedule a time each week when you experiment with new techniques or new equipment. Julia Cameron, author of *The Artist's Way* (Penguin Group) calls this an "Artist's Date." When I do this, I limit myself to one or two lenses and I often visit familiar territory. When you photograph a familiar place and the goal is to enhance your creativity, do things differently. Shoot from a different vantage point and use a different lens than you'd normally use for the subject.

When I was out on a recent Artist's Date, walking on a secluded beach with my wife, I saw a wonderful pattern of sea vegetation. Many photographers would put a wide angle lens on the camera and create a documentary image of the scene. I decided to use my Lensbaby Composer (http://lensbaby.com) with an optic that would create a sweet spot of focus that I could move to a specific area where I wanted to draw my viewer's attention to. I converted the image to black and white and added a sepia tone for a yesteryear look (see Figure 8-1).

Great photos always inspire me to get out the camera and take some pictures. Great photos can also help you become more creative. When you see a really great photo, dissect the image and try to figure out what the photographer did to make it so compelling. Was it a camera technique, or did the photographer do some editing after the fact to make the image pop? You can find great photos on the Internet in lots of places. One of my favorite places is http://photo.net. At this website, you'll find many types of inspirational photographs from portraits to drop-dead gorgeous landscapes. You can even join Photo.net and upload your own images. Next time you need something to spark your creativity, look at some great photographs.

You can enhance your creativity while you're taking pictures. Stretching the envelope is a wonderful way to create interesting photographs. The following points can help you stretch your creativity:

✔ **Simplify the scene to its lowest common denominator.** A great way to do this is to use a large aperture (small f-stop value) and focus your camera on the most important part of the scene. Or you can compose your picture so the viewer's eye is drawn to a single element in the image.

✔ **Look for patterns.** Patterns are everywhere. For instance, migrating birds in flight create a unique pattern, scattered leaves in the gutter create interesting random patterns, and flower petals create compelling symmetrical patterns. Of course, nothing says you have to compose an image symmetrically, either.

✔ **Don't fall in love with your first shot.** Before moving on, think of other ways you can capture the scene. Perhaps you can move to a different vantage point, switch lenses, or select a different aperture. Milk a scene for all it's worth and remember to look down. An interesting photograph may be beneath your feet. For that matter, turn around and look where you've been. Sometimes you can get a much better image of a scene by turning around and capturing the scene with a different light.

✔ **Explore your favorite subject and create a theme of photographs.** For example, if you're a cat lover, photograph your cat and then photograph the neighborhood cats. When you photograph the same subjects or places frequently, you think of new ways to create interesting pictures. Your creative juices start flowing and before you know it, you see your favorite subject in a different way. Photographing your favorite subjects and photographing them often helps you master your camera, and also helps you create better images of your favorite subjects.

My favorite subject happens to be landscapes. I live near the ocean and not very far from a picturesque river and several beautiful state parks, so lately this has been my theme.

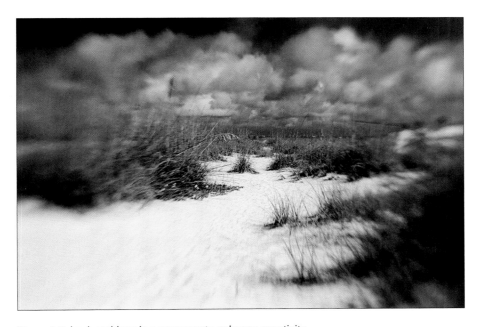

Figure 8-1: Look at things in a new way to enhance creativity.

Composing your images

A photographer's job is to create a compelling image, an image that makes the viewer take more than a casual glance. When you compose an image properly, you draw your viewer into the image. Lots of rules exist for composing a photo. I mention many of them in this section. Your job as a photographer is to figure out which one best suits your subject. This section is designed to make you think about composition when you look through the viewfinder of your SL1/100D or the LCD monitor when you photograph in Live View mode. You can use one of the Live View grids as a visual reference, or visualize a grid in the camera viewfinder. For more information on the Live View grid, see Chapter 5.

When you compose an image, look for naturally occurring curves that you can use to draw your viewer into the photograph. Curves are everywhere in nature: Birds have curved necks, and roads and paths have curves. The trunk of a tree curves to cope with Mother Nature like the trees in the tundra regions of the Rocky Mountain National Park. Look for naturally occurring curves and compose your image so that the curve draws the viewer's eye into the picture.

Many photographers take pictures in *landscape* format — the image is wider than it is tall. When you're photographing a scene like a waterfall, a person, or anything that's taller than it is wide, rotate the camera 90 degrees to shift into *portrait* format. The photograph of the anhinga (bird) in a pine tree (see Figure 8-2) is an example of shooting in portrait format. A few other compositional elements are in this picture: The branch leads your eye into the photo, the bird's beak is diagonal to the other elements in the picture, and then there's the lovely curve of the bird's neck. . . .

Many photographers place the horizon line smack-dab in the middle of the picture. Boring! When you're photographing a landscape, take a deep breath and look at the scene. Where is the most important part of the scene? That part of the scene

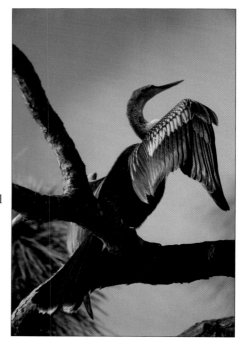

Figure 8-2: Use curves as part of your composition.

should occupy roughly two-thirds of the image. For example, if you're photographing a mountain, the mountain base should be in the lower third of the image. When you're photographing a sunset, place the horizon line in the lower third of the image to draw your viewer's attention to the sky. In Figure 8-3, I wanted to draw the viewer's eye to the massive thunderhead in the distance, so I placed the horizon line in the lower third of the image.

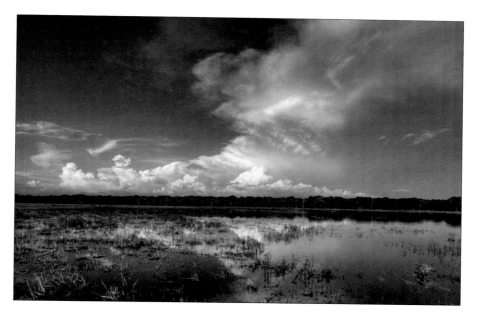

Figure 8-3: Place the horizon line for visual interest.

When you're composing an image, draw the viewer's eye to a center of interest in your photo. In a compositional rule known as the *Rule of Thirds,* imagine your scene is divided into thirds vertically and horizontally, creating a grid, as shown in Figure 8-4. Compose your picture so a center of interest intersects two gridlines. Figure 8-4 shows a grid overlay inside a facsimile of your SL1/100D viewfinder. Notice where the boy is placed in the sunset image. The middle of his body intersects two gridlines. This image, therefore, is composed according to the Rule of Thirds.

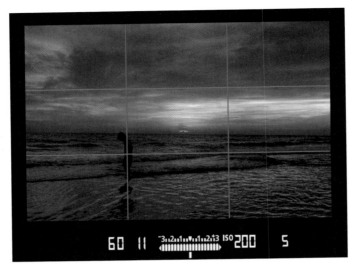

Figure 8-4: Align images according to the Rule of Thirds.

Visualizing your images

Anybody can point a camera at something or somebody, press the shutter button, and create a photograph. The resulting photograph may or may not be good, but that's not really photography. True photography is studying your subject and then visualizing the resulting photograph in your mind's eye. When you visualize the photograph, you know the focal length needed to capture your vision, the camera settings to use, and the vantage point from which to shoot your image.

Seeing, thinking, and acting

To take a good picture, you need a great camera like the SL1/100D, but even that doesn't guarantee you'll get a good, or even mediocre, picture. Getting a good picture is all about you: Your unique personality, vision, and creativity are what separate your photographs from those taken by the guy down the street who also owns an SL1/100D. Have you ever looked at two photographs of the same subject, yet they look completely different? That's where the skill and unique vision of each photographer comes into play as well as the photographer's comfort level with his equipment. Compare Ansel Adams's fine-art photographs of Yosemite to tourist snapshots from the same location, and you'll see what I mean.

Being in the moment

Some people think of photography as a religion. They approach their equipment and their subject with reverence, awe, and wonder. I'm sure you've seen photographs that have brought out those feelings in you. There's no reason you can't create your own jaw-dropping images. One of the best skills you can develop is *being in the moment* — experiencing the present moment and not thinking about anything else but the subject you're about to photograph.

If you're distracted by things you have to do later, you can't devote your total focus to the subject you're photographing. When you aren't thinking about anything in particular but are instead observing what's around you, you notice things that'd normally pass you by. When you're in the moment, you notice small details, such as the photogenic pile of leaves in the gutter or the way the sun dapples through the leaves to create an interesting pattern on the wall. You get better pictures when you're focused on what you're doing and not fretting about what you're going to cook for dinner or wear to work the next day.

Practicing 'til your images are pixel-perfect

If you use your camera only once in a blue moon, your pictures will show it. Letting your gear gather dust in the closet won't help you become a better photographer. Instead, use your camera every chance you get. Consider joining a local camera club because networking with other photographers is a wonderful way to get new information and stimulate your creativity. You may also find a mentor there. Simply strike up a friendship with an experienced photographer and tell her you want to tag along the next time she goes on a photo shoot. When you work with another photographer, notice the things that attract her attention and the subjects she uses for her images. She may photograph things you'd never think of photographing and create great pictures, or may photograph the same subjects as you but in a unique and different way.

The best way to practice photography is to take pictures of people, places, and things that interest you every chance you get. Practice your photography when you see something that inspires you, such as a compelling image in a magazine or a picture on the web. With that inspiration fresh in your mind, grab your camera and take lots of pictures of similar subjects.

I often do a photo walkabout. I grab one or two lenses, my trusty camera, and my imagination and then go to a part of town I haven't photographed. I start exploring. This photo walkabout gives me a chance to learn how to use a new piece of gear or experiment with a new technique, which enhances my creativity. Figure 8-5 shows an image I created with a 90mm macro lens.

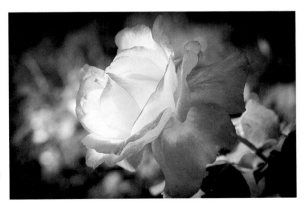

Figure 8-5: Practice makes perfect.

Becoming a student of photography

When you decide to seriously pursue photography, you can find a lot of resources. Great portrait photography is all around you. For instance, you'll find compelling portraits of the rich and famous in magazines like *People* and *US Weekly,* or you can find great pictures of breathtaking scenery in magazines like *Outdoor Photographer* or *National Geographic.* You can find great pictures of things in magazine advertisements. Your local newspapers and magazines are also great resources for great images.

When you see an interesting image in a magazine, study it carefully. Try to determine the type of lens the photographer used and then try to determine whether the photographer shot the picture in Aperture Priority or Shutter Priority mode. After you ascertain which shooting mode the photographer used:

- **In Shutter Priority mode,** try to determine whether the photographer used a fast or slow shutter speed.

- **In Aperture Priority mode,** try to determine whether the photographer used a large or small aperture.

Also try to determine how the photographer illuminated the subject. Did he use available light, camera flash, or fill flash? If you study great images carefully, you can get a rough idea of the settings the photographer used to take the picture.

Another great way to understand portrait photography is to study the masters:

- **Annie Leibovitz or Greg Gorman:** If you're into portrait photography, study their work.

- **Arnold Newman:** Study him if you like the work of the old portrait-photography masters. He created some wonderful environmental portraits.

- **Henri Cartier-Bresson:** If you like the gritty style of street photography, he's your man.

- **Ansel Adams or Clyde Butcher:** If you enjoy landscape photography, study their work. Clyde Butcher is affectionately known as the "Ansel Adams of The Everglades."

As I mention earlier, you can find lots of examples of great photography at www.photo.net. Other photography sites such as Flickr (www.flickr.com) or 500PX (http://500px.com) can be sources for inspirational photography.

Never leave home without a camera

You can't ask a photo opportunity to wait while you go home to get your camera. Photo opportunities happen when you least expect them. Therefore, never leave home without a camera.

Developing a style

Photographers are attracted to different subjects and do things in different ways. Casual photographers tend to produce similar images, but die-hard photographers like to do things differently. Die-hards have a different way of seeing things, and therefore, produce different-looking images, even when they photograph the same subjects. They experiment with different lenses, different vantage points, different lighting, and so on.

Each year thousands of photographs are taken of Yosemite National Park, yet most of them pale in comparison with the memorable images photographed by Ansel Adams. The key to developing your own style is to study the work of the masters. If you're a landscape photographer, check out Ansel Adams's work. If you like the gritty, down-to-earth, street-journalism style of photography, look at Henri Cartier-Bresson's work. The next step is to shoot what you love as often as you can.

If you're nervous about taking your expensive SL1/100D with you wherever you go, I don't blame you. I actually feel the same way. That's why I bought a relatively inexpensive point-and-shoot camera that I carry with me everywhere I go. When I see something I want to photograph, I reach in the glove box of my car, grab my trusty point-and-shoot camera, and snap the picture.

Canon makes the PowerShot G15, which is a wonderful point-and-shoot camera with professional features; it's a great camera to augment your SL1/100D. The G15 won't fit in your shirt pocket, but it will fit in your pants pocket, coat pocket, or your glove box. The Canon PowerShot S110 is another great option for a second camera.

Some photographers think smartphone cameras are a joke. However, if you have one of the new smartphones, you may have a competent camera. The newer iPods and iPads also have good cameras. If your portable device doesn't have a great camera, you can still use it to create a digital sketch of a scene you want to photograph at a later date with your SL1/100D. As one photographer is fond of saying, "The best camera is the one that's with you."

I also recommend carrying a small notebook with you. When you create a digital sketch with your point and shoot, you can add notes about the location and time of day you think would be best to photograph it. You can also jot down notes and ideas you get when you network with other photographers. A Moleskine Cahier notebook is small and will easily fit in your camera bag.

Waiting for the light

Landscape photographers arrive at a scene they want to photograph and often patiently wait for the right light or until a cloud moves into the frame to get the perfect picture. Sometimes they'll backtrack to a spot at a time when they know conditions will be better. Good landscape photographers are very patient, which is a virtue that all photographers need to cultivate. When you arrive at a beautiful scene but the light is harsh, stick around a while or come back later when you know the lighting will be better.

Also wait when you're shooting candid pictures. Minutes may pass with nothing exciting happening, but don't put away the camera yet. If you wait patiently, something will happen that piques your interest and compels you to press the Shutter button.

Defining your goals

Before you snap the shutter, get a clear idea of what the final image will look like. If you don't have a goal for the picture or the photo shoot, you're wasting your time — and if you're photographing a person, you're wasting your time and your subject's time. Of course, the goal doesn't have to be a great image. You can go on a photo shoot to experiment with new ideas, master a new technique, or experiment with a new lens. After all, practice makes perfect.

When you know why you're taking the picture, you'll know what settings to use, how to light the photo, which lens to use, and so on. If you're creating an image for a friend or a client, adhere to the standard rules of composition, but also take a couple of pictures using a unique vantage point or a slightly different composition than you'd normally use; you may end up with some interesting pictures your client will like. However, if you're creating photographs for yourself, the sky's the limit, and you can get as creative as you want. You can shoot from different and unique vantage points, tilt the camera, break the composition rules, use an unorthodox lens, and so on.

What's your center of interest?

When you create a picture of a person or place, decide what the main point of interest is and how you'll draw the viewer's eye there. For some photos, the point of interest may be a person's face or a landmark, such as the Lincoln Memorial. If you're creating a portrait of a pianist, a picture of him playing the piano would be appropriate and your center of interest could be his hands on the keys.

Sometimes, you have more than one center of interest. When this occurs, you can compose the photo in such a manner that one center of interest leads the viewer's eye to the other center of interest. For example, if you're photographing a cellist on a beach near San Francisco's Golden Gate Bridge, you have two centers of interest — the musician and the bridge. Your job is to marry these two centers of interest to create a compelling image and guide your viewer's eye through the photo. You also need to compose the photo so that one center of interest doesn't dominate the other.

What's your best vantage point?

The decision you make on your best vantage point depends on what you're photographing. In most instances, you want to be eye-to-eye when photographing a person. If you're photographing a landscape and the sky or a mountain is the dominant feature, choose a vantage point that causes the sky or mountain to dominate the upper two-thirds of the image. If you're photographing a scene in which a lake or the ocean is the dominant feature, lie on your belly and compose the photo so that the water feature occupies the bottom two-thirds of the image. Yup. The old Rule of Thirds is at work. Figure 8-6 shows a unique vantage point for an image of a historic district in Sarasota, Florida.

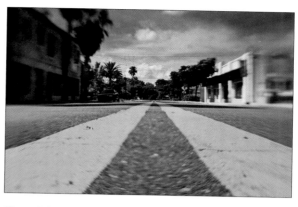

Figure 8-6: Using a unique vantage point to add interest to an image.

What else is in the picture?

You have to notice everything in the viewfinder or LCD monitor. The only time you aren't bothered by other objects is when you shoot a portrait against a solid color background, such as a wall or a cloth backdrop. If your subject's too close to the background, though, you may notice wrinkles from a cloth backdrop or texture from a wall. If this happens, ask your subject to move forward and then shoot the picture in Aperture Priority mode with your largest available aperture. Focus on your subject, and the bothersome details in the background will be out of focus.

When you're taking pictures on location, you often have unwanted objects, such as telephone poles in the background. Sometimes you have to decide whether to include the distracting elements in the image and then delete them in an image-editing application, but that takes time. If you can move your subject slightly and make the distracting elements disappear, that's always your best option. You can also move to a different place in the same general area with a pleasing background and no distracting elements.

When you're photographing a landscape, take a careful look in the frame. Are power lines visible? Are ugly buildings or trash in the frame? If so, move slightly until the distracting elements are no longer in it.

The genius of digital photography

Immediacy is the genius of digital photography. The old days of waiting for your film to be developed and returned from the lab are gone. You know if you got the shot as soon as it appears on your camera's LCD monitor. You also never have to pay for film again. Ever.

With these advantages comes a curse: If you're not careful, the very genius of digital photography can turn you into a bad photographer. You don't pay for film, so you tend to shoot more images, which is a good thing if you take good photographs. If you just shoot everything that pops up in front of your camera, you're going to get a lot of bad photos that end up in the trash.

To fully take advantage of the genius of digital photography, be in the moment and do your best to make every image a keeper. Practice using the myriad features your SL1/100D has to offer, and get it right in the camera. Don't rely on image-editing applications to fix a bad image. Image-editing applications like Photoshop are designed to enhance a correctly exposed, well-composed image and make it better. I cringe when I hear a photographer say, "I'll Photoshop it." As I've said before, Photoshop is not a verb; it's a noun.

Practice also enters into the equation. When you know your camera like the back of your hand and you apply all your attention to your photography, you're well on the way to utilizing the genius of digital photography to its fullest and capturing compelling photographs.

Choosing the Optimal Settings for Great Photographs

Your camera has settings for every conceivable type of photography. In the early chapters of this book, I show you the SCN modes, where the camera takes the bull by the horns and uses automatic settings. However, your camera doesn't really know if you're photographing a pet rock or the Grand Canyon. When you take off the training wheels and start using the really cool SL1/100D features and Creative Shooting modes, you're in control, and with practice (plus the sage advice of your friendly author), you'll create some great images.

All you need to do is attach the right lens to the camera to be ready for action. You can take pictures of just about any object, from a small insect to a racing car traveling at a high rate of fuel consumption. The trick is knowing what settings to use for a specific picture-taking situation. For example, say you're photographing your significant other and want her to be the center of attention with a soft blurry background. That's easy to achieve with the right camera setting and the right lens.

In addition to the right settings, you have to be creative so your photograph of a known person, place, or thing doesn't look like someone else's photograph of the same person, place, or thing. To take great pictures, you have to examine everything in the viewfinder and determine whether it's something you should include in the photograph. As I mention elsewhere, with a bit of thought and keen observation, you'll notice that light pole sticking out of your significant other's head and ask her to move to a different position (or you'll move to a different position).

Photographing action

Your camera is well equipped to photograph action, whether your subject is a flock of flying birds or the Blue Angels in formation. When you photograph an object in motion, your goal is to portray motion artistically. The camera settings and lens you use depend on the type of subject you're photographing. If you're photographing a marathon runner, you want to depict the beauty and grace of his fluid stride and athletic body. If you're photographing a racecar, your goal is the same. You want to depict the magnificence of a beautifully sculpted racecar at speed. So the type of settings you use depends on whether your subject is moving toward you or parallel to you, and whether your subject is moving very fast or very slow.

Photographing fast-moving subjects

When people see my photographs of racecars, they always assume I'm using a fast shutter speed because the car looks so clear, and they can see every detail, including the driver's name on the side of the car. I do just the opposite, though. I shoot with a relatively slow shutter speed when the car is traveling parallel to me using a technique called panning. You can do this with the kit lens if you're close to your subject. However, if you're not close to the faster-than-a-speeding-bullet object you want to photograph, consider purchasing a longer telephoto lens, or renting one. To photograph a fast-moving subject by panning, use these steps:

1. **Attach a telephoto lens to your camera.**

    The focal length of the lens depends on how far away your subject is. When I photograph racecars, I use a Canon 70–200mm f/4 lens. The 18–135 f/3.5–5.6 IS STM is another excellent choice for photographing race cars with your SL1/100D. (You can read about lenses like this in Chapter 1.) If the cars are relatively close to me, I can zoom out and still get the whole car. If they're far away, I zoom to 200mm, which brings the action to me.

2. **Point the camera where your subject will be when you take the picture and then zoom in.**

    If you're photographing an automobile race, you can compose your picture a lap before you take it. I generally zoom to almost fill the frame with the car and then zoom out a little, leaving a little distance in front of the car to give the impression that the car is going somewhere.

3. **Press the Quick Control button and use the cross keys to highlight the current autofocus mode. Then rotate the Main dial to switch to AI Servo focus mode (see Chapter 7) so that your camera focuses continually on your subject as it moves toward or away from you.**

   If your camera has a hard time keeping fast-moving subjects in focus, you can focus manually on the spot where the object will be when you take the picture.

4. **Switch to a single autofocus point in the center of the frame.**

   When you use multiple autofocus points, the camera may focus on an object other than the one you want to photograph. For more information on choosing an autofocus point, see Chapter 7.

5. **Rotate the Mode dial to Tv (Shutter Priority mode) and then press the shutter button and rotate the Main dial to select a shutter speed of 1/160 second.**

   You may have to use a slightly higher shutter speed if you're using a lens with a 35mm equivalent focal length of 200mm or longer. The aperture really doesn't matter with this technique. The background is stationary, but the car and camera are moving at the same relative speed. Therefore, the background will be a blur caused by the motion of the camera relative to the background. However, if you're photographing a race on an overcast day, and the f-stop value is lower than f/6.3, increase the ISO setting until you have an f-stop of f/6.3 or smaller. If you shoot with too large of an aperture, the side of the car will be in focus, but the driver's helmet will be out of focus.

6. **Spread your legs slightly and move your elbows to the side of your body. Cradle the barrel of the lens with your left hand and position your right forefinger over the shutter button.**

   This helps stabilize the camera as you pan with your subject. In this position, you're the human equivalent of a tripod.

7. **Pivot from the waist toward the direction from which your subject will be coming.**

8. **When your subject comes into view, press the shutter button halfway to achieve focus.**

   Sometimes the camera has a hard time focusing on a fast-moving object, such as a fighter jet traveling at several hundred miles per hour. If this is the case, switch to One-Shot AF mode, switch your lens to manual focus, and focus on the place where your subject will be when you press the shutter button. Press the shutter button just before your subject reaches the spot on which you've focused.

9. **Pan the camera with your subject to keep it in frame.**

   When you're photographing an object in motion, keep more space in front of the object than behind it. This shows your viewer the direction in which your subject is traveling.

10. Press the shutter button when your subject is in the desired position and follow through.

If you stop panning when you press the shutter button, your subject won't be sharp. Figure 8-7 is a photograph of a racecar racing through a corner. I used the panning technique to catch the essence of speed. At this point, the car was traveling well over 100 mph.

Don't get discouraged when you photograph fast-moving subjects, and your shots don't turn out how you want. You'll end up with a fair share of duds, but with practice, you'll start getting some sharp images. If 25 percent of your pictures shot using this technique are in sharp focus, you're doing well.

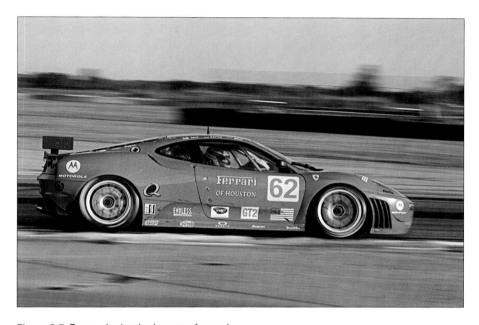

Figure 8-7: Pan to depict the beauty of speed.

Freezing action

When your subject is traveling toward or away from you at a fast rate of speed, your goal is to freeze the action. Another time you want to freeze action is when you want the photo to depict the beauty and grace of your subject. An example of this is a close-up of a tennis player with the ball just leaving her racket or a water-skier slicing through the water. To freeze action

1. Attach a telephoto lens to your camera.

The focal length of the lens depends on how far away your subject is. I generally use a focal length that is the 35mm equivalent of 300mm or longer when photographing racecars coming toward me. This puts some distance between me and the subject. A telephoto lens also does a great job of compressing the background. For example, if you're photographing a gaggle of racecars, a long focal length makes them look like they're closer to each other than they actually are.

2. **Point the camera where your subject will be when you take the picture and then zoom in.**

   When you compose the picture, leave some room in front of your subject to give the appearance that it's going somewhere. I generally try to include some of the background to give viewers an idea of the locale in which the photograph was taken.

3. **Press the Quick Control button and use the cross keys to highlight the current AF mode. Then rotate the Main dial to switch to AI Servo focus mode so that your camera focuses continually on your subject as it moves toward or away from you.**

   Your camera may have a hard time focusing on a fast-moving vehicle. I had this problem recently when photographing the start of an automobile race. The cars were traveling well over 100 mph at the place I wanted to photograph them, so I switched to manual focus and focused on an expansion joint. I snapped the shutter just before the car crossed the expansion joint. (For more information on switching focus modes, see Chapter 7.)

4. **Press the shutter button halfway, press the AF Point Selection/Magnify button, and then use the Main dial to select the single autofocus point in the center of the frame.**

   With multiple autofocus points, the camera may focus on something other than your subject. (For more information on switching to a single autofocus point, see Chapter 7.)

5. **Rotate the Mode dial to Tv (Shutter Priority mode), press the shutter button halfway, and then rotate the Main dial to choose a shutter speed of 1/1000 second.**

   Choose a higher shutter speed when trying to freeze the motion of something like a pitcher throwing a fastball. When you set the shutter speed, make note of the f-stop. If you can get a 5.6 or 7.1 f-stop, the background will be recognizable but not in sharp focus. You may have to experiment with different ISO speed settings to achieve the optimal shutter speed and aperture combination. Note that if you're shooting in low ambient light, you may see the maximum aperture (smallest f-stop number) blinking in the viewfinder, which means the image will be underexposed at the current shutter speed. Either choose a slower shutter speed, or increase the ISO until the aperture stops blinking.

6. **Press the Quick Control button, use the cross keys to highlight the current drive mode, and then rotate the Main dial to switch to Continuous Shooting mode.**

   With this mode, you can capture a sequence of images as long as your finger is on the shutter button at approximately 4 fps (frames per second). This is a great way to capture a sequence of your dog catching a Frisbee. For more information on choosing a drive mode, see Chapter 6.

7. **Press the Shutter button halfway to achieve focus.**

   A green dot appears on the right side of the viewfinder when you achieve focus. When shooting in AI Servo autofocus mode, the camera updates focus as your subject moves toward or away from you.

   If the dot is flashing, the camera can't achieve focus. You may experience this when you try to focus on a subject that's traveling very fast. If this happens, switch to One-Shot AF mode, switch the lens to manual focus, and then prefocus on the place your subject will be when you take the picture.

8. **Press the shutter button fully to take the picture.**

   If you switched to manual focus, press the shutter button just before the subject moves to where you focused. Figure 8-8 was photographed at the start of an automobile race. In this case, I switched to manual focus and focused on an expansion strip in the race track (which began life as a WWII airport).

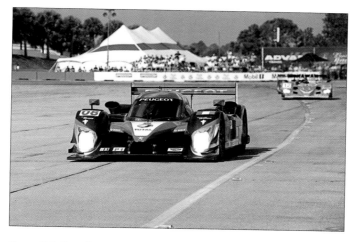

Figure 8-8: Freezing motion.

To get the knack of this technique, photograph a family member bouncing a ball or throwing a knuckleball at baseball practice.

Photographing slow-moving subjects

I cover freezing motion and capturing the essence of speed in previous sections in this chapter. Here I show you techniques to photograph subjects that move slower, such as horses, runners, and bicyclists. When you freeze the motion of subjects like these, the end result is kind of boring. When you photograph slow-moving subjects like runners or cyclists, you can use blur creatively to capture a compelling photograph of your subject. This technique also works great for photographing birds in flight. To photograph slow-moving objects

1. **Attach a telephoto zoom lens to your camera.**

   You can do this technique with a lens with a shorter focal length that's the 35mm equivalent of 50mm. However a longer focal length compresses the background. I like to use my 70–200mm lens when photographing slow-moving subjects.

2. **Point the camera where your subject will be when you take the picture and zoom in.**

3. **Press the Quick Control button, use the cross keys to highlight the current autofocus mode, and then rotate the Main dial to switch to AI Servo autofocus mode.**

   After the camera locks focus, your camera updates focus continually as your subject moves toward you. (For more information on switching autofocus modes, see Chapter 7.)

4. **Press the shutter button halfway, press the AF Point Selection/Magnify button, and then rotate the Main dial to switch to a single autofocus point in the center of the frame.**

   When you use multiple autofocus points, the camera may inadvertently focus on an object other than the one you want to photograph. (For more information on switching to a single autofocus point, see Chapter 7.)

5. **Rotate the Mode dial to Tv (switch to Shutter Priority mode), press the Shutter button halfway, and then rotate the Main dial to select a shutter speed of 1/30 second or slower.**

   This shutter speed is a good starting point, but don't be afraid to choose a slower shutter speed. I often photograph runners and bicyclists at a shutter speed of 1/6 second.

6. **Spread your legs slightly and move your elbows to the side of your body.**

This stabilizes the camera, which is important when you're shooting at a slow shutter speed.

7. **Pivot from the waist toward the area from which your subject will be coming.**

8. **When your subject comes into view, press the shutter button halfway to achieve focus.**

   A green dot appears in the right side of your viewfinder when you achieve focus. When you shoot in AI Servo autofocus mode, the camera updates focus as your subject moves.

9. **Pan the camera with your subject and then press the shutter button when your subject is at the desired spot.**

   Remember to follow through.

When you use this technique, certain parts of your subject are in relatively sharp focus, but body parts, such as a runner's arms and legs, are a blur of motion (see Figure 8-9).

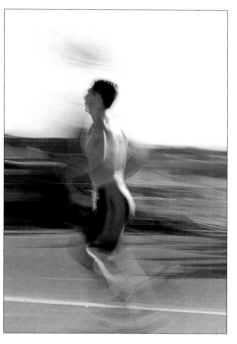

Figure 8-9: Using motion blur creatively.

Photographing landscapes

If you live in an area similar to the paradise in which I live, you can discover lots of lovely landscapes — thank you, Joni — and create compelling pictures of the landscapes with your camera. Landscape photography is a time-honored tradition. The fact that you own a camera capable of capturing images with an 18MP resolution means that you can create some very big prints of your favorite landscapes. My home is decorated with photographs I've shot since moving to the Gulf Coast of Florida. To photograph landscapes

1. **Attach a wide-angle zoom lens to your camera.**

   When you're photographing landscapes, you want to capture the wide expanse. Use a lens that can zoom out to a focal length that is the 35mm equivalent of 28mm or less. My favorite lens for shooting landscapes has a focal length that is the 35mm equivalent of 24mm.

2. **Rotate the Mode dial to Av (Aperture Priority mode), press the shutter button, and then rotate the Main dial to choose the smallest aperture (highest f-stop value) possible for the lighting conditions.**

A small aperture gives you a large depth of field. When you're photographing something like the Grand Canyon, you want to see everything from foreground to background. When I photograph landscapes, I use an aperture with a value of f/11.0 or smaller. Keep in mind that you may have to increase the ISO speed setting when photographing in cloudy or overcast weather. For more information on Aperture Priority mode, see Chapter 6.

3. **Press the shutter button halfway to achieve focus.**

   A green light appears in the viewfinder when the camera achieves focus. Take note of which autofocus points glow red. In spite of the large depth of field you get with a small aperture, you don't want the camera focusing on items in the foreground.

4. **Press the shutter button fully to take the picture.**

Landscape photography is rewarding. The preceding steps get you started in the right direction, but the time of day is also very important. If you think morning is for eating breakfast and the time before sunset is for eating dinner, you have it all wrong. These are the times you need to be chasing the clouds with your camera in hand. And yes, I do mean "chasing the clouds" because clouds add interest to any landscape.

If you have a still body of water into which the clouds can reflect, you have an even more compelling picture. The light in the morning just after sunrise and the light just before sunset are warm, almost golden in color. That's why the hour after sunrise and the hour before sunset are the *Golden Hours*. This is when you need to photograph your landscapes (see Figure 8-10).

Composition is a very important part of photography, especially when you photograph a landscape. Your goal is to draw your viewer into the image. For more information on composing your photographs, check out the earlier "Composing Your Images" section in this chapter.

Photographing the sunset

Sunset is an awesome time of day for photographers. The sun is low on the horizon, casting warm orange light. Add clouds to the equation and you have the recipe for great sunset pictures. When you photograph a sunset, the sun is obviously a key player, but you need other ingredients, such as clouds and an interesting landscape, for a great shot. Without clouds, you have a boring picture of an orange ball sinking in a cerulean blue sky. You can take pictures of sunsets with the skyline of your town in silhouette. You can get an even better sunset shot when you have a body of water such as a lake, a river, or an ocean. The water will reflect the colorful clouds. If the water is still, you have a wonderful mirror reflection of the clouds and the setting sun. If the water is choppy, the sun and clouds still cast a wonderful glow on the waves.

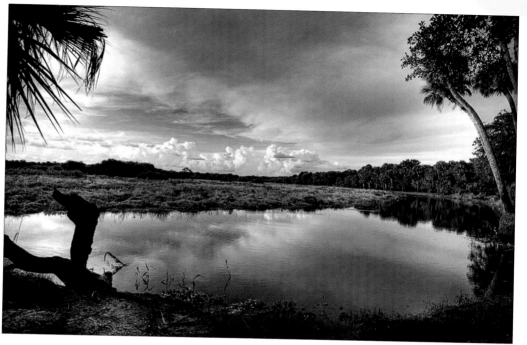

Figure 8-10: Photographing landscapes in the Golden Hour.

You can get some great sunset pictures in the final few minutes before the sun sets. After the sun sets, many photographers pack up their gear and head home. This is a mistake. As long as the clouds don't go all the way to the horizon, the sun will reflect warm colors on the underside of the clouds for about 10 to 15 minutes after setting. If you want really great sunset pictures, wait a few minutes after the sunset and get ready to take some pictures when the clouds are bathed in giddy shades of pink, orange, and purple (see Figure 8-11).

The camera settings for a sunset are almost identical to those you use for landscapes, with the exception of lens choice. If you're going for the grand view, use a wide-angle lens with a minimum focal length that is the 35mm equivalent of 28 mm or less, and choose the smallest possible aperture for a large depth of field. Sometimes you may need to go the other route and choose a telephoto focal length and a fairly large aperture for a limited depth of field.

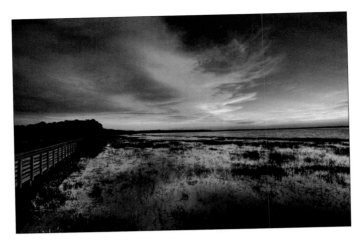

Figure 8-11: Catching the perfect sunset.

Recently I photographed a sunset at a picturesque beach a few minutes from my home. I used my Canon 24–105mm F 4.0 L lens and zoomed to 105mm, with an aperture of f/7.1. You can get similar results with the 18–135mm f/3.5–5.6 STM IS lens. I focused on some nearby sea oats. The sea oats were in silhouette and in sharp focus. Due to the relatively large aperture, the clouds were a little soft, and the sun was a soft out-of-focus orange orb, as shown in Figure 8-12. Because I was using a relatively long focal length, the sun is somewhat large in the resulting photo, which makes it clear I took the photo as the sun was setting.

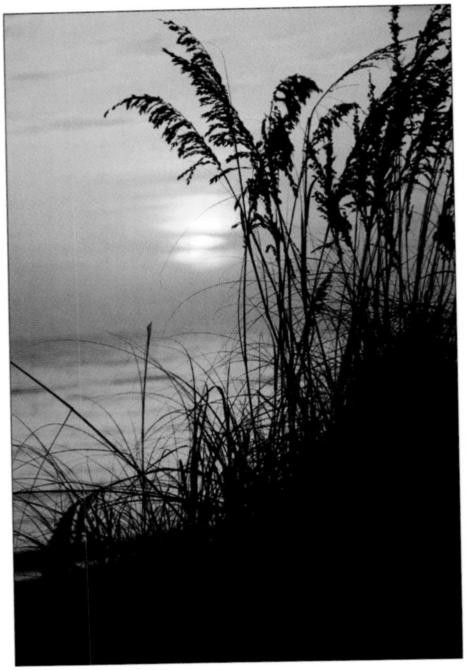

When you photograph a sunset, the camera metering system may make the scene much brighter than it actually is. If you notice this when reviewing the image on the camera LCD monitor, lock exposure on the sky and then take the picture. Alternatively, you can use exposure

Figure 8-12: Photographing the sunset.

compensation to reduce exposure by one stop or more. (For more information on exposure compensation and locking focus, see Chapter 6.)

When you photograph the sun, don't look directly at the sun through your viewfinder or you may damage your vision. If you photograph sunsets with Live View mode or with the mirror locked, don't point the camera at the sun for a long period of time because you may damage some of the sensitive components in your camera.

Photographing people and things

Photographing people and the world around you is another way to get the most out of your great camera. When you photograph people and things, your goal is to create a compelling photo of the object or person, a portrait if you will. In the upcoming sections, I offer some advice for photographing people, pets, flowers, and more.

Photographing people and pets

With the right lens, your camera can capture stunning photos of people or pets. You can photograph formal or candid portraits, or use Live View mode to shoot from the hip. When you photograph people and pets, here are some things to keep in mind:

- Use a telephoto lens with a focal length that is the 35mm equivalent of 85mm or longer.

- Switch to Aperture Priority (Av) mode. (For more information on Aperture Priority mode, see Chapter 6.)

- Switch to a single autofocus point or the middle autofocus zone. (For more information on modifying autofocus, see Chapter 7.)

- Choose your largest aperture (smallest f-stop value). Choosing a large aperture gives you a small depth of field. Your subject is in focus, but the background is a soft, out-of-focus blur.

- If you're photographing a group of people in rows, switch to a smaller aperture for a larger depth of field to ensure that all the people in the image will be in focus. If the resulting shutter speed is too slow, you'll have to increase the ISO setting, or mount your camera on a tripod.

- If you're taking the picture indoors, photograph your subject against a solid color wall. You can also tack a solid color bed sheet to a wall and use that as a backdrop.

- If you're photographing your subject outdoors, photograph her against a nondescript background, such as distant foliage. If you photograph your subject with a telephoto lens with a large aperture and shoot *wide open* (photographer-speak for using your largest aperture), the background will be a pleasant out-of-focus blur that won't distract your viewer's attention from your subject (see Figure 8-13).

✔ If possible, don't use a flash when photographing people because this produces a harsh light that isn't flattering for portraits. Available light from a window is your best bet if you photograph indoors and diffuse shade is best if you photograph the portrait outdoors. Photographing portraits on a cloudy overcast day is also ideal. If you do use a flash, use it with a diffuser, which spreads the light out and makes it appear as though your subject is illuminated with a larger light source. You can find flash diffusers at your favorite camera retailer, or purchase them online. LumiQuest (`www.lumiquest.com`) manufactures a line of very portable and very affordable flash diffusers.

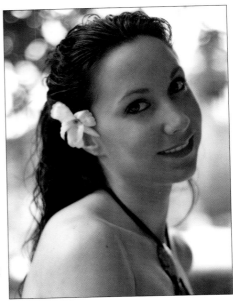

Figure 8-13: Find a pleasing background that doesn't detract from the subject.

✔ If you use an auxiliary flash to illuminate your subject, mount it in the hot shoe and then bounce it off a white surface, such as a wall or the ceiling. When you bounce the flash off a large surface, you end up with a soft diffuse light similar to that of a cloudy day.

✔ When using flash to illuminate your subject, make sure she's not too close to the wall; otherwise, you'll get a nasty shadow.

✔ When you're shooting portraits of a friend, relative, or your pet, take lots of pictures. Your subject will give you more natural expressions as he becomes comfortable with you taking pictures and relaxes.

✔ Use Live View mode when you want candid shots of friends or your pet. After enabling Live View, place the camera on a table with the end of the lens just off the table. When you see something interesting happen, take a picture. Your friends won't be as intimidated by the camera on the table as they would if you held the camera to your face.

✔ Never photograph pets with flash. The bright light scares them, and the light reflecting from the back of their eyes makes them look like they're possessed.

✔ When you photograph a person or a pet, make sure the eyes are in focus.

   1. Switch to a single autofocus point when photographing a head-and-shoulders portrait.

> *2. In the viewfinder, align the autofocus point with the person's (or pet's) eye that is closest to the camera, and press the shutter button halfway to achieve focus.*
>
> *3. Recompose the shot and take the picture.*
>
> Remember that the eyes are the windows to the soul.

You need to consider lots of things when you photograph people and pets, much more than I can include in this book. If you want more information on portrait photography, check out *Digital Portrait Photography For Dummies* by yours truly.

Exploring selective focus

When you own a camera like the SL1/100D and a lens with a large aperture with an f-stop value of 2.8 or smaller, you can create some wonderfully artistic photos by using the *selective focus* technique. When you take pictures with the largest aperture on a lens with a focal length that is the 35mm equivalent of 85mm or longer, you have a wonderfully shallow depth of field. You can use this to your advantage by focusing on one spot that will be your center of interest. The rest of the image will be out of focus, and your viewer's attention will be drawn to the point in sharpest focus. Here's how to create images with this technique:

1. **Switch to a single autofocus point and Aperture Priority mode.**

   See Chapter 7 for more on autofocus points and Chapter 6 for more on the Aperture Priority mode.

2. **Look through the viewfinder and position the autofocus point over your center of attention.**

3. **Press the shutter button halfway to achieve focus and then move the camera to recompose the image.**

   I photographed Figure 8-14 with a Canon 85mm f/1.8 lens. I switched to a single autofocus point and focused on the Harley Davidson badge.

Exploring macro photography

Extreme close-up photography, also known as *macro photography,* can be a tremendous source of enjoyment. With a macro lens, you can get close to small insects, flowers, and other objects that look interesting when magnified to life-size proportions. Keep the following in mind when working with macro photography:

✔ **Get a good macro lens.** Canon makes a wonderful lens for macro photography — the 100mm EF f/2.8 lens — which works on your SL1/100D. You can also choose from lots of third-party macro lenses available for your camera. Tamron makes a great 90mm macro lens and 180mm macro lens.

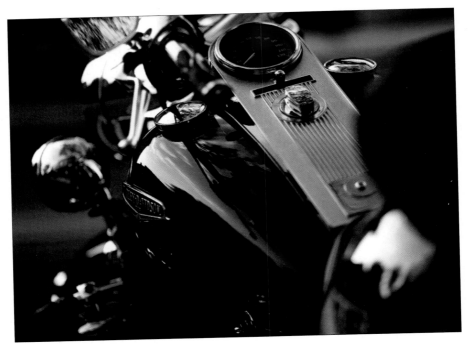

Figure 8-14: The selective focus technique with a telephoto lens and a large aperture.

- ✓ **Focus, focus, focus.** Focus is extremely important because when you use a macro lens and get very close to your subject, you're dealing with a very limited depth of field.

- ✓ **Avoid the wind.** Macro photography is almost impossible to do when the weather is windy because your subject keeps moving in and out of focus. If it's not too windy, switch the autofocus mode to AI Focus. If the camera achieves focus and the item you're photographing moves, the camera switches to AI Servo and updates focus.

- ✓ **Outsmart the wind.** When it's windy and your camera fails to achieve focus using the AI Focus mode, switch to One Shot AF mode and focus manually on a point in the middle of your subject's range of motion. Switch to continuous drive mode and capture several images of your subject. One or more of them are bound to be in focus.

- ✓ **Use aperture priority.** When you decide to get small and go macro, shoot in Aperture Priority (Av) mode (see Chapter 6) and choose the smallest aperture possible for the lighting conditions. This gives you a slightly larger depth of field.

- ✓ **Flash can be your friend.** When you shoot close-ups of subjects like flowers, use built-in camera flash to add a splash of light to your subject, especially if the flowers are in shade or you're shooting on a cloudy overcast day. Use flash exposure compensation to reduce the power of the flash so that you're adding a kiss of light to the image. The flash helps freeze motion and warms up the image.

✔ **Use a tripod.** A good tripod is a handy accessory when shooting macro photography because it keeps the camera steady. When you shoot with a tripod, switch to the drive mode that has the 2-second time delay. The slight delay causes any vibration that occurred when you pressed the shutter button to subside. If you're not using a tripod, shoot at a higher shutter speed than you normally would, keep as steady as possible, focus, and gently squeeze the shutter button when you exhale.

Photographing wildlife

With a camera like the SL1/100D, you can capture stunning photos of wildlife, whether the animals are moving or standing still. Photographing wildlife can be challenging, but the results are extremely rewarding. When you shoot wildlife with a camera and get a great shot, the animal lives to see another day and you have a wonderful trophy to matte and frame. The following sections offer some tips for photographing wildlife in different locations.

Photographing animals at state parks

Good spots to photograph wildlife near your home are state parks. Search online for **state park** followed by the name of the town or county in which you live to find parks near you.

Another good source for information is the people in your local camera store or camera club. Be nosy and ask them where their favorite wildlife photography spots are. Make friends with them and ask whether you can tag along on one of their photo shoots. I live in an area that has many state parks. When I moved to my current stomping grounds, I had the good fortune to find a photography buddy who has shown me many of the wonderful wildlife hot spots near my home.

Here are some things I've figured out about photographing wildlife in a state park:

✔ **Photograph animals with a long lens.** Unless you're photographing large animals, you'll need a long lens with a focal length that is the 35mm equivalent of 300mm or greater. This may be quite a handful on a small camera like the SL1/100D but is still manageable. State parks are animal sanctuaries. Even though the animals are protected, they're wary of humans. A long lens is the only way you can get close-ups of the animals.

✔ **Switch to Shutter Priority (Tv) mode (see Chapter 6) and choose the proper shutter speed.** When you're photographing wildlife with a long lens, camera shake due to operator movement is magnified. Choose a shutter speed that's equal to the reciprocal of focal length of the lens you're using. For example, if you're using a lens with a focal length the

35mm equivalent of 300mm, you have to choose a shutter speed at least 1/300 second. If your lens has image stabilization, enable it when photographing wildlife. You may have to increase the ISO speed (see Chapter 7) to get the proper shutter speed, especially if you're photographing wildlife in a forest or in dense foliage. A tripod is also useful to stabilize the camera.

✔ **Use a large aperture (small f-stop number) when you create wildlife portraits.** The shallow depth of field you get with a large aperture ensures that your viewer's attention is drawn toward the animal, and not the background (see Figure 8-15). To get the desired f-stop when you want to use a specific shutter speed, change the ISO setting.

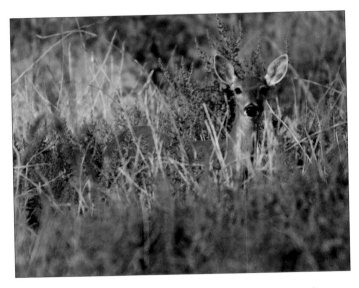

Figure 8-15: Use a large aperture when creating wildlife portraits.

✔ **Switch to a single autofocus point (see Chapter 7) and focus on the animal's eyes.** If the eyes aren't in focus, you've missed the shot. When you're shooting wildlife with a long lens and using a large aperture, you have a very shallow depth of field, which makes accurate focus a necessity. If the animal's eyes are in focus, your viewer assumes the entire animal is in focus.

✔ **Always travel with a photo buddy.** Many of the animals in state parks are fairly benign. However, some of the inhabitants can be dangerous if you're not careful. Many state parks have bears, alligators, and other animals that can be hazardous to your health when provoked. While you're in the moment photographing a bird, your buddy can watch your back and make sure a dangerous animal like an alligator isn't sneaking up on you. An alligator can pop out of the water like a rocket.

Stabilizing the camera when using long telephoto lenses

When you photograph wildlife with a long telephoto lens, any operator movement is magnified. The simple act of pressing the shutter button, no matter how gently you do it, vibrates the camera. The vibration degrades the resulting images slightly; it doesn't appear to be tack-sharp. A tripod is a huge help when using a long lens, but it doesn't stop the vibration. Here are two techniques you can use to minimize the vibration transmitted after you press the shutter button.

Stabilizing the camera with the self-timer

An easy way to stop vibration from reaching the camera is to delay the shutter opening after you press the shutter button. You do this with the camera's self-timer as follows:

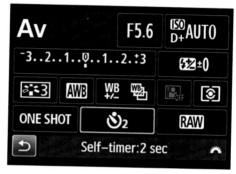

Figure 8-16: Stabilizing the camera with the 2-Second timer.

1. **Press the Quick Control button.**

2. **Use the cross keys to select the current drive mode and rotate the Main dial until the 2-Second Timer icon appears (see Figure 8-16).**

3. **Mount the camera on a tripod.**

4. **Compose your scene and press the shutter button halfway to achieve focus.**

   When the camera focuses on your subject, a green dot appears in the viewfinder.

5. **Press the shutter button fully.**

   Press the shutter button gently; don't stab it with your finger. After you press the shutter button, the timer counts down. When you press the shutter button gently, 2 seconds is enough time to stabilize any vibration transmitted to the camera.

Using mirror lockup to stabilize the camera

Your camera can also lock the mirror in the up position before the picture is taken. This helps minimize the transmission of any vibration that occurs when the mirror moves up prior to opening the shutter. This vibration can cause your image to be less than tack sharp. You can enable Mirror Lockup using a custom function as follows:

1. **Press the Menu button.**

   The previously used menu displays.

2. **Use the cross keys to navigate to the Camera Settings 4 tab (or just tap its icon).**

3. **Use the cross keys to highlight Custom Functions (C.Fn) (the left image in Figure 8-17) and then press the Set button.**

   The Custom Function menu is displayed.

4. **Use the cross keys to highlight C.Fn III: Autofocus/Drive Mirror Lockup (see the right image in Figure 8-17) and then press the Set button.**

   You can now enable mirror lockup.

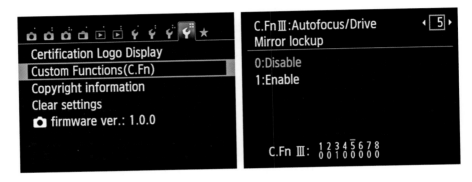

Figure 8-17: Enable mirror lockup here.

5. **Use the cross keys to highlight Enable and then press the Set button.**

   Mirror lockup is enabled.

6. **Press the shutter button halfway to return to shooting mode.**

7. **Compose the scene and then press the shutter button halfway to achieve focus.**

   A green dot appears in the right side of the viewfinder.

8. **Press the shutter button fully.**

   The mirror locks up.

9. **Press the shutter button again.**

   The picture is taken, and the mirror drops down.

When you're using mirror lockup in bright conditions, press the shutter button as soon as possible after the mirror locks up. Excessive exposure to bright light or the sun can damage the sensor. Make sure you disable mirror lockup as soon as you no longer need it.

Photographing animals at the zoo

If you live in a big city or don't have any nearby nature reserves or parks, you can still get some great shots of wildlife at your local zoo. Visit the zoo on an off day when there will be fewer crowds to contend with and get there just before feeding time. The animals are likely to be more active prior to feeding time.

When you find an animal you want to photograph, make sure no humans (or other signs that you're at a zoo) are in the frame. Switch to Aperture Priority (Av) mode (see Chapter 6) and choose your largest aperture. Move around to compose the best possible picture and then zoom in on the animal. Patiently wait until the animal does something interesting and then take the picture. Stick around for a few minutes, and the animal may do something else that's interesting or amusing. If possible, compose your image so that no telltale signs, such as fence posts or signs, give away that the image was shot at a zoo. If you're forced to take pictures with these objects, crop them out in your image-editing program.

Photographing birds

Birds run the gamut from downright ugly (the turkey vulture comes to mind) to beautiful and graceful. If you've ever witnessed a snowy egret preening, you've seen a truly elegant bird. When you photograph birds, it's almost like shooting a portrait of a person. Here are some tips for photographing birds with your SL1/100D:

- **If you're photographing flying birds, switch to the middle autofocus zone and switch to AI Servo autofocus mode (see Chapter 7).** When the camera achieves focus, it updates the focus as the bird flies.

- **If you're photographing flying birds, switch to Shutter Priority (Tv) mode (see Chapter 6), and choose a shutter speed of 1/250 second or faster.** This freezes the bird's motion. You can also go the other way and choose a slow shutter speed of 1/30 second. If you choose the slower shutter speed route, pan the camera with the bird. That way, the bird's wings will be blurred in your shot, giving you an artistic photograph of a bird in flight.

- **Photograph birds in the morning or late in the afternoon.** The light is warmer and more pleasing at these times of day. The harsh midday sunlight isn't a good light for any subject, even your fine feathered friends.

- **Use a long telephoto lens with a focal length the 35mm equivalent of 200mm or greater.** If the lens has a large aperture (small f-stop value), you're in business. The telephoto lens gets you close to your subject without spooking the bird. Even protected birds in a city park are unnerved by the sight of a human at close range. Shooting in Aperture Priority (Av) mode (see Chapter 6) and choosing a large aperture helps to blur the background. After all, you want photographs of birds, not the buildings in the background.

✔ **Crouch down to the bird's level for a more natural-looking photograph.** This often means kneeling in wet grass. Wear a pair of old jeans when you photograph wildlife and watch where you kneel; you may kneel in a great blue heron's bathroom.

✔ **Photograph birds on a cloudy day or a foggy morning.** You'll have beautiful diffuse light that won't cast harsh shadows. If the sky is completely overcast, you have no shadows. Photograph birds in heavy fog, and you have no signs of civilization (see Figure 8-18). When you photograph birds in low light, you may have to increase the ISO speed setting to get a shutter speed fast enough to take pictures while hand-holding the camera. Alternatively, you can use a tripod.

✔ **Take one shot and then move closer.** Get as close as you think you can without spooking the bird and then take a picture. With one picture in the bank, move closer and take another picture. If you approach the bird cautiously, you won't spook him and may end up getting an extreme close-up.

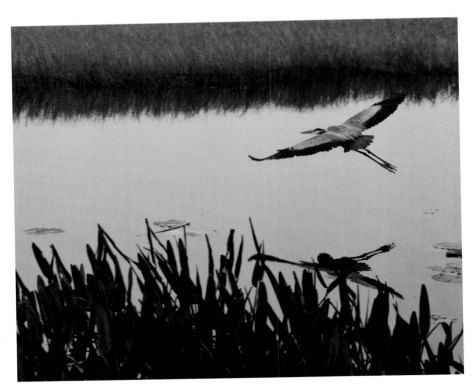

Figure 8-18: Photograph birds when it's cloudy or foggy.

Part III
Editing and Sharing Images

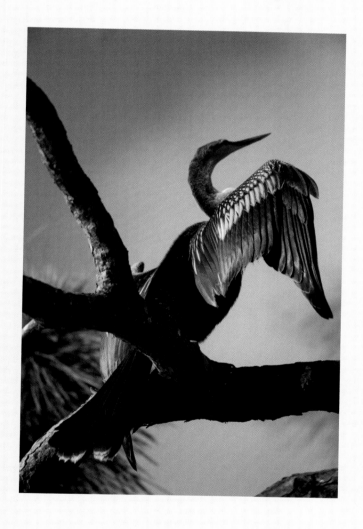

Check out the article "Customizing Buttons to Make Auto Exposure Lock Easier" online at www.dummies.com/extras/canon.

In this part . . .

- ✔ Learn how to use Canon software to edit your images.

- ✔ Discover how to edit JPEG files with ImageBrowser EX.

- ✔ Get familiar with editing Raw files in Canon Digital Photo Professional.

- ✔ Find out how to print files from ImageBrowser EX and Canon Digital Photo Professional.

9

Editing Your Images

In This Chapter

▶ Getting to know the Canon ImageBrowser EX

▶ Downloading and organizing images

▶ Rating, keywording, and commenting on images

▶ Changing your view

▶ Backing up your images

▶ Editing JPEG images in ImageBrowser EX

▶ Editing RAW files in Digital Photo Professional

*W*hen it comes time to edit your photos, you can use third-party software, such as Adobe Photoshop Lightroom, Apple's Aperture, Adobe Photoshop Elements, or Adobe Photoshop. If you don't have an image-editing application on your computer, you can install *ImageBrowser EX,* which is the software that Canon provides with your camera. This free application isn't as powerful as Lightroom or Photoshop, but you can still do a lot of things with it.

You have a two-pronged attack for organizing and editing your work. Use ImageBrowser EX to download and organize your work as well as edit JPEG files. And if you've used the RAW format to capture your images, bring in the heavy artillery and use Canon Digital Photo Professional 3.13, which also ships with your camera. In this chapter, I show you how to use both applications.

Note: As I discuss further in Chapter 10, if the colors in your monitor are slightly off, what you see on your monitor is not what you will get when you print the image or send the image to a third-party printer. The best way to ensure consistent and accurate color is to calibrate your monitor.

Introducing the Canon ImageBrowser EX

The Canon ImageBrowser EX application is your first weapon for organizing images: perfect for downloading your images, rating and renaming them, and more. If you can't get 'er done in ImageBrowser EX, though, you can rely on Canon Digital Photo Professional. Both applications are on the Canon EOS Digital Solution Disk included with your camera. Just install the software, and you're ready to play. Figure 9-1 shows the Canon ImageBrowser EX in all its glory.

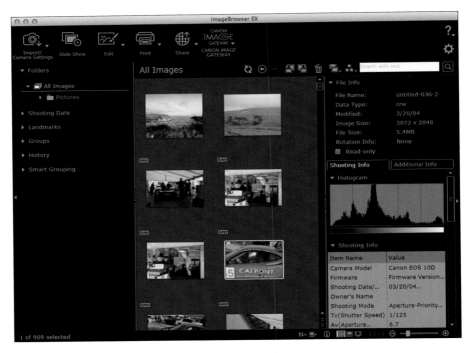

Figure 9-1: The Canon ImageBrowser EX interface.

ImageBrowser EX shows thumbnails of your images in a main window. The top of the application contains task buttons that you use to organize and edit your images. The main window is divided into three sections:

- **Left:** Navigate images and folders.
- **Middle:** Display image thumbnails.
- **Right:** Display image information.

You can change the view of the middle window to suit your workflow, as I show you in upcoming sections.

Downloading Your Images

The first step in your image-editing journey is to download your images. You can download images directly from the camera or from a memory card reader. I suggest the latter because a memory card reader gets the job done faster. Another reason I favor downloading images from a card reader is that downloading images from your camera saps juice from the battery.

To download images to your computer from the camera

1. **Launch ImageBrowser EX.**

2. **Turn your camera on, and connect the USB (Universal Serial Bus) cable supplied with your camera to your computer and to the camera (see Figure 9-2).**

3. **Click the Import/Camera Settings button, which is on the left side of the workspace.**

   The button expands to show the available tasks (see Figure 9-3).

4. **Click the Connect to EOS Camera option.**

   The EOS Utility SL1 application appears in the ImageBrowser EX window (see Figure 9-4).

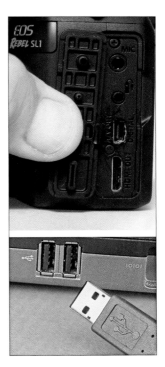

Figure 9-2: Connect your camera to the computer.

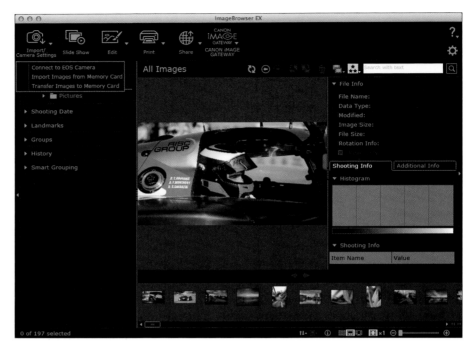

Figure 9-3: The Import/Camera Settings commands.

The dialog box in Figure 9-4 automatically appears when you insert a memory card in a card reader, or connect your camera to the computer, even if the ImageBrowser EX application isn't open. After the images are downloaded, ImageBrowser EX opens by default.

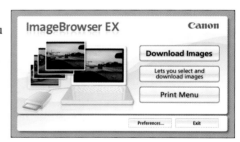

Figure 9-4: Downloading with the EOS Utility application.

5. **Click the desired option.**

- *Download Images:* The images will be downloaded into your computer's default location for downloading images, which is not necessarily a good thing because they're just dumped in with everything else in the folder.

- *Lets You Select and Download Images:* I recommend using this option, which gives you the option of creating the folder into which the images are downloaded. If you follow my advice, the dialog box shown in Figure 9-5 appears.

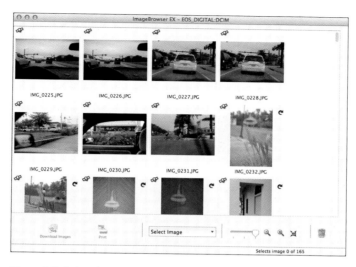

Figure 9-5: Select images to download.

6. **Select the images you want to download.**

   - *Pick some.* At this stage, you can just click a single image that you want to download; the images you don't download will get lost in pixel heaven when you reformat the card. However, this can be rather tedious, so I suggest you choose the next option.

   - *Pick 'em all.* I suggest that you choose Select All from the drop-down menu in the bottom-center of the screen. It's much easier to decide whether to delete an image when you can see it full-size on your computer screen.

7. **Click the Download Images button.**

   The Download Images Dialog box appears (see Figure 9-6). This dialog box shows the default settings for downloading images.

   Notice the option to open ImageBrowser EX after the download is completed. This is for photographers who just insert a card into a card reader, or connect a camera with a card to the computer, which opens the download utility. Also notice that the images are downloaded into the default folder for images on your computer. This is all well and good if you shoot only a couple of hundred pictures per year, but I have the feeling that you bought this camera because you want to shoot lots of pictures. Therefore, I recommend sorting your images into specific folders, by month, week, or individual photo shoot.

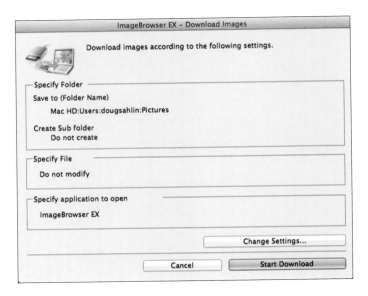

Figure 9-6: Downloading images.

8. **Click the Change Settings button.**

   The Change Settings dialog box appears (see Figure 9-7). By default, images are downloaded into the Pictures folder, but you have the option to specify a different folder. The option to download the images into a subfolder is the option I suggest you take. This organizes the images in a folder based on the month, day, and year the images were photographed.

9. **Specify the desired folder or choose the option to create a subfolder.**

   Note the option that enables you to create a subfolder. After you enable the Create Sub Folder check box, open that drop-down menu and choose the desired option. I suggest you choose Shooting YearMonthDate (see Figure 9-8). This option lets you store the images in a subfolder that you can easily identify. There is also an option to give the image a new name.

   You might think giving an image a new name is wise, but if you choose this option, you'd download only one image — because then all images will have the same name. Not good. I show you how to give the image a meaningful name in the next step.

10. **Click the Specify File Name tab at the top of the dialog box.**

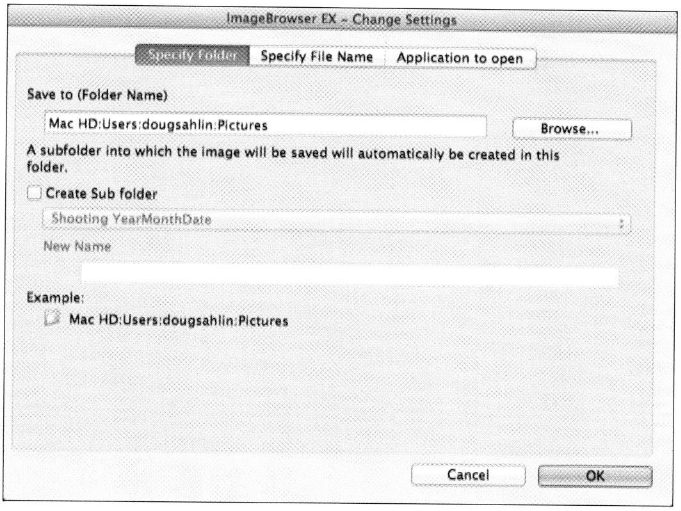

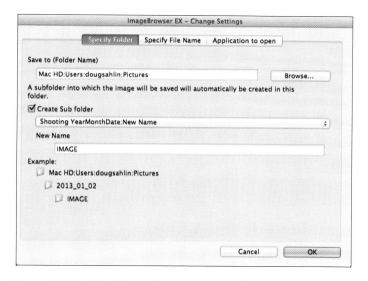

Figure 9-7: Change download settings here.

Figure 9-8: Specify a folder where to store your downloaded images.

11. **Fine-tune the filename by choosing Shooting YearMonthDate + Prefix + Sequence Number from the drop-down menu.**

    The default prefix is IMG, which stands for "image," but you can change that:

a. Select IMG.

b. Enter a prefix name that makes sense to you and will help you identify the person or place in the photographs.

Figure 9-9 shows the new name for a card full of images I created at Myakka State Park.

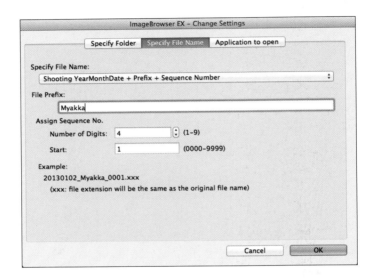

Figure 9-9: Rename your images to better identify them later.

12. **Click OK to exit the Change Settings dialog box.**

The Download Images dialog box appears with all the settings you have changed.

13. **Click Start Download.**

A dialog box appears, showing you the progress of the download. The access lamp on your camera flashes while the images download.

After the download is complete, the images appear in the ImageBrowser EX main window (see Figure 9-10).

Thumbnail mode is the default viewing mode. You can switch to a different viewing mode by clicking the desired icon at the bottom of the window. Any images or movies you've protected in the camera have a lock icon above them, indicating they're protected in ImageBrowser EX as well.

You will have to change the settings as outlined in this section to specify the desired prefix each time you download images. This may seem like a lot of work, but it beats hunting for a needle in a haystack.

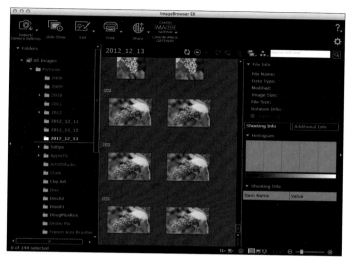

Figure 9-10: Downloaded images appear in the main window.

 If you plan to do all your image management with ImageBrowser EX, do not move images to different folders by using your computer operating system. If you do, ImageBrowser EX won't know where they are. (Later in the chapter, in the "Organizing Your Images" section, I show you how to create folders, move images, and delete them from within ImageBrowser EX.)

Using external card readers

The USB cable that ships with your camera makes it possible to download images to your computer; however, downloading images uses your camera's battery power. If you attempt a download with a low battery, you run the risk of corrupting the images or the memory card if the battery exhausts its power during a lengthy download. So, I recommend downloading your images with an external card reader. Downloading from a card reader is quicker, and it doesn't sap the juice from your camera battery. Connect an external card reader to a computer USB port, and you're ready to download images with ImageBrowser EX or a different application. Many card readers accept multiple image-card formats. Choose a card reader that has a port for the SD cards your camera uses.

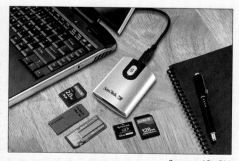

Courtesy of SanDisk

The only time you can rename more than one image with ImageBrowser EX is upon import. I strongly advise you to give each of your images a meaningful name when you download them.

After you download images to your computer, a dialog box may appear asking you whether you want to format the card. Don't accept this option. You should always format cards in the camera, not in the computer.

Rating and Keywording Images

If you download images how I suggest in the previous section, ImageBrowser EX downloads your images into folders arranged by the date they were photographed and adds the prefix you specify upon download. This upfront admin will prevent you from having to find the proverbial needle in the haystack. (IMG_90842? What's that?) You can also rate images and add keywords to images, which make them easier to find as well.

The first thing I do after downloading images from a photo shoot is to rank them and add keywords. In the days of film, photographers would put their slides on a light box and give them a rating from one to five stars, with five-star images being the best of the lot. Jump to the digital age, and it's the same concept. You can assign each image a rating of up to five stars with ImageBrowser EX.

Using keywords ("tags" in ImageBrowser EX) is another method of identifying images. You can add a keyword to an image that reflects the type of photography, the place in which the image was photographed, the name of the person in the photograph, and so on.

You may be tempted to skip adding keywords to images after you download them and do something more entertaining like recycle your cat's hairballs, but it's always best to add keywords right after you download. Your memory is fresher, and you'll save the drudgery of having to keyword four or five shoots in one sitting.

If you're like me, you shoot a lot of images at the same place, and they have the same basic keywords. To help refine your digital filing system, you can add keywords to multiple images — and multiple keywords, too, as follows:

1. **Click the folder into which the images were downloaded.**

   You find the folders listed by date in the Folders tab.

2. **Select the images for which you want to add keywords.**

   You can select contiguous images in the ImageBrowser EX window by pressing the Shift key, clicking the first image you want to select, and then clicking the last image you want to select. Select noncontiguous images by pressing and holding the Ctrl key (Windows) or the Command key (⌘; Mac) and then clicking the desired images.

3. **After selecting the desired images, right-click.**

The context menu appears (see Figure 9-11).

4. **Choose Add Tag.**

The ImageBrowser EX dialog box appears (see Figure 9-12).

5. **In the Tag Name text box, type a keyword that helps you identify the image.**

You can assign multiple keywords to the selected images.

Place a comma and a space between each keyword and the next.

I generally start by adding the town where I shot the image.

6. **Click OK.**

The keyword is added to the properties of each image.

7. **(Optional) Repeat Steps 5 and 6 to add any additional keywords that help describe the photographs.**

You could add the person's name, the word *sunset* if it were a sunset shot, and so on.

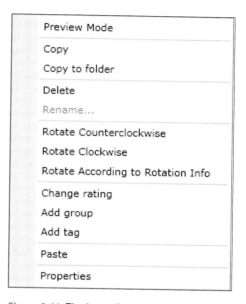

Figure 9-11: The ImageBrowser EX context menu.

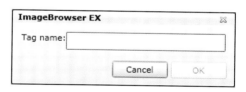

Figure 9-12: Add a keyword (or more than one) to multiple images.

Another manner in which you can sort images is by ranking them. You can rank an image from 1 to 5 Stars. To rank images

1. **Click the folder into which the images were downloaded.**

You find the folders listed by date in the Folders tab.

2. **Select the images that you want to rank.**

   You can select contiguous images in the ImageBrowser EX window by pressing the Shift key, clicking the first image you want to select, and then clicking the last image you want to select. Select noncontiguous images by pressing and holding the Ctrl key (Windows) or the Command key (Mac) and then clicking the desired images.

3. **Right-click.**

   The context menu appears (refer to Figure 9-11).

4. **Pause your cursor over Change Rating.**

   The rating submenu appears (see Figure 9-13). You can assign a rank of 1–5 to the selected images, or reject them. All images you mark as rejects can be found later and then deleted in one fell swoop.

5. **Click the desired rating.**

   ImageBrowser EX assigns the keywords and ranks the images, which makes them easier to find in the future.

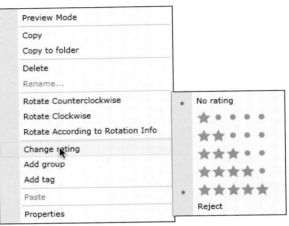

Figure 9-13: Rating images, how rank.

Adding Comments to Images

You can also add comments, which appear as *metadata* with the Additional Info of your images. *Metadata* is data that's recorded with the image when you shoot it, and data you add, such as keywords and comments. You can add whatever comments you want to help you remember the image. To add a comment to an image

1. **Select the image in ImageBrowser EX and then click the Additional Info tab in the right pane.**

2. **Scroll down until you see the Comments text box (see Figure 9-14).**

3. **Type the comment.**

   The comment is applied to the image.

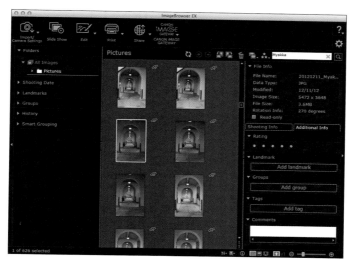

Figure 9-14: Apply a comment to an image here.

You can apply a comment to only one image at a time.

Adding Information to Images

Metadata is very powerful. When you add metadata to an image, you leave yourself bread crumbs to help you find it — or remember it. The information can also be used if you decide to branch out and try to sell images to stock-photo agencies. The more metadata you have, the easier it is to find a specific image. Applying tags to multiple images is definitely the efficient way to work. However, sometimes you need to add information to special images. If your images end up listed in a stock agency, the information you add can help people find your photographs. To add information to a single image

1. **Launch ImageBrowser EX and then navigate to the image to which you want to add additional information.**

   As a rule, I find this easier to do right after a photo shoot when all the information is fresh in my mind. After you select the image, the shooting information is shown on the Shooting Info tab (see Figure 9-15).

2. **Click the Additional Info tab (see Figure 9-16).**

   Here, you can add the following information to the image metadata:

   - *Rating:* You can assign a rating from 1 to 5 to selected images.

   - *Landmark:* Enter the name of the landmark here to create a new folder in the Landmarks section of the Folders tab. After creating the folder, you then drag the applicable images into the folder. This applies the landmark information to each image and creates a bookmark in the landmark folder, which you can use to quickly locate images you've taken of the landmark. To me, this seems redundant. If you do a good job of adding keywords (which I describe earlier), you can easily find any image you want no matter how many images you download to your computer.

   - *Groups:* Here's another way for you to further segment your images. When you create a group, you create a folder into which you can drag images. The images still stay in their original folders, but the group folder is a bookmark to all images you add to a specific group. For example, if you do pet photography, you can

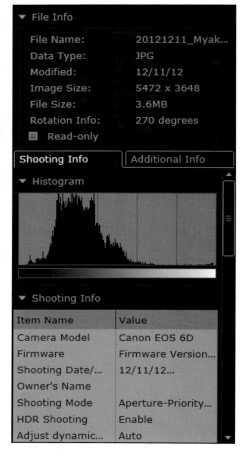

Figure 9-15: All the shooting info that's fit to print.

create a group for Dogs and a group for Cats and whatever other type of image you photograph. (A word of caution, though: If you plan to photograph venomous snakes, do so with a 500mm lens. It takes the fear out of getting close.) But seriously, the group option seems redundant to me as well. It's another step you don't have to take if you do a good job of adding keywords to your images.

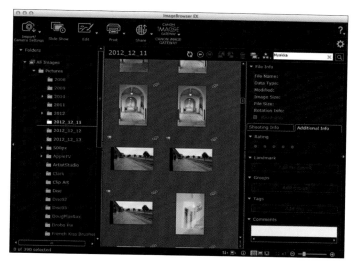

Figure 9-16: Add metadata to images with the Additional Info tab.

- *Tags:* This is very important metadata you should add to each image. I include the town in which the image was photographed, the state in which the image was photographed, and any other pertinent information I think should be added. For example, if the image is a photograph of wildlife, I add *wildlife* as a tag. Remember that you can use more than one keyword; just separate each tag with a comma. At the risk of being redundant, if you do a good job of keywording (tagging) your images, you'll be able to find them easily.

- *Comments:* Here's another useful metadata tag you can add to images. You can add a comment that will help you remember the weather conditions that were prevalent when you created the image, other photographers you were with, and so on.

3. **Keep going for the images you want to add information to.**

Changing Your View

ImageBrowser EX is quite versatile. You have three different ways to view your images: Thumbnail mode, Preview mode, or Full Screen mode. The mode you choose depends on the task you're performing. You can perform all tasks in Thumbnail and Preview modes. In Thumbnail mode, you can perform changes to multiple images. In Preview mode, you work on one image at a time.

To view images in Thumbnail mode

1. **Click the Thumbnail Mode icon.**

   The view shows very small thumbnails (see Figure 9-17). Click the thumbnail to reveal information about the image.

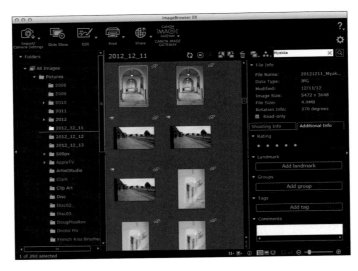

Figure 9-17: Viewing images in Thumbnail mode.

2. **Drag the Zoom slider to increase magnification.**

3. **Click the Information icon to hide the image information and view thumbnails only (see Figure 9-18).**

   The larger images make it easier for you to decide which images you're going to edit and which images need additional information.

4. **Double-click the thumbnail to view it in Preview mode (see Figure 9-19).**

   Preview mode shows one large image and a filmstrip of thumbnails below it. Some photographers find it useful to *winnow* (photographer-speak for choosing which images to keep and which ones to toss in the trash can) images in Preview mode. When you view images in Preview mode, you can use the left

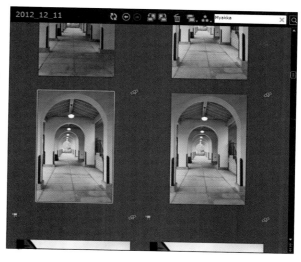

Figure 9-18: The better to see you, my lovely thumbnail.

and right arrow keys above the filmstrip to preview different images in the folder. You can also click the Preview Mode icon to view images in Preview mode.

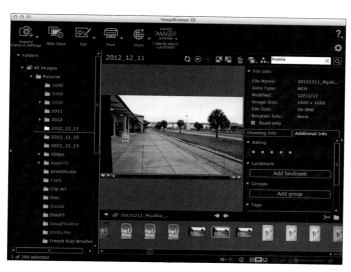

Figure 9-19: And now for your viewing edification: Preview mode.

Backing Up Your Work

You work hard to capture great photographs with your EOS SL1-100D. Your work in ImageBrowser EX and Canon Digital Photo Professional fine-tunes your images, but a computer crash or hard drive failure will wipe out all your images in a heartbeat. You can save images to a CD, but that's 700MB, less storage capacity than a memory card.

Invest in a good external hard drive and use an application to back up your work. After you back up images to the external hard drive, take it offline, which minimizes wear and tear on the hard drive.

I know some photographers who leave their external hard drives online all the time. And some of them have paid the price when the drive crashed and burned. Do an online search for a backup program for your operating system. Most companies that sell backup programs will let you download a fully functional trial version of the software. Try a couple, and when you find one you like, buy it. Unfortunately, I'm not in a position to make a recommendation because I use proprietary software to back my images up to an 8TB external hard drive array.

Organizing Your Images

By default, your images are downloaded into the Pictures folder. You can, however, organize your work by creating new folders, moving images into different folders, and deleting images.

To create a new image folder

1. **In the ImageBrowser EX Folders tab on the left side of the workspace, select the root folder in which you want to create a subfolder.**

2. **Right-click and then choose New Folder from the context menu.**

   A new folder is born.

3. **Enter a name for the folder, as I've done in Figure 9-20, and then click OK.**

   Your new folder is empty, but I show you how to fill it if you read further.

To move images to your new (or another) folder

1. **Click the Thumbnail icon to switch to Thumbnail mode.**

   Your new folder and the images in the root folder display.

2. **Drag images from the root folder into the new folder.**

   Alternatively, you can select an image and drag it into the desired folder, as displayed on the Folders tab.

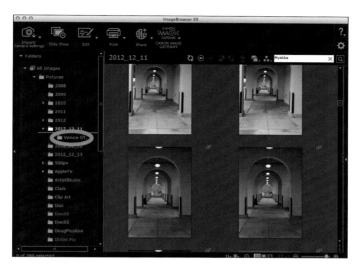

Figure 9-20: Creating a new folder.

To delete one or more images

1. **Select the images and press the Delete key, which looks like a trash can.**

   A dialog box appears asking you to confirm deletion.

2. **Click OK.**

   The images are deleted.

Editing JPEG Images in ImageBrowser EX

You can view all the images you download in ImageBrowser EX, but you can only edit JPEG images. If you shot RAW images, select them in ImageBrowser EX and then edit them in Canon Digital Photo Professional. When editing a JPEG image in ImageBrowser EX, you can correct red-eye, adjust sharpness, crop the image, apply an auto-adjustment, and insert text. I can't cover all the image-editing tools in ImageBrowser EX — doing so is beyond the scope of this book. However, in the following sections, I cover the most important ones.

When editing an image, you can compare the edited image with the original by selecting the Show Original Image check box, in the lower-left corner of each editing task's dialog box. See Figure 9-21.

Adjusting brightness and saturation

You can adjust the color of a JPEG image in ImageBrowser EX. You can also change the brightness and saturation. You can even adjust the RGB (red, green, blue) channels and levels as well as use the Tone Curves Adjustment menu option to adjust brightness for different tone values. Use the brightness adjustment to make an image darker or lighter, and use the saturation adjustment to make the colors more vibrant (add saturation) or less vibrant (decrease saturation). If you remove all saturation from an image, it becomes monochrome, or black and white.

To adjust image color in a JPEG

1. **Select the image you want to edit and then click the Edit button.**

   The menu drops down to reveal the editing options.

2. **Click Edit Image.**

   The Edit drop-down menu appears (see Figure 9-22).

3. **Select Adjust Color and Brightness.**

   The Color/Brightness Adjustment dialog box appears (see Figure 9-23).

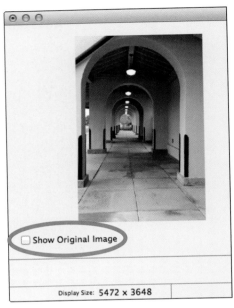

Figure 9-21: Add a check mark to compare edits to original.

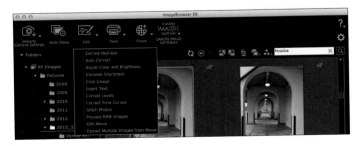

Figure 9-22: Editing an image in ImageBrowser EX.

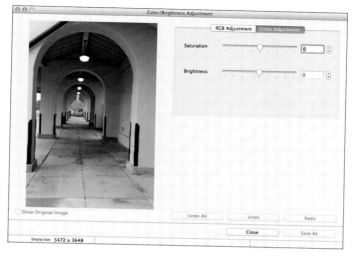

Figure 9-23: Adjust image brightness and saturation here.

4. Drag the sliders to adjust brightness and saturation.

TIP

The settings you choose are a matter of personal taste. Don't go too far over the top with saturation though because you might create some colors that can't be printed. It's also a good idea not to increase saturation when editing images of people. When you increase saturation, you amp up all colors including the red tones, which affects the skin color of people in the photograph.

5. Click the Save As button.

A dialog box appears, telling you that some shooting information might be lost.

6. Click OK.

When the Save As dialog box appears (see Figure 9-24), you can save the image only as a JPEG file. However, you can rename it and specify the folder where to save the edited image.

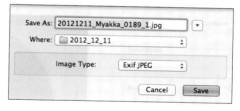

Figure 9-24: Saving your edited image.

7. Enter a filename and specify the folder where the image will be saved.

WARNING!

Because you change the original image, image editing is destructive, which means it makes changes to the original image that can't be undone, destroys some pixels, and changes other pixels forever. This is why I urge you to give the image a different filename and store it in a different folder. That ensures you'll have the original image to edit at a later date.

In addition to adjusting the brightness and saturation, you can adjust the color for the RGB channels by choosing an option from the RGB Adjustment tab (refer to Figure 9-23). This is fairly advanced image editing, as is another option on the list, Correct Levels.

Toning your curves

The Tone Curve Adjustment option lets you adjust tonality in specific brightness ranges. This option is useful and fairly easy to master. Adjusting the tone curve can also add more contrast to an image.

To adjust the tone curve of a JPEG image

1. **Select the image you want to edit and then click the Edit button.**

   The menu drops down to reveal the editing options.

2. **Select Correct Tone Curves.**

   The dialog box refreshes to show the Tone Curve Adjustment dialog box (see Figure 9-25). The diagonal line is the tone curve. The line isn't a curve now because it's applying brightness information in a linear fashion: from shadows (the left side of the curve), to midtones (the middle section of the curve), and then to highlights (the right end of the curve). When you add points for different tonal values along the curve and drag them to adjust brightness, you see a curve.

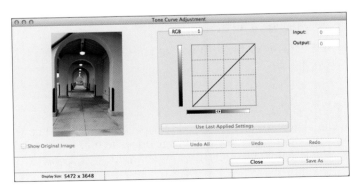

Figure 9-25: The Tone Curve dialog box.

3. **Click a point on the curve to make an adjustment for that tonal value.**

   Click a point near the bottom of the curve to modify the brightness of shadow areas, a point in the middle of the curve to change the brightness of the midtones, and a point near the top of the curve to change the brightness level for highlights. After you click a point, you see values in the Input and Output text boxes (see Figure 9-26).

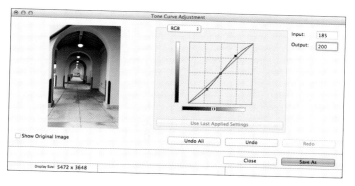

Figure 9-26: Adjusting the tone curve.

4. **To adjust a point, drag it up to make the tonal range brighter or down to make the tonal range darker.**

   You can also change the value in the Output text box. A typical use for a tone curve is to apply more contrast to the image, with one point near the bottom of the curve, one point in the middle of the curve, and one point near the top of the curve. Study Figure 9-26 and note the input and output values for the shadow, midtone, and highlight points. I haven't changed the value for the middle point, which is smack-dab in the middle of the tonal value range. Doing so would increase the overall brightness of the image. Brightening the highlights and darkening the shadows increases image contrast.

5. **Click the Save As button.**

6. **In the Save As dialog box that appears, follow the prompts to save the image.**

Sharpening an image

You can also sharpen an image in ImageBrowser EX. When you sharpen an image, the application locates image edges and applies additional contrast to make the image appear sharper. To sharpen a JPEG image

1. **Select the image you want to edit and then click the Edit button.**

   The menu drops down to reveal the editing options.

2. **Select Increase Sharpness.**

   The Sharpness dialog box appears (see Figure 9-27).

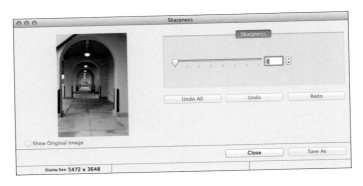

Figure 9-27: Sharpening an image.

3. Drag the slider to sharpen the image.

Take care not to oversharpen an image. As you drag the slider, pay attention to the edges. If you see something that looks like a halo or a white spot on an edge, you've gone too far.

Working with RAW Files in Digital Photo Professional

When you capture an image with the RAW file format, you have more data to work with. The images have a greater bit depth than JPEG images, which means that you have more colors to work with. I use Adobe Photoshop Lightroom to edit and sort my RAW images. I find it very intuitive, and I can edit a massive amount of images in a short amount of time. Adobe Photoshop and Adobe Photoshop Elements have a Camera RAW editor in which you can edit RAW images. If you're just experimenting with the RAW format or don't have one of the aforementioned applications, you can edit your work in Canon Digital Photo Professional.

When you install Canon software, several shortcuts are sprinkled on your desktop. To open Digital Photo Professional, you can either click its shortcut on the Windows desktop or the Macintosh Dock, or launch the application from your computer menu. In Windows, you'll find Digital Photo Professional in the Canon Utilities Folder on your Start menu. If you use a Macintosh computer to edit your images, you'll find the application icon in the Canon Utilities folder in the Applications folder. Alternatively, you can select a RAW image in ImageBrowser EX and then choose Edit➪Process Raw Images.

Note: A soup-to-nuts tutorial of Digital Photo Professional is beyond the scope of this book; however, the following steps show you how to process and tweak a RAW image in the application. The application offers help that you can use if you decide to explore some of the more esoteric commands.

You can jump from ImageBrowser EX directly to Canon Digital Photo Professional, or launch the application by itself and begin editing. The following steps show you how to edit RAW files in Canon Digital Photo Professional:

1. **Launch Digital Photo Professional.**

   The application opens (see Figure 9-28) and displays thumbnails for all images that reside in the same folder as the image you select in ImageBrowser EX.

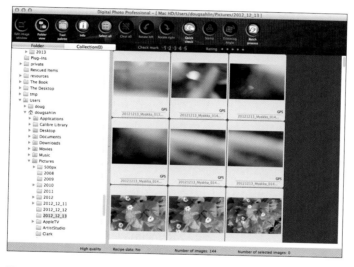

Figure 9-28: Editing Raw images in Digital Photo Professional.

2. **Select the image you want to edit.**

   The images you download with ImageBrowser EX are stored in sub-folders of the Pictures folder. The default name of the folder is the date that the image was photographed. (Of course, you might have already changed the folder name, as I discuss earlier.) You'll find the folders on the left side of the interface.

3. **Click the Edit Image Window button.**

   The image opens in another window. Notice the editing icons on top of the Edit window (see Figure 9-29). Use the Stamp tool to clone pixels from one part of the image to another. There's also an icon to launch the Tool palette, which appears on the right side of the window.

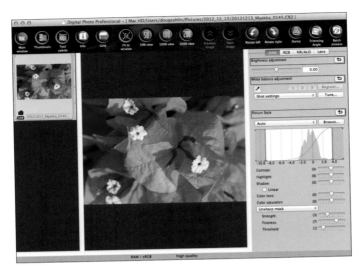

Figure 9-29: Editing an image in the Edit window.

Here are a few things you can edit:

- **Brightness adjustment:** Drag the slider to brighten or darken the image. As you drag the slider, you see the image change in real time.

- **White balance:** Click the eyedropper in the White Balance Adjustment section, and then click an area inside the image that should be pure white, black, or gray. After you click inside the image, the white balance changes. If you don't like the results, click again.

  Alternatively, you can click the drop-down arrow and choose an option from the White Balance Adjustment drop-down list. You can choose Shot Settings to return the image to the white balance as determined by the camera or choose Auto to let Digital Photo Professional adjust the white balance. On the drop-down menu, you find the same white balance options found on your camera — Daylight, Cloudy, Shade, and so on — are also found in this drop-down list.

- **Colorcast:** If you're really adventurous, click the Tune button (under White Balance Adjustment) to open a color wheel that you use to fine-tune the white balance and remove any colorcast. You may not get great results, so use this at your own risk.

- **Picture style:** You can choose a different picture style from the drop-down list to change the look of the image. Choose a style from this drop-down list, and the picture style the image was photographed with displays on the Picture Style button. Because these are RAW files, you can almost literally fold, spindle, and mutilate them. Alternatively, you can click Browse, which opens a folder of Picture Styles created by those wild and crazy engineers at Canon. As always, if you don't like the preset you choose, you can always revert to Auto, or whichever style you used to capture the image by clicking the curved arrow to the right of the style currently listed in the Picture Style window.

✔ **Tonal area fine-tuning:** Drag the Contrast, Highlight, and Shadow sliders to fine-tune these tonal areas. You can increase or decrease contrast for all tonal ranges. As you make your changes, the image updates in real time, and the curve in the window above the sliders updates as well.

✔ **Color tone and color saturation:** Drag the sliders while reviewing the thumbnail. When what you see is what you like, stop dragging the sliders.

✔ **Image sharpness:** Use the Unsharp Mask option. The amount of each option you use varies depending on the image you're editing. If you're not happy with the results, click the drop-down menu, choose Sharpness, and then drag the slider to increase image sharpness.

After you make your adjustments, click the Tool Palette button to hide the Tool palette and display the edited image in the main window.

Digital Photo Professional doesn't store the changes after you close the application. Therefore, save your changes by saving the image in another file format. When you launch Digital Photo Professional again, you can apply different edits to the RAW file and save the image with the new changes using a different filename. To save your edited work:

1. **With the image you just edited still selected, choose File⇨Convert and Save.**

   The Convert and Save dialog box appears (see Figure 9-30).

2. **Enter a filename and location for the edited image.**

   If desired, you can use the same filename — although now the file will eventually have a different file extension (see the next step). The file format in which you can save the image won't overwrite the RAW file. You can save the new file in the same folder or create a new folder in which to store your edited images.

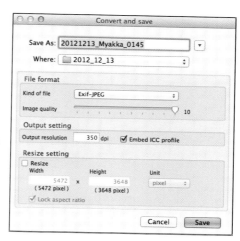

Figure 9-30: Convert an edited file to a different format and save it.

3. **Choose a file type.**

   You can save the file in any of the following formats:

   - *Exif-JPEG:* Saves the edited image as a JPEG file.
   - *Exif-TIFF (8Bit):* Saves the edited image as an 8-bit TIFF file.
   - *TIFF (16Bit):* Saves the edited image as a 16-bit TIFF file. The file size of this format is considerably larger than the 8-bit TIFF format, but you have more information to work with if you edit the image in an application like Photoshop.
   - *Exif-TIFF (8Bit) + Exif-JPEG:* Saves an 8-bit TIFF file and a JPEG file.
   - *TIFF (16Bit) + Exif-JPEG:* Saves a 16-bit TIFF file and an 8-bit JPEG file.

   If you choose a JPEG option, you can specify the quality.

4. **Accept the default JPEG image quality of 10 or drag the slider to specify a different quality.**

   The default setting of 10 produces a high-quality image but at the expense of a large file size. If you specify a lower quality, the image quality is poorer, but the file size is smaller. When you specify a lower quality, Digital Photo Professional compresses the file, and data is lost.

5. **Accept the default resolution of 350 dpi (dots per inch) or enter a different resolution.**

   With most printers, you can get by with a resolution of 300 dpi.

6. **Accept the default option to embed the ICC (International Color Consortium) profile or select the check box to reject the option.**

   Your best option is to embed the profile with the image. If you don't embed the profile with the image, a generic profile will be assigned to the image when you print it, which may result in an image with colors that look nothing like the original.

7. **(Optional) Select the Resize check box.**

   If you use this option, the Width and Height text boxes appear with the current dimensions of the image. The Lock Aspect Ratio check box is selected by default. If you deselect this option and change one value, the other value won't change, and the image won't look right.

8. **(Optional) Enter a new value for width or height.**

   When you enter one value, Digital Photo Professional does the math and supplies the other value as long as you enable the Lock Aspect Ratio option. (You did enable it, didn't you?)

9. **Click Save.**

   Your changes to the image(s) are saved.

Creating Prints from Your Images

*P*rinters have come a long way. Back when I started printing my own images, printer ink cartridges had three inks. Then printers graduated to cartridges with six inks. Now the really good printers have as many as 12 cartridges that enable you to print stunning color as well as black-and-white prints. You can also get prints made at a wide variety of sources, from your local drugstore or supermarket to online printers that specialize in creating beautiful prints in sizes from 4 x 6 inches to as large as 30 x 20 inches.

Your camera has an 18-megapixel (MP) capture, which means you can create very large prints. In this chapter, I explore the wonderful world of printing the images you capture in your SL1/100D.

Deciding to Print at Home or Go to a Printer

Modern photo-quality printers are a wonderful thing. They print rich, wonderful colors with crisp delineation among them. But good photo-quality printers don't come cheap, and neither do the ink cartridges. Modern printers have multiple cartridges. If you've been printing a lot of images that use, say, red or cyan ink, you'll exhaust that cartridge much sooner than the other cartridges in your printer. And you never seem to have a spare cartridge of the color that runs out.

Calibrating your monitor

When you edit images for print, you rely on your monitor to preview the image. If the colors in your monitor are slightly off, what you see on your monitor is not what you will get when you print the image or send the image to a third-party printer. The best way to ensure consistent and accurate color is to calibrate your monitor. A monitor calibrator (*colorimeter* in techno-speak) is attached to your computer screen, and a software program generates colors and shades of gray. The colorimeter measures the colors displayed on your computer screen and compares them to the values in the software program. When the calibration process is completed, the software generates a profile that adjusts the colors on your screen to match the known values generated by the software. If you decide to calibrate your monitor, do so every couple of months because the colors in your monitor change as it ages. As of this writing, X-Rite's ColorMunki Smile (`http://xrite photo.com`) is a good device with a reasonable price tag.

In addition to the problem of running out of ink at an inopportune moment, don't forget the expense involved. If you use a third-party fine-art paper, it soaks up ink like a sponge. Then, when you run out of one color in one cartridge in the middle of a print job, you have a double whammy: You've wasted lots of ink and a sheet of very expensive paper.

Fortunately, you can get good color prints in lots of other ways. The following list shows a few options:

- ✔ **Superstore printing services:** Many superstores, such as Costco and Sam's Club, have do-it-yourself printing. Simply bring a memory card to the store, put it in the machine, and review the images on the card. Many of the in-store kiosks have basic editing options, such as cropping images to a specific size. After you select images from your card, just place your order. In many instances, you can do your shopping in-store and come back an hour later for your prints.

- ✔ **Drugstores:** Many drugstores offer printing of digital images. Simply bring your memory card to the store, insert it in their machine, choose the images you want to print, and place your order.

- ✔ **Online printing services:** Lots of online printing services offer many options in addition to standard prints. If you want standard prints, no problem. A full online printing service can print anything from wallet-size images to huge wall posters. You say you want to put a picture of your cat on a coffee mug? No problem. Upload the image, and you'll get your cat's mug on a mug within a matter of days. Other services include photo books, images on mouse pads, and so on. One of my favorite online printing sources is Mpix (www.mpix.com), which offers all the aforementioned services and much more. Most online printers require that your images be exported as JPEG images with the sRGB color space.

Finding Images

After you download your images and edit them, you end up with lots of images in lots of folders. Even though the folders are organized by date, and each one has the date as the actual folder name, and even though you've renamed the images, looking for a single image (or group of images) is like looking for the proverbial needle in the haystack — unless you took the time upfront to rank them and tag them with keywords. (I show you how in Chapter 9.) If you did, you can easily search images by image type, star rating, and keywords, choosing any or all those criteria. When you need to find images of Aunt Millicent, you can easily find them with ImageBrowser EX by following these steps:

1. **Launch ImageBrowser EX and select the root folder for your images.**

   There's no place to start like the start.

2. **Click the Filter by File Category icon and then choose an option from the drop-down menu (see Figure 10-1).**

3. **Click the Filter by Rating icon to search for images by star rating.**

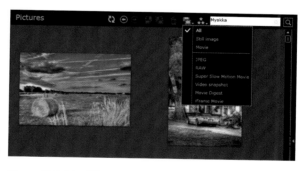

Figure 10-1: It's all in your file.

   From the drop-down list that appears, choose to search for one-, two-, three-, four-, or five-star images. You can also choose to filter by <star rating> or More, in which case ImageBrowser EX will display images of the rating you choose and higher, or choose to filter by <star rating> or Less, in which case

ImageBrowser EX will display the images of the star rating you choose and lower.

4. Enter the desired keyword in the Search with Text text box.

You can only enter one keyword at a time.

5. Click the Search icon that looks like a magnifying glass.

The images that match your criteria are displayed in the window as thumbnails.

Chapter 9 gives you the grand tour of ImageBrowser EX, including how to add keywords to and rate your images.

Leaving Some Breathing Room

Your SL1/100D produces images with an aspect ratio of 3:2, which is perfect if you print your images on 4 x 6" photo paper. However, if you print your images on different size papers, the aspect ratio of those papers doesn't match the aspect ratio of your camera. For example, if you print images on 8 x 10" paper, the aspect ratio is 4:5. So, if you take a picture and don't leave any breathing room at the edges, you can't crop to 8 x 10 without cutting out part of your subject.

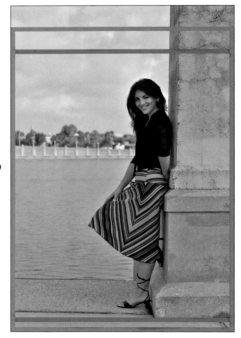

Figure 10-2: Leave a little wiggle room for different aspect ratios.

When you take pictures, keep this in mind: Leave a little breathing room so you can crop to different aspect ratios without losing important parts of your image. Figure 10-2 shows an image that has plenty of breathing room. The complete image is perfect for a 4 x 6 print. The red rectangle shows the image cropped for a 5 x 7" print, and the blue lines show the image cropped for an 8 x 10" print. Breathing room is a wonderful thing.

Creating photo books at Blurb

If you want to see your images in a custom photo book, you can make this a reality by visiting Blurb (www.blurb.com). Blurb is a popular website for creating and selling photo books. You can create a great-looking photo book with Blurb's free BookSmart software, which you can download free from www.blurb.com/booksmart. After you use the software to create your book, you can upload the photos to Blurb directly from the BookSmart software. You can also create a custom book in an application like Adobe InDesign and then upload it to Blurb as a PDF (Portable Document Format). After you upload the book, you have 14 days to order at least one copy of it. If you don't order a copy within 14 days, Blurb removes it from the website. Blurb offers hardcover and softcover books in the following

sizes (in inches): 7 x 7, 8 x 10, 10 x 8, 12 x 12, and 13 x 10. You can also upgrade to premium paper, which looks absolutely stunning with high-resolution images. The minimum number of pages is 20, and the maximum number of pages you can put in a book is 440. You can put multiple photos on a page with BookSmart templates.

You can also choose to make your book public after you order one copy. When you make a book available to the public, you can specify the selling price. The following image is a copy of the book cover I created from images I shot at a local car show. Quite a few copies of this book have been ordered online. When your book sells, Blurb sends you the difference between your selling price and its established price minus a small handling fee.

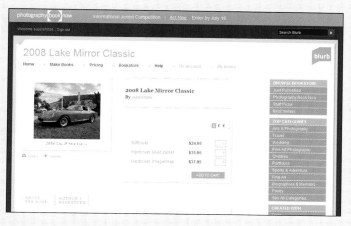

Cropping an Image in ImageBrowser EX

More often than not, you need to crop an image. Understandably, because you're losing pixels when you crop, you end up with a smaller (digital) image size as well. To crop an image in ImageBrowser EX

1. Select the image you want to edit and then click the Edit button.

The menu drops down to reveal the editing options.

2. **Select Crop Image.**

   The Cropping dialog box appears (see Figure 10-3). You have two methods of trimming an image.

   - *Manual:* The first method is to simply drag the handles until you crop away unwanted pixels. This method is fine when you create an image for the web or to send via e-mail.

   - *Aspect ratio:* When you want to print an image on photo paper with set dimensions, you need to crop to an aspect ratio from the Advanced Options choices menu. (More on this option in a bit.)

   The following steps show you how to crop manually.

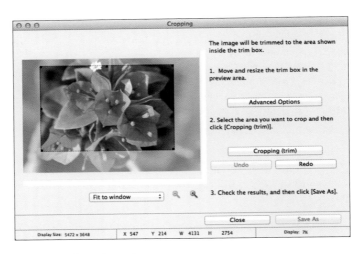

Figure 10-3: Cropping an image.

3. **Drag the handles.**

   Drag any handle to trim the image to a different size. Click inside the trim box and then drag to move the box to trim to a different area of the image.

4. **Click the Cropping (Trim) button.**

   The image trims to size. If you don't like the results, click the Redo button.

5. **Click the Save As button.**

6. **In the Save As dialog box, follow the prompts to save the image.**

Image size and resolution considerations

When you're printing an image, make sure to size the image appropriately to print on the media size you choose. Also important: Match the resolution of the printer as closely as possible. To find the ideal resolution, check with the company that's doing your printing, or check your computer printer manual. If you're printing the image, a resolution of 200 dots per inch (dpi) gives you acceptable results. If you choose a resolution of 300 dpi, you'll get a better-looking image because the pixels are smaller, and you'll get a better color variation.

So how does this equate to image size? If you want to print an 8 x 10" image at 200 dpi, the image dimensions must be 1600 x 2000 pixels, and of course, the image must have a resolution of 200 dpi. If you want to print an 8 x 10" image at

300 dpi, your image must be 2400 x 3000 pixels. To do the math for a different image resolution, multiply the size in inches by the resolution to get the document size in pixels. Your image should be larger than this.

Unfortunately, neither ImageBrowser EX nor Digital Professional Pro has a menu command to change the image size. If you have Photoshop Elements, though, you can easily perform this task. If you decide to invest the paltry sum Adobe charges for Photoshop Elements, *Photoshop Elements 11 For Dummies* (Barbara Obermeier and Ted Padova) is a good book to reference. If you own an earlier version of Photoshop Elements, Wiley has *Photoshop Elements For Dummies* books dating all the way back to version 2.

Cropping an image in ImageBrowser EX is an inexact science, but you can add precision to cropping if you use the Advanced Options and follow these steps:

1. **Select the image you want to edit and then click the Edit button.**

   The menu drops down to reveal the editing options.

2. **Select Crop Image.**

   The Cropping dialog box appears (refer to Figure 10-3). I show you how to crop manually in the preceding set of steps. Now it's time to add precision to cropping.

3. **Click the Advanced Options button.**

   The Advanced Options for cropping images appears (see Figure 10-4).

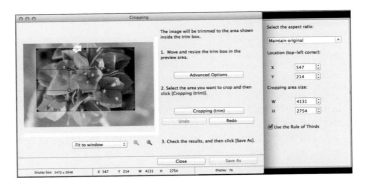

Figure 10-4: Advanced cropping options.

4. **Choose an option from the Select the Aspect Ratio drop-down menu.**

   You can maintain the original aspect ratio, or choose one that matches the media on which you're going to print the image. Your options are Manual, Maintain Original, 1:1, 3:2, 2:3, 4:3, 3:4, 16:9, or 9:16. If you're not familiar with aspect ratio, it compares the proportion of the width to the height. When you choose 3:2, for example, the image is cropped to a size that is 3 units high and 2 units wide. For example, if you wanted to print the image on 6 x 4" paper, you'd choose the 3:2 aspect ratio. Oddly, there is no aspect ratio that matches the popular 10 x 8 print size.

5. **(Optional) If you want to crop the image according to the Rule of Thirds, select the Use the Rule of Thirds check box.**

   This places an overlay of nine rectangles on top of the cropping rectangle. If you're not familiar with this rule of composition, a *Rule of Thirds power point* is where the edges of two rectangles intersect. In Figure 10-4, you can see four small squares where the rectangles intersect. If you crop your image so that a center of interest (an object or a person) appears on one of the small squares, your viewer (in theory) will be drawn toward the center of interest.

6. **Enter Location values for the X and Y coordinates for the upper-left corner of the cropping rectangle.**

   If you use ImageBrowser EX to do your cropping, you'll have no idea where these coordinates are. My recommendation is to use the cropping rectangle handles to crop the image by eye. The X and Y coordinates appear in these text boxes after you crop manually. You can then tweak the position of the upper-left corner of the cropping rectangle by changing the values slightly until you can see the results you're after.

7. **Enter the Cropping Area Size.**

   This is the dimension in pixels of the cropped image. This requires a bit of math on your part. Your camera has a default resolution of 240 pixels per inch (ppi). Therefore, you have to multiply the desired width and height by 240 and enter these values in the W and H text boxes. For example, if you want to print a 6 x 4 image, you enter 1440 (6 inches x 240) in the W text box and 960 in the H text box. Unfortunately, even if you choose the desired aspect ratio, you can't enter the width and have ImageBrowser EX automatically figure the height. For this type of sophistication, you'll need a full-fledged image-editing application like Adobe Photoshop or Adobe Photoshop Elements.

8. **Click the Cropping (Trim) button.**

   The image is cropped to your specifications.

9. **Click the Save As button.**

   The Save As dialog box appears. The image is saved using the JPEG file format.

10. **Enter a name for the image and then specify the folder in which to save the image.**

    Use a different name for the image, especially if you're cropping a JPEG image. If you use the same name and save it in the same folder, you overwrite the original, which is not a good thing.

Printing an Image

If you're printing an image on your local printer — that is, your desktop or personal printer — you can do so from within ImageBrowser EX or Digital Photo Professional. You can print a single image or a contact sheet of multiple images. I show you how to do both in the upcoming sections.

Printing an image from ImageBrowser EX

You can print images in ImageBrowser EX on your local printer, and you'll get the best results when printing JPEGs. If you attempt to print a RAW image from within ImageBrowser EX, the application uses an embedded JPEG thumbnail designed to be used as an image preview. And if you try to print large images from RAW files, you probably won't be happy with the results. You get the best results when you print RAW images from within Digital Photo Professional.

To print an image from ImageBrowser EX

1. **Launch ImageBrowser EX and select the image you want to print.**

   You can select the image while viewing a folder in Thumbnail or Preview mode.

2. **Click the Print button and then select Print Images.**

   The Photo Print dialog box appears (see Figure 10-5).

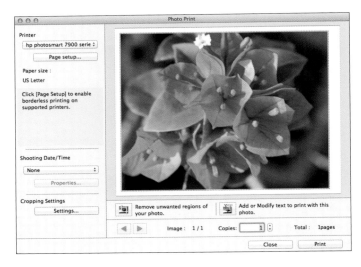

Figure 10-5: Printing an image.

3. **Click the Printer drop-down arrow and choose the desired printer.**

   Your default printer appears on the button. If you have more than one printer, you'll find them on this drop-down list.

4. **Click the Page Setup button.**

   A dialog box with properties for your printer appears. Use this to match the media size to what you have in your printer tray, specify page layout, and so on. The options vary depending on the printer you use. Choose the desired options and close the dialog box.

5. **(Optional) To display the shooting date and time on the image, click the Shooting Date/Time drop-down menu.**

   You have the following options: None (the default), which does not print the date and time; Date/Time, which prints the date and time; Date; or Time. Personally, I never print the date and time on a photo. The date and time are already included with the image metadata. If you choose this option, a preview of the date and time appear on the preview of what the final print looks like.

6. **(Optional) If you choose to display the date on the image, click the Properties button.**

This opens the Shooting Date/ Time Settings dialog box (see Figure 10-6). The options, which enable you to change the text outline, text color, time and date separator, and the position where the date and time appear on the image, are fairly self-explanatory. I'll do my bit to help save a rain forest by not wasting paper to record the obvious.

7. **(Optional) Click the Settings button to trim the image.**

The Cropping Settings dialog box opens. From this dialog box, you can choose to automatically crop the image, which eliminates a white border around the image, or choose not to crop the image.

8. **(Optional) Add text to the image.**

    a. *Click the Insert Text button.*

The Insert Text dialog box opens (see Figure 10-7).

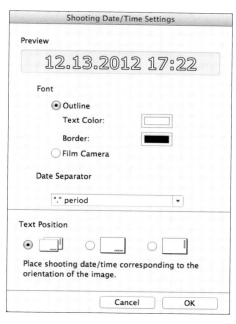

Figure 10-6: Modify how the date and time appear on the image.

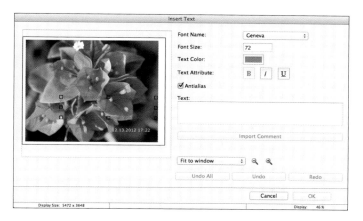

Figure 10-7: Add text to your printed image.

    b. Click inside the image where you want the text to appear and then type the text in the text box that appears.

      Four handles appear around the text box. The text box resizes while you type. After you click inside the image, you can enter text atop the image, and the options to change the font type, size, and color appear.

    c. Accept the default font type as well as size and color, or specify different options.

    d. If you added comments to the image, click the Import Comment button to add the comments to the text box.

    e. Click inside the text box, drag it to the desired position, and then click OK.

      You return to the Photo Print dialog box.

9. Specify the number of copies to print.

    The default is one copy; however, you can print additional copies by entering the desired amount in the text box or by clicking the spinner buttons.

10. Click the Print button.

    The selected printer prints the image.

Printing an image in Digital Photo Professional

If you want to print RAW images, use Digital Photo Professional. The process is pretty straightforward. You can specify the printer and then modify the printer properties to suit the media you're using. To print an image from Digital Photo Professional

1. Launch Digital Photo Professional, select the image you want to print, and then choose File➪Print.

    The Print dialog box appears (see Figure 10-8).

2. Choose the desired printer from the Printer drop-down list.

    This menu shows every available printer on your computer or in your network.

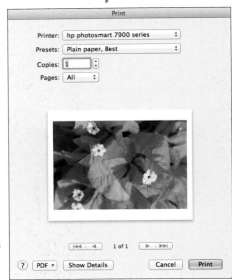

Figure 10-8: Printing an image from Digital Photo Professional.

3. Choose the desired preset from the Presets drop-down menu.

This menu shows the various paper options available for your printer. When you choose a preset, the printer sends the proper amount of ink to create the best possible print for the paper you choose.

4. Specify the number of copies to print.

Enter a value in the text box or use the spinner buttons.

5. Click Print.

The selected printer prints your image.

You can also save the image in PDF format by clicking the PDF button and choosing the desired options from the drop-down menu.

Printing a Contact Sheet in ImageBrowser EX

Many photographers print and file *contact sheets,* which are collections of thumbnails (many images on one print) that serve as handy references with information about each photo. Contact sheets are also useful for showing images to prospective clients. After all, looking at an image tells you a lot more than looking at a filename.

If you choose RAW images, ImageBrowser EX uses the thumbnail image for the contact sheet because ImageBrowser EX can't decode RAW files. This may result in poor image quality. If you primarily shoot RAW images, skip to the next section.

To print an contact sheet in ImageBrowser EX

1. Launch ImageBrowser EX and select the images you want to include on the contact sheet.

2. Click the Print button and then choose Contact Sheet.

The Print Contact Sheet dialog box appears (see Figure 10-9).

3. Choose a printer from the Name drop-down list.

Your default printer is listed on the button, and any additional printers connected to your computer appear on the drop-down list.

4. Click the Page Setup button.

A dialog box with the printer properties appears. The properties differ depending on what type of printer you use.

5. Specify the desired options from the Page Setup dialog box and then click OK.

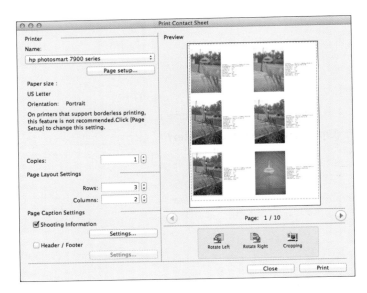

Figure 10-9: Printing a contact sheet.

6. **Back in the Print Contact Sheet dialog box, enter the number of copies in the Copies text box.**

   Alternatively, click the spinner buttons to specify the number of copies.

7. **In the Page Layout Settings section, enter the desired number in the Rows and Columns text boxes.**

   This setting determines how the images display on the sheet. The default setting gives you three rows and three columns. If you choose a larger number, the images will be smaller.

8. **Decide whether to show shooting information, such as filename and copyright.**

   - *No:* Deselect the Shooting Information check box (it's enabled by default) so that only images appear on the sheet.

     If you deselect this check box, skip to Step 9.

   - *Yes:* If you want the shooting information to print, click its Settings button. After the Shooting Information Settings dialog box appears (see Figure 10-10), follow the next two substeps.

   a. *Select the shooting settings you want displayed under each image and optionally select the Comment check box to print any image comments on the contact sheet.*

b. *Accept the default font (Geneva) or choose a different font from the drop-down list, set the font size, and then click OK.*

The Shooting Information Settings dialog box closes.

9. **(Optional) Select the Header/ Footer check box to include a header and footer on each sheet.**

If you don't select the Header/ Footer check box, skip to Step 10.

a. *Click its Settings button.*

The Header/Footer Settings dialog box appears (see Figure 10-11).

b. *Type the desired text in the Header and Footer text boxes, change the font if desired, print page numbers if desired, and then click OK.*

The Header/Footer Settings dialog box closes.

10. **(Optional) To change the orientation of, or crop, an individual image, click it and then click one of the icons below the preview window.**

You can rotate the image right or left, or crop it. The third option seems rather foolish to me given that the object of a contact sheet is to show a thumbnail version of the complete image, not a cropped copy. If you do choose to crop the thumbnail, a dialog box opens with a preview of the image and cropping handles you can drag to crop the thumbnail.

11. **Click the Print button.**

The selected printer prints the contact sheet.

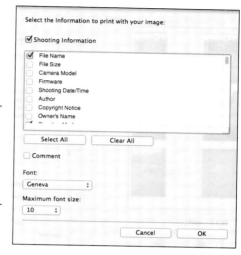

Figure 10-10: Modifying Shooting Information options.

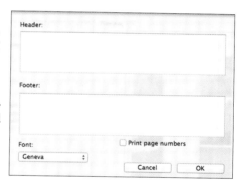

Figure 10-11: Enter information for the header and footer.

Printing a Contact Sheet in Digital Photo Professional

If you need to print a contact sheet of RAW images, opt for Digital Photo Professional. You can specify how many rows and columns are on the sheet and much more. To print a contact sheet in Digital Photo Professional

1. **Launch Digital Photo Professional and then choose File⇨Print Contact Sheets.**

   The Contact Sheet dialog box appears (see Figure 10-12).

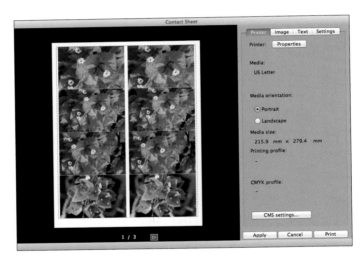

Figure 10-12: Printing a contact sheet of RAW images.

2. **Click the Properties button.**

   The Page Setup dialog box appears (see Figure 10-13).

3. **Open the Format For drop-down list.**

   A list of printers connected to your computer appears.

4. **Select the desired printer from the drop-down list.**

5. **Accept the default paper size (8 1/2 x 11) or open the Paper Size drop-down list to select the desired paper size.**

6. **Accept the default orientation (Portrait) or select Landscape.**

This option determines whether the sheet is taller than it is wide *(portrait),* or wider than it is tall *(landscape).*

7. **Accept the default scale (100%) or enter a different value.**

   If you enter a larger value, part of the contact sheet will be cut off.

8. **Click OK to apply the settings and exit the Page Setup dialog box.**

9. **Specify a printer profile or CMYK (cyan, magenta, yellow, black) simulation profile.**

   a. *Click the CMS Settings button.*

   The Color Match Settings dialog box opens.

   b. *Select the desired options from the drop-down list.*

   c. *Click OK to exit the Color Match Settings dialog box and return to the Contact Sheet dialog box.*

10. **Set how you want images laid out on the contact sheet.**

    a. *Click the Image tab (see Figure 10-14).*

    The size and formatting options for the contact sheet are displayed.

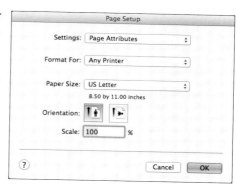

Figure 10-13: Choose page setup options here.

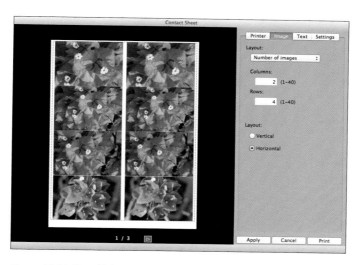

Figure 10-14: Specify layout options.

b. *From the Layout drop-down list, choose one of the following:*

- *Number of Images:* The default option sizes the contact sheet to the page. If you accept the default option, enter the desired value in the Columns and Rows text boxes. This determines how many columns and rows of images are displayed on each page of the contact sheet.

- *Size:* Specify the size of the contact sheet, which determines how much of the page is contact sheet and how much is blank. The default unit of measure is millimeters. If you want to use the Size option and prefer to set the size in inches, go to Step 12 to open the Settings tab, and then choose inches as the unit of measure.

c. *Choose the desired layout.*

Your options are Vertical or Horizontal.

11. **Set header, footer, and caption information.**

a. *Click the Text tab (see Figure 10-15).*

b. *Enter the desired information in the Header and Footer text boxes.*

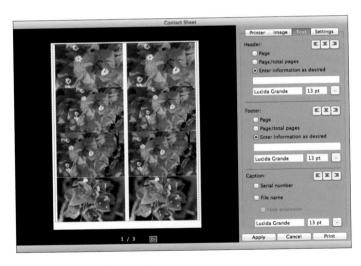

Figure 10-15: Specifying text options.

Alternatively, you can display the page number, or you can display the page number and the total number of pages.

c. *Accept the default font face and size for the header/footer, or click the ellipsis (. . .) button to the right to specify a different font face and size.*

    d. (Optional) Choose an option in the Caption section. If you don't choose a Caption option, skip to Step 12.

- You can display the serial number or the filename.

- Accept the default font face and size for the caption, or click the ellipsis (. . .) button to specify a different font face and size.

12. Finish on the Settings tab (see Figure 10-16).

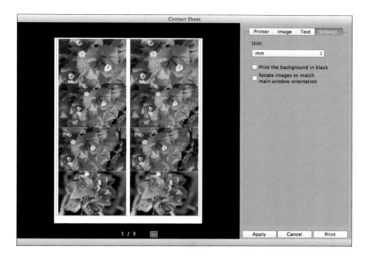

Figure 10-16: Specifying the final settings.

    a. (Optional) Click the Unit drop-down list. Choose between

- *Inches*

- *Millimeters*

    b. (Optional) Select the Print Background in Black check box.

    Choose this option, and the background behind the images is black.

    c. (Optional) Select the Rotate Images to Match Main Window Orientation check box.

    If you don't use this option, images aren't rotated if they don't have the same orientation.

13. Click the Print button.

The selected printer prints the contact sheet.

Using third-party papers

Lots of companies manufacture paper for printing digital images. Some papers are more economical than those available from your printer manufacturer, and others are more expensive and suitable for creating fine art prints. For example, papers with a high rag content make your images look like artwork instead of photos.

When you print images from an application such as Photoshop Elements, the printer determines how much of each ink is laid on the paper to create the resulting image. However, when you use *third-party* paper (paper not manufactured by the company that made your printer), your printer has no way of knowing how much ink to lay on the paper to replicate what you see on your computer screen. When this is the case, you need to get an ICC (International Color Consortium) profile for the paper and your printer. Many manufacturers of fine-art photo paper, such as Ilford and Hahnemühle, have profiles you can download for your printer and their paper. They also supply instructions on where the profile needs to be stored on your system and how to use the profile with many popular image-editing applications, such as Photoshop and Photoshop Elements. An ICC profile tells the printer how much ink to use for the paper with which the profile is matched. When you use a paper supplied by the printer manufacturer, you don't have to worry about ICC profiles; you simply choose the appropriate paper from a drop-down list. When you use a third-party paper, you let the image-editing application manage the printer and choose the appropriate ICC profile from a drop-down list to match the paper you're using. For more information about ICC profiles, refer to your image-editing application manual.

Part IV
The Part of Tens

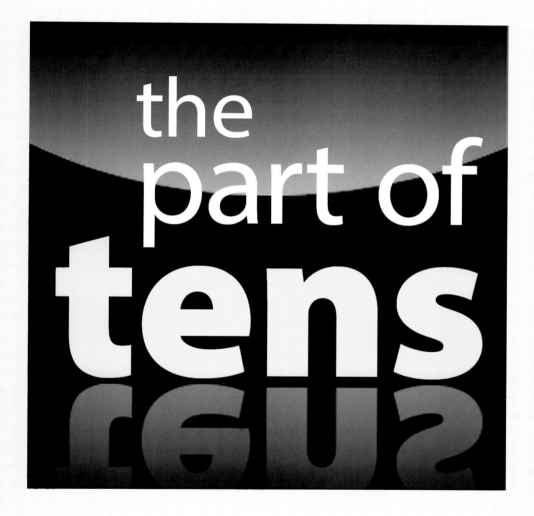

Enjoy an additional Part of Tens listing ten cool features of your camera online at www.dummies.com/extras/canon.

In this part . . .

- ✔ Create custom menus that contain your favorite commands.
- ✔ Find out how to register user settings.
- ✔ Add copyright information to images.
- ✔ Use the Creative Filters to apply special effects in-camera.
- ✔ Discover cool projects you can do with your camera.

Ten Tips and Tricks

*W*hen the weather is dismal and you're fresh out of ideas for shooting macro or still-life photography in your house, you can always photograph your pet rock. Or better yet, you can do some cool things with your camera, such as creating a custom menu or a custom picture style. In this chapter, I show you some cool tips and tricks that you can do on a rainy day.

Creating a Custom Menu

Do you have a set of menu commands you use frequently? How cool would it be not to have to sift through all 4,000 commands in your camera menu? That's right; you can cut to the chase and create your own custom menu with your very own favorite commands. If I've piqued your curiosity, read on. To create a custom camera menu

1. **Click the Menu button.**

   The last used menu displays.

2. **Use the cross keys to navigate to the My Menu Settings tab (the left image in Figure 11-1).**

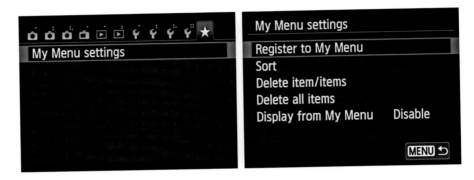

Figure 11-1: Gonna make your very own menu.

3. **Press the Set button.**

   The My Menu Settings screen displays. The Register option is highlighted when you first open the menu (the right image in Figure 11-1).

4. **Press Set.**

   A list of menu commands displays (see the left image in Figure 11-2).

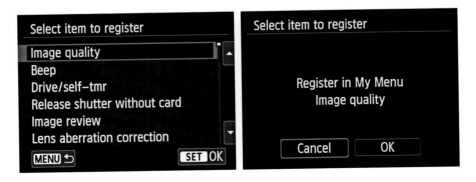

Figure 11-2: Choose commands to register.

5. **Use the cross keys to highlight a command and then press Set to register it.**

   A confirmation window appears asking whether you want to register the command in your custom menu (the right image in Figure 11-2).

6. **Use the right cross key to highlight OK and then press Set.**

   The command is grayed out on the list.

7. **Repeat Steps 5 and 6 to add other commands to your menu.**

8. **After registering commands to your menu, press the Menu button.**

   You're returned to the My Menu Settings window (refer to the right image in Figure 11-1). You have the following commands at your disposal:

   - *Register to My Menu:* Register additional commands to your custom menu.

   - *Sort:* Press Set to make your menu commands display. Select a menu command and press Set to display an up-and-down arrow next to the command. Use the cross keys to reorder the command in the list and then press Set. Repeat for other commands you want reordered. Tap the Menu button when finished.

   - *Delete Item/Items:* Press Set to display all commands on your menu. Use the cross keys to highlight a command and then press Set to delete it from the list. This opens a dialog box asking you to confirm deletion. Use the right cross key to highlight OK and then press Set. Tap the Menu button to return to the My Menu Settings dialog box.

   - *Delete All Items:* Press Set to reveal a confirmation screen for deletion of all registered items. Use the right cross key to highlight OK and then press Set.

   - *Display from My Menu:* Press Set to reveal the options. Use the cross keys to highlight Enable and then press Set. The My Menu tab is selected. The last menu used opens first by default. However, if you put all your frequently used commands on a custom menu, you won't have to use the other menu tabs as often. The right image in Figure 11-3 shows a custom menu.

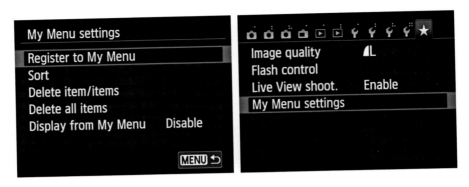

Figure 11-3: Setting My Menu Settings options.

Adding Copyright Information to the Camera

You can add your copyright information to the camera. The data you enter will be added to the EXIF metadata recorded with each image. To add copyright information to the camera

1. **Press the Menu button.**

   The last used menu displays.

2. **Use the cross keys to navigate to the Camera Settings 4 tab.**

3. **Use cross keys to highlight Copyright Information (see the left image in Figure 11-4) and then press the Set button.**

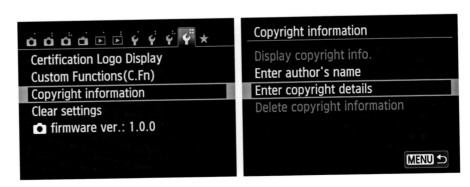

Figure 11-4: Add your copyright to the camera.

The Copyright Information menu displays.

4. **Use the cross keys to highlight Enter Copyright Details (the right image in Figure 11-4) and then press Set.**

   The Enter Copyright Details screen appears (left image in Figure 11-5).

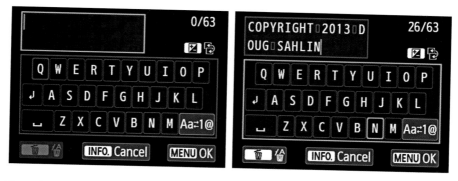

Figure 11-5: Enter copyright information here.

5. **Enter your copyright detail information.**

6. **Press the Aperture/Exposure Compensation button to navigate to the character section of the dialog box.**

   Use the Aperture/Exposure Compensation button to navigate between the text box and the text selection box (which looks like a standard keyboard).

7. **Use the cross keys to highlight a letter, character, or number, and then press Set to add it to your copyright information.**

   Continue until you've entered the desired text and year.

8. **Press the Menu button to approve the changes (the right image in Figure 11-5).**

   A confirmation screen appears, telling you that the screen will close after the text that was entered is saved to the camera.

9. **Use the right cross key to highlight OK and then press Set.**

   You return to the copyright menu (see the left image in Figure 11-6).

10. **Use the cross keys to highlight Display Copyright Info and then press Set to check your info.**

    Your copyright information is displayed (the right image in Figure 11-6).

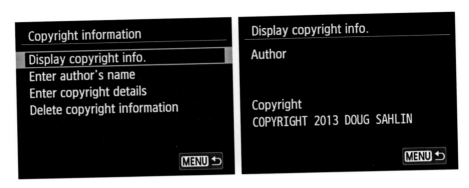

Figure 11-6: Reviewing your copyright information.

To edit your copyright information, follow the previous steps. When you get to Step 4, and your current copyright information displays, tap the Erase button to delete letters, and then enter the revised information, using the cross keys to select letters. Press Set to add each letter to your copyright information.

Adding Author Name to the Camera

You can also add your name as the author of each image you capture with your camera. The information is added as EXIF data to each picture you take. To register your author information with the camera:

1. **Press the Menu button.**

   The last used menu displays.

2. **Use the cross keys to navigate to the Camera Settings 4 tab.**

3. **Use the cross keys to highlight Copyright Information (see the left image in Figure 11-7) and then press the Set button.**

   The Copyright Information menu displays.

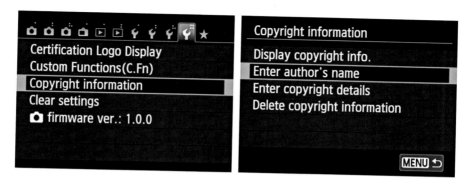

Figure 11-7: Add your name to the camera information.

4. **Use the cross keys to highlight Enter Author's Name (the right image in Figure 11-7) and then press Set.**

   The Enter Author's Name screen appears (the left image in Figure 11-8).

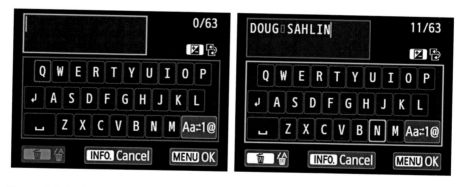

Figure 11-8: Register your name with the camera.

5. **Press the Aperture/Exposure Compensation button to enter the text selection box.**

   Use the Aperture/Exposure Compensation button to navigate between the text box and the text selection box (essentially, an onscreen keyboard).

6. **Use the cross keys to navigate to a letter, character, or number.**

   The character is highlighted with a gold rectangle.

7. **Press Set.**

   The character appears in the text box.

8. **Continue adding characters to complete your name.**

   Your completed author information appears in the text box (refer to the right image in Figure 11-8).

9. **Press the Menu button.**

   A confirmation screen appears, telling you that the screen will close after the text that was entered is saved to the camera.

10. **Use the right cross key to highlight OK and then press Set.**

    You return to the copyright menu. You can edit your name with the techniques from the preceding section.

Creating and Registering a Picture Style

If you like to use Picture Styles in your photography, you'll be glad to know that you can customize your favorite style. Then you can register it as a User Defined style so it's available whenever you want. To customize a Picture Style

1. **Press the Menu button.**

   The last used menu command is displayed.

2. **Use the cross keys to navigate to the Shooting Settings 3 Tab.**

3. **Use the cross keys to highlight Picture Style (see the left image in Figure 11-9) and then press Set.**

   The predefined Picture Styles are displayed.

4. **Use the cross keys to highlight a user-defined (User Def.) picture style (the right image in Figure 11-9).**

   You can have up to three custom picture styles (User Def. 1, and so on).

5. **Press Set.**

   The Picture Styles menu displays.

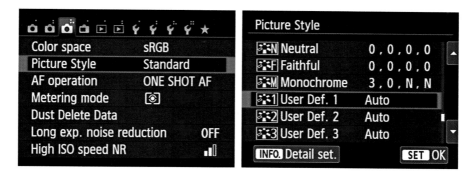

Figure 11-9: Customize a Picture Style here.

6. Use the cross keys to highlight User Def. 1 and then tap Info.

The selected Picture Style displays at the top of the screen, with the settings you can modify (the left image in Figure 11-10).

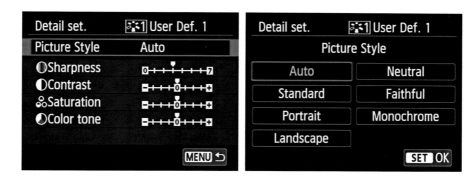

Figure 11-10: Customizing a picture style.

7. Press Set.

The Picture Style menu appears showing the preset styles you can modify (the right image in Figure 11-10).

8. Use the cross keys to select a preset Picture Style to modify into a custom style and then press Set.

For example, if you're a portrait photographer, use Portrait as the basis for your custom style. The details for the picture style display (the left image in Figure 11-10). You can customize the following:

- *Sharpness:* Increase or decrease image sharpness.
- *Contrast:* Increase or decrease the amount of contrast.
- *Saturation:* Increase or decrease color saturation.
- *Color Tone:* Change the skin tone: more yellow by moving the indicator to the left, or more red by moving the indicator to the right side.

9. **Customize image sharpness (the first on the list), or use the cross keys to highlight another detail, and then press Set.**

   The selected detail appears. You can now customize it.

10. **Use the cross keys to increase or decrease the amount of the detail.**

    Use the left cross key to decrease the amount of detail or the right cross key to increase it. As you make a change, the old setting appears as a dimmed-out pointer (see the left image in Figure 11-11).

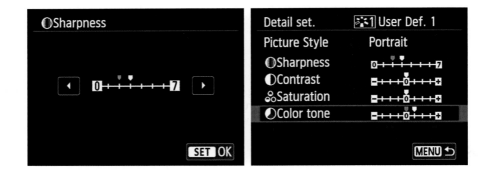

Figure 11-11: Customizing a picture style.

11. **Press Set.**

    The change is applied, and you returned to the Detail Set menu.

12. **Repeat Steps 6–11 to customize the other details in the Picture Style.**

    Customize the details that make sense to the style you're customizing. For example, you wouldn't change Color Tone when customizing for Landscape. The right image in Figure 11-11 shows a customized set that's ready to be registered with the camera.

13. **Press the Menu button.**

    Your custom picture style is registered. The text above the style shows the style on which your style is based; it also shows the changes you've made to the base style, in blue.

14. **Press Set to choose the custom Picture Style.**

    The custom Picture Style appears in the Picture Style menu and will be applied to all images until you choose a different picture style.

    You can also customize a Standard picture style. Follow the preceding steps but instead of selecting one of the User Defined styles, select one of the Standard styles and then press the Info button. Follow Steps 9–11 to customize the picture style to suit your taste.

Updating Your Camera's Firmware

Canon is constantly making changes to make its cameras better. Canon locates any potential problems based on user input and its own tests, and then takes this information and modifies the camera's *firmware,* which is like the OS for your computer. If you've registered your camera, Canon notifies you by e-mail when a firmware update is available. Register your camera online or by mailing the card provided with the camera documents. If you mail the card, make sure you fill in the E-Mail section of the form to be notified of any changes.

When you get an update notification, follow the link to the firmware and follow the prompts to download the information to your computer. You then transfer the firmware program to an SD card to install it on your camera. Canon posts detailed instructions on how to install the firmware on one of the web pages associated with the download.

Make sure you have a fully charged battery in your camera when you update firmware. If the battery exhausts itself during the firmware upgrade, you may permanently damage your camera.

Restoring Your Camera Settings

Sometimes you need to do some spring cleaning and wipe the slate clean. If you've enabled more settings on your camera than you care to deal with, no longer use, or even know about, you can restore camera settings to factory defaults.

Restoring to factory defaults wipes out *all* your menu changes, your custom menu, and any Picture Styles you registered or customized, so think twice before doing this.

To restore your camera settings to the factory defaults

1. **Press the Menu button.**

   The last used menu displays.

2. **Use the cross keys to navigate to the Camera Settings 4 tab.**

3. **Use the cross keys to highlight Clear Settings (the left image in Figure 11-12) and then press Set.**

   The Clear Settings menu appears (the right image in Figure 11-12).

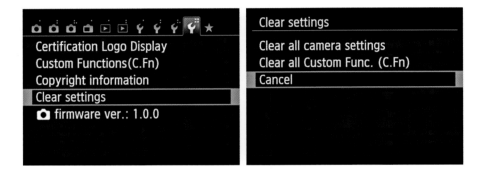

Figure 11-12: Clear all your camera settings here.

4. **Use the cross keys to highlight one of the following options:**

   • *Clear All Camera Settings:* This option clears all camera settings except Custom Functions (C.Fn.).

   • *Clear All Custom Func. (C.Fn.):* This option clears Custom Functions only.

   • *Cancel:* This is your Hail Mary in case you decide not to clear camera settings.

5. **Press Set.**

   A progress screen appears, telling you the camera is busy. When it stops, the camera settings are cleared.

Disabling Shooting without a Card

The default option of your camera is to enable shooting without a card —
which, in my humble estimation, is dangerous. If after downloading images
to your computer, you forget to put the card back in the camera, with the
default option, you'll be able to release the shutter without a card. Granted,
you get a warning on the LCD monitor that there is no card in the camera
after you press the shutter, but you may lose a precious picture because of
the default option. To disable releasing the shutter without a card

1. **Press the Menu button.**

   The last used menu displays.

2. **Use the cross keys to navigate to the Shooting Settings 1 tab.**

3. **Use the cross keys to highlight Release Shutter without Card (the left
   image in Figure 11-13) and then press Set.**

   The Release Shutter without Card options display (the right image in
   Figure 11-13).

4. **Use the cross keys to highlight Disable and then press Set.**

   You can no longer release the shutter without a card in the camera.
   When you press the shutter button without a card in the camera, the
   word *Card* flashes in the viewfinder and the shutter does not release.

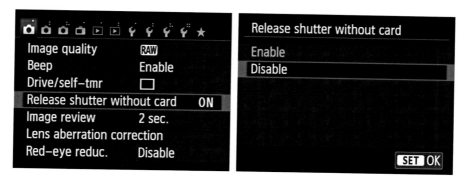

Figure 11-13: Disable releasing the shutter without a card.

Enabling Red-Eye Reduction

Red-eye is the disease that made flash photography unpopular. If you've ever seen a picture of a person taken with a pop-up flash and their eyes are redder than a Ferrari, you've seen red-eye. Fortunately, a setting in your camera can reduce red-eye by firing the red-eye reduction lamp just before the flash fires. To enable red-eye reduction

1. **Press the Menu button.**

   The last used menu displays.

2. **Use the cross keys to navigate to the Shooting Settings 1 tab.**

3. **Use the cross keys to highlight Red-eye Reduc. (the left image in Figure 11-14) and then press Set.**

   The red-eye reduction options display.

4. **Use the cross keys to highlight Enable (the right side of Figure 11-14) and then press Set.**

   Red-eye reduction is enabled. Now when you take a picture with flash, the red-eye reduction lamp will fire just before the flash does.

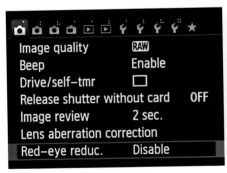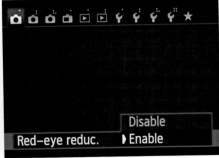

Figure 11-14: Enable re-eye reduction here.

Creating a Makeshift Tripod

Your SL1/100D can capture images in very low-light conditions. However, at times, you absolutely can't get a blur-free shot without using a tripod. But what do you do when you've left home without one? — say, you're on vacation and don't have the room to carry a tripod in your baggage. Here are some ways you can steady your camera without a tripod:

- ✔ **Switch to Live View mode and place the camera near the edge of a table.** If you can see the tabletop on the LCD monitor, move the camera closer to the edge.

- ✔ **Hold the camera against a wall.** Use this technique when you rotate the camera 90 degrees (also known as *Portrait mode*).

- ✔ **Lean against a wall and spread your legs slightly.** Now you are a human tripod. Exhale before shooting and then press the shutter button gently.

- ✔ **Use a small beanbag to steady the camera.** You can just throw the beanbag in your camera bag; it doesn't take up much space. Place your camera on the beanbag and move it to achieve the desired composition. You can purchase beanbags at your local camera store.

  As an alternative to a bean bag, you can carry a baggie filled with uncooked rice (cooked rice is messy and will spoil) in your camera bag. Place your camera on the bag and move it until you achieve the desired composition.

In addition to using one of these techniques, use the 2-Second Self-Timer. This gives the camera a chance to stabilize from any vibration that occurs when you press the shutter button.

Disabling the Camera Beeper

If you photograph wildlife, or take candid photographs of people, disabling the camera beeper is a good option to enable. When you disable the camera beeper, you can still verify focus in the viewfinder, the LCD monitor when shooting Live View, or with Touch Shutter, but the camera doesn't make the beeping noise, which would alert animals to your presence, or let people know that you are taking their picture. To disable the camera beeper:

1. **Press the Menu button.**

   The last used menu displays.

2. **Use the cross keys to navigate to the Shooting Settings 1 tab.**

3. **Use the cross keys to highlight Beep (see the left image in Figure 11-15) and then press Set.**

   The Beep options are displayed (see the right side in Figure 11-15).

4. **Use the cross keys to highlight one of the following:**

- *Enable:* The default option, which makes a beeping noise.
- *Touch to (muted speaker icon):* Disables the beep during touch-screen operations.
- *Disable:* Disables the beep when focus is achieved, or when using the countdown timer.

5. **Press Set.**

The option is enabled.

6. **Press the shutter button halfway to return to shooting mode.**

When you press the shutter button to achieve focus, the beep is not heard. Silence is golden.

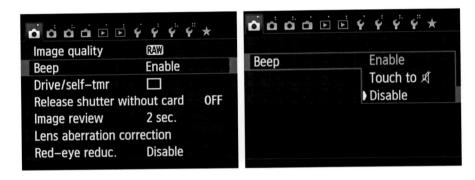

Figure 11-15: Adjusting beep options.

Ten Cool Projects

*A*h, another Part of Tens chapter. You guessed it — a list about stuff you can do with your camera, your images, and the software that came with it. In this chapter, I show you some interesting things, such as using Creative Filters, creating abstract images, editing your images, and more. So if you're up for extra bits of useful information, prop up your feet, get comfortable, and read on.

Cropping JPEG Images In-Camera

If don't have image-editing software installed on your computer, or you're on vacation with a laptop with no image-editing software, you'll be happy to know that you can do minimal editing in your camera. One editing option you have is to crop away unwanted pixels and then save the edited image as a new file. To crop an image in-camera (JPEG only, not RAW images or movies)

1. **Press the Menu button and then use the cross keys to navigate to the Playback Settings 2 tab, as shown in Figure 12-1.**

2. **Use the cross keys to highlight Cropping (see the left image in Figure 12-1) and then press the Set button.**

   The images that can be cropped are displayed on the LCD monitor (see the right image in Figure 12-1). Note that only JPEG images can be cropped. You can press the AE Lock/FE Lock/Index/Reduce button to view four or nine thumbnails. Movies have a filmstrip icon around the border of the thumbnail and cannot be cropped.

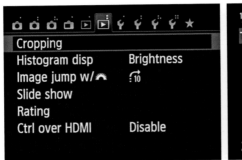
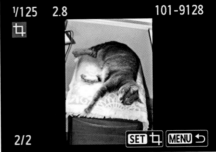

Figure 12-1: Snip, snip. Looking for an image to crop.

3. **Use the cross keys to select the image you want to crop and then press the Set button.**

   The image is displayed with cropping tools.

4. **Rotate the Main dial to change the aspect ratio of the image.**

   As you rotate the dial, the green cropping frame changes to display how the different aspect ratios will crop the image. Your choices are 3:2, 16:9, 4:3, or 1:1.

5. **Press the AF Point Selection/Magnify button to crop the image at the selected aspect ratio.**

As you press the button, the green frame shrinks to show the area to which the image will be cropped. If you go too far, Press the AE Lock/FE Lock/Index/Reduce button to increase the size of the cropping frame. You can also press the Info button to switch from a horizontal crop (Landscape mode) to a vertical crop (Portrait mode).

6. **Use the cross keys to move the cropping frame to the desired part of the image (see the left image in Figure 12-2).**

   The frame shows what will remain after cropping. You can also press the Aperture/Exposure Compensation button to see the image as it will appear when cropped.

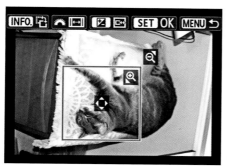 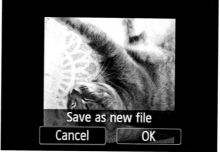

Figure 12-2: Yikes. I'm gonna be cropped.

7. **Press the Set button.**

   A window appears showing you the cropped image and prompting you to save the file as a new image, as shown in the right image in Figure 12-2.

8. **Press the right cross key to highlight OK and then press the Set button.**

   A message window appears telling you the folder to which the image will be saved.

9. **Press the Set button to save the cropped image as a new file.**

Resizing Images In-Camera

Most photographers resize their images in an image-editing application, such as Photoshop Elements or Picasa. However, if you don't have any image-editing software on your computer, or you're on vacation with just a laptop and minimum software, you can resize JPEG images in-camera. To resize an image using your camera

1. **Press the Menu button and then use the cross keys to navigate to the Playback Settings 1 tab, as shown in Figure 12-3.**

2. **Use the cross keys to Highlight Resize (see the left image in Figure 12-3) and then press the Set button.**

   Images that can be resized are displayed. You can resize JPEG images only.

3. **Use the cross keys to select the desired image and then press the Set button.**

   The sizes to which the image can be resized are displayed (see the right image in Figure 12-3).

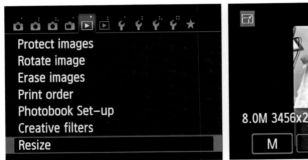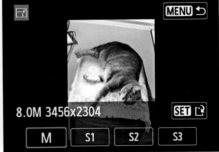

Figure 12-3: Resizing images in-camera.

4. **Use the cross keys to highlight the desired size and then press the Set button.**

   When you highlight a size, the dimension in pixels is displayed plus the file size. You are prompted to save the image as a new file.

5. **Use the right cross key to highlight OK and then press the Set button.**

   The resized image is saved as a new file.

Editing Movies In-Camera

When you review movies in your camera, you can also do a little trimming. You can cut footage from the beginning or end of a movie clip in the camera by following these steps:

1. **Use the cross keys to navigate to the movie you want to edit.**

   You can press the AE Lock/FE Lock/Index/Reduce button to view four or nine thumbnails. Movies have a filmstrip icon around the border of the thumbnail.

2. **Select the movie you want to edit and then press the Set button.**

   The playback controls display.

3. **Use the cross keys repeatedly to highlight the Edit icon that looks like a pair of scissors (see the left image in Figure 12-4) and then press the Set button.**

   The editing controls display (see the right image in Figure 12-4). Cut Beginning is the first tool, which enables you to trim footage from the beginning of the movie clip.

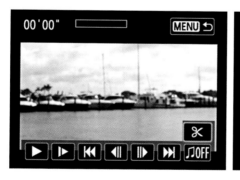 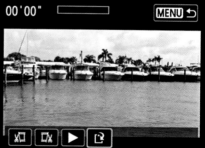

Figure 12-4: Editing a movie in-camera.

4. **Press the Set button.**

   The Cut Beginning edit tool is available.

5. **Press and hold the right cross key to fast-forward to the spot where you want the clip to begin and then press the Set button.**

   The icon that indicates where the movie begins displays above the clip.

6. **Use the cross keys to highlight the Cut End tool and then press Set.**

   The tool for trimming from the end of the movie is highlighted.

7. **Press and hold the left cross key to rewind the movie to where you want the clip to end and then press the Set button.**

   The revised starting and ending points for the movie display above the clip (refer to the left image in Figure 12-5).

8. **Use the right cross key to highlight Save and then press the Set button.**

   The Save button is the icon to the right of the Play button in the image on the left image in Figure 12-5. After pressing the icon, a confirmation screen appears asking whether you want to create a new file or overwrite the existing file (see the right image in Figure 12-5). If you still have footage on the original file you want to keep, make sure you create a new file.

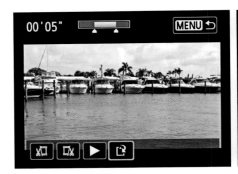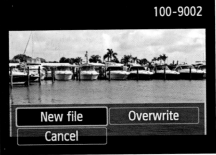

Figure 12-5: Trimming the beginning and ending of a movie clip.

9. **Use the cross keys to highlight the desired option and then press the Set button.**

   After choosing the desired option, yet another screen appears asking you to confirm the action.

10. **Press the right cross key to highlight OK and then press the Set button.**

    Your movie clip is on the cutting-room floor.

Using Creative Filters

If you don't own an expensive set of filters for your camera, or have an all-singing all-dancing image-editing application with more filters than there are Smiths in the NYC phone book, you can easily create some pretty cool images in-camera with the Creative Filters. The following list describes each filter:

- *Grainy B/W:* Creates a black-and-white image with grain that looks like it was photographed with film.

- *Soft Focus:* Creates a soft image reminiscent of the effect you get when applying a soft focus filter to a lens. You control the amount of softness by adjusting the blur.

- *Fish-eye:* Creates an image that looks like it was created with a fish-eye lens.

- *Art-Bold:* Creates an image that looks like an oil painting. You control the effect by adjusting contrast and saturation.

- *Water Painting:* Makes an image look like a watercolor painting with soft muted colors.

- *Toy Camera:* Applies a vignette to the corner of the image and changes the color tone to make it look like the image was photographed with a toy camera.

- *Miniature:* Creates an image with a diorama effect. You determine the area of the image that is sharp.

Creative filters are fun. You can apply them to RAW images or JPEG images. After you apply a filter to a photograph, the resulting image is saved as a JPEG file. The steps for applying each filter are similar as shown next:

1. **Press the Menu button.**

   The last used menu is displayed.

2. **Use the cross keys to navigate to the Playback Settings 1 menu tab.**

3. **Use the cross keys to highlight Creative Filters (see the left image in Figure 12-6) and then press the Set button.**

   An image is displayed.

4. **Use the cross keys to navigate to the image you want to edit (see the right image in Figure 12-6).**

   You can press the AE Lock/FE Lock/Index/Reduce button to display thumbnails.

5. **Press Set to begin editing the image.**

   The Creative Filter icons are displayed below the image (see the left image in Figure 12-7).

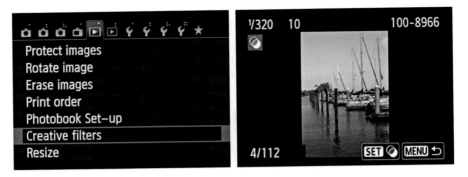

Figure 12-6: Applying a Creative Filter to an image.

6. Use the cross keys to highlight the desired filter and then press the Set button.

As you navigate between filters, the name of the filter is displayed on the monitor. After you select a filter, it is applied to the image with the default settings. The right image in Figure 12-7 shows the Grainy B/W filter with the default filter effect.

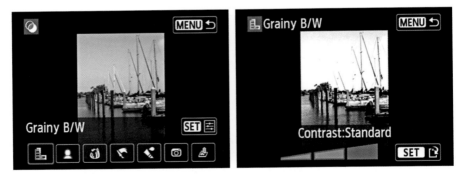

Figure 12-7: Choose a filter and then choose its setting.

7. (Optional) Use the cross keys to select the desired filter setting and then press the Set button.

Most filters have three settings, which are Low, Standard or High. The only filter that has a slightly different effect is Miniature. When you apply this filter to an image, a white rectangle appears in the image (see the left image in Figure 12-8). Use the cross keys to place the rectangle. This is the area of the image that will be the sharpest. Press the Info button to switch the white rectangle from horizontal to vertical.

After you apply the setting, a screen appears prompting you to save the edited image (see the right image in Figure 12-8).

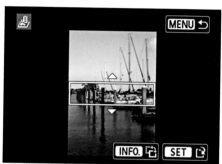 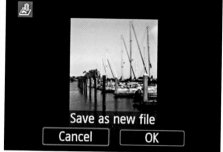

Figure 12-8: Saving the edited image.

8. **Use the right cross key to highlight Save and then press the Set button.**

   Another screen appears showing the folder and filename.

9. **Use the right cross key to highlight OK and then press the Set button.**

   The image is saved.

Strutting Your Stuff Online

Everybody likes to show off their work, and you can do this online in quite a few places. The granddaddy of photo-sharing sites is Flickr (www.flickr.com). This site enables you to post your images online, but it's more than just a photo-sharing site: It's a community as well. You can send your Flickr URL to other photographers to show off your work. The site boasts a gallery design. Other members of the Flickr community can comment on your work. You can set up a free account with 1 terabyte (TB) of storage, with ads and no stats, and start uploading images to your personal gallery. Or, you can upgrade to an Ads Free account for $49.95 per year. Figure 12-9 shows your friendly author's Flickr account.

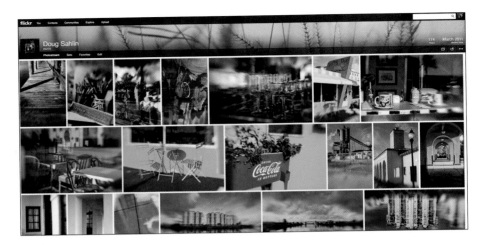

Figure 12-9: Showing your stuff on Flickr.

Another great photo-sharing site is 500PX (see Figure 12-10). 500PX (`http://500px.com`) is a lively community of photographers. To test the waters, you can sign up for a free account and (as of this writing) upload 20 images per week. If you like what you see, you can upgrade to a Plus membership for $25 per year, which gives you the option of selling your images online, with unlimited uploads per week. Such a deal! There is also an Awesome membership, at $75 per year, which allows you to set up a custom portfolio website and more.

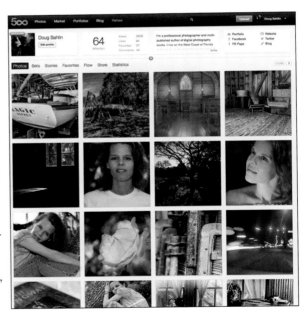

Figure 12-10: Strut your stuff at 500PX.

Uploading Images to Your Facebook Page

Another place where you can show off your work online is at Facebook. If you have a Facebook page (and who doesn't?), you can upload images from ImageBrowser EX while creating an album for your Facebook Home page (or Timeline: what used to be called your Wall). Here's how you do it:

1. **Launch ImageBrowser EX. (See Chapter 9.)**

2. **Select the images you want to upload to your Facebook Home page.**

3. **Click the Share button and then choose Upload to Facebook Album.**

   The Canon Utilities Uploader for Facebook appears (see Figure 12-11).

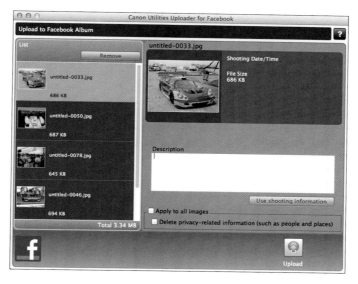

Figure 12-11: I'm going to show my Facebook friends some cool images.

4. **Select an image and enter a description for the image.**

   This call's on you, Lou. Write whatever you normally write when you create a Facebook album of your images. You have the option to apply the same description to all images in the album.

5. **(Optional) Click the Use Shooting Information button.**

   This adds shooting information to the description. Included are the camera model, shutter speed, aperture, and ISO. Upload this information at your own risk; other photographers may glean some wisdom from your post and steal your thunder.

6. **(Optional) Select the Delete Privacy-Related Information (Such as People and Places) check box.**

   This disavows all records of the innocent or guilty parties in the image, which is useful if you shoot pictures of people who are part of a witness-protection program. Kidding!

7. **Review the information before uploading to Facebook.**

   If you change your mind and decide to not upload an image to Facebook, select it from the left column and click the Remove button.

8. **Click the Upload button.**

   When you upload for the first time, you'll be asked a series of questions regarding your Facebook page and Canon's Utilities application. It's all standard stuff. After you go through that rigmarole, you'll see the Upload Confirmation dialog box (see Figure 12-12).

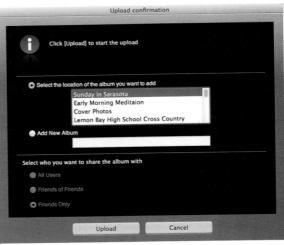

9. **Select the album to which you want to add the images, or enter the name of a new album.**

Figure 12-12: Set your controls for the heart of the sun.

   In most instances, you'll choose the latter. When you do, the utility creates the new album for your Facebook Home page.

10. **After choosing an album, or entering the name of a new album, choose an option that determines who will see the album.**

    You can choose to make the album visible to all users, friends of Friends, or Friends only.

11. **Click the Upload button.**

A progress status window appears, informing you about the upload. After the upload is complete, a message window appears, telling you the upload is complete.

12. **When the Upload Is Complete window appears, click OK.**

This closes the Canon Utilities Facebook Uploader, and you can now edit more images, upload more images, or visit Facebook and review the album (see Figure 12-13).

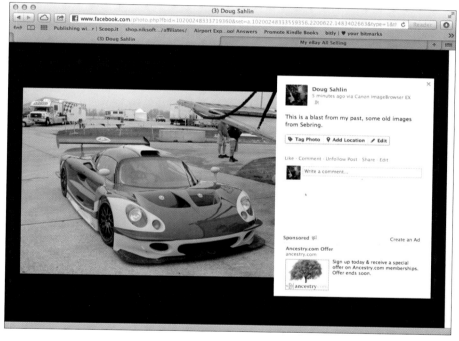

Figure 12-13: An album uploaded to Facebook is a thing of beauty.

Creating Abstract Images In-Camera

When you stretch the envelope, you can create some very cool images with your camera. A technique I like to use is controlled motion blur when photographing vertical objects, such as tree trunks. If you're a nature photographer, this technique will spice up your portfolio. To create an abstract image

1. **Attach the desired lens to the camera.**

   Choose a lens with a focal length of 80mm or greater. If you're using the kit lens, zoom to 55mm.

2. **Rotate the Mode dial to Av (Aperture Priority).**

   You're using the aperture to control how long the shutter is open.

3. **Press the ISO button and then rotate the Main dial to set the ISO speed to 100.**

   You want the shutter to be open for a long time. The lowest ISO setting makes the camera less sensitive to light, thus requiring a longer shutter speed.

4. **Rotate the Main dial to specify the smallest aperture (highest f-stop value) for the lens you're using.**

   This ensures that the shutter will be open for a long time.

5. **Find an interesting subject.**

   Closely spaced trees or tall grass are ideal subjects for this technique.

6. **Aim your camera at the base of the subject and then press the shutter button halfway.**

   The camera achieves focus.

7. **Press the shutter button fully and slowly move the camera up.**

   The shutter opens, and the picture is taken. Depending on the ambient light, your lens may be open for several seconds. When you slowly move the camera up, you create abstract patterns of nature (see Figure 12-14).

8. **Edit your pictures.**

   When you edit images in an application like Photoshop or Photoshop Elements, you can use filters to tweak the images. Figure 12-15 shows an abstract image created using this technique, as it appears after being edited in Photoshop.

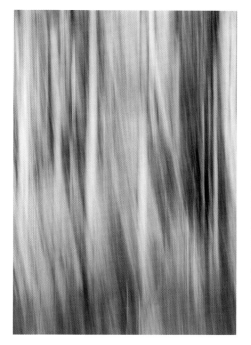

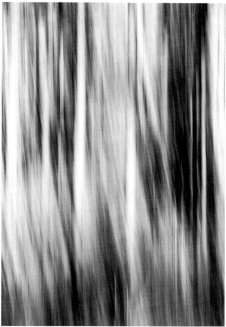

Figure 12-14: Creating an abstract image in camera.

Figure 12-15: A tweaked abstract image.

Editing Your Images in Photoshop Elements

The software that Canon provides with your SL1/100D will get the job done. If you want a more powerful image-editing application but you're on a beer budget, consider purchasing Adobe Photoshop Elements 11.0. This image-editing powerhouse gives you the power to manage your images, work with multiple keywords, find images, and much more. And that's just the Organizer. Elements is also a three-pronged image editor. You can edit images using the Guided Edit panel, Edit Quick mode, or Full Edit mode. If you're new to image editing, the Guided Edit panel guides you through the image-editing process. If you want the quick, down, and *Dirty Harry* version of the Editor, use Edit Quick mode. As the title implies, this version enables you to quickly edit an image. If you want the full-course treatment from soup to nuts, edit your images in the Full Edit mode.

Photoshop Elements 11 gives you the power to crop, resize, color correct, adjust your image, and much more. If you're in an artsy-fartsy state of mind, you'll find a plethora of filters you can use to edit your images. You can also use third-party filters, such as Nik Software, Alien Skin, and so on. Photoshop Elements 11 is too cool for school (see Figure 12-16). As of this writing, the application sells for a meager $99.99. So much power for such a small investment is a great deal, Lucille.

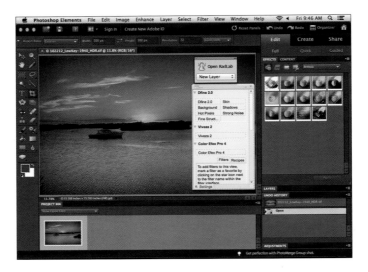

Figure 12-16: Editing images in Photoshop Elements.

Creating Video Albums and Snapshots

Video is cool. Your camera can capture high definition (HD) video, and it has a few more tricks up its sleeve. You can also create video snapshots and compile them into an album. And you don't need expensive software, either. All you need to know is a couple of menu commands to create little video snippets of people or places and combine them into an album. Each snapshot can have a duration of 2, 4, or 8 seconds. To create a video album

1. **Use the cross keys to navigate to the Video Settings 2 tab, use the cross keys to highlight Video Snapshot (see the left image of Figure 12-17), and then press the Set button.**

   The Video Snapshot options are displayed (see the right image of Figure 12-17).

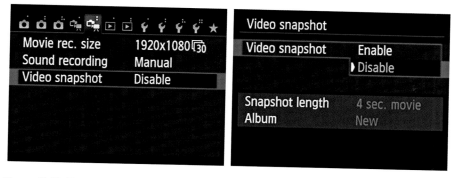

Figure 12-17: Enable Video Snapshots here.

2. **Use the cross keys to highlight Enable and then press the Set button.**

   The Video Snapshot menu displays (see the left image of Figure 12-18).

3. **Use the cross keys to highlight Album Settings and then press the Set button.**

   The Album Settings appear (see the right image of Figure 12-18).

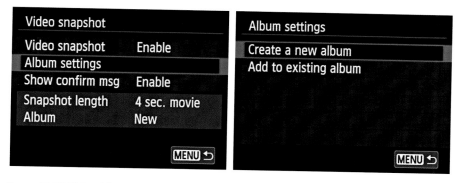

Figure 12-18: Video Album Settings.

4. **Use the cross keys to highlight Create a New Album and then press the Set button.**

   The current Snapshot Length setting displays (see the left image of Figure 12-19).

6. **Use the cross keys to highlight Snapshot Length and press the Set button.**

   The Snapshot Length setting options display (see the right image in Figure 12-19).

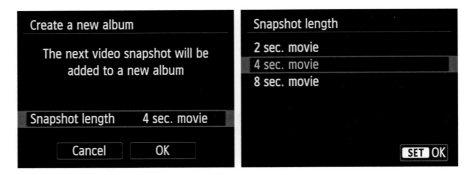

Figure 12-19: Choosing the snapshot length.

7. **Use the cross keys to highlight the desired snapshot duration and press the Set button.**

    All videos captured until you disable video snapshots will be added to this album and be the duration you specify. The screen refreshes, and you have the option to cancel the settings or approve them.

8. **Use the right cross key to highlight OK and then press the Set button.**

    You return to the Video Shooting Settings 2 tab.

After you specify the settings for the video album, it's time to create some video snapshots and add them to the album. You can add as many snapshots as you want to the album and then edit the album after creating it. To create the video snapshot album

1. **Press the shutter button halfway to return to shooting mode and then move the power switch to Video.**

    You're now ready to create video snapshots and add them to the album.

2. **Compose the scene on your LCD monitor and then press the Live View Shooting/Movie Shooting button.**

    As the video is captured, a blue progress bar appears on the LCD monitor. When the blur bar reaches the end, the camera stops capturing video, and the first frame of the video snapshot is displayed on your monitor.

3. **Use the right cross key to highlight Save as a New Album (see the left image in Figure 12-20) and then press the Set button.**

    The video snapshot is saved to a new album.

4. **Press the Live View Shooting/Movie Shooting button.**

    The camera records another video snapshot. After the snapshot is captured, the first frame of the snapshot is displayed on the LCD monitor.

5. Use the cross keys to highlight Add to Album (see the right image in Figure 12-20) and then press the Set button.

The video snapshot is added to the album. If you create a clip that you think would be better suited to a new album, click the Save as New Album icon. Continue adding snapshots to the album.

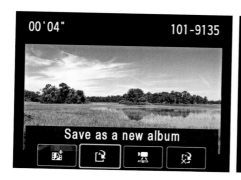 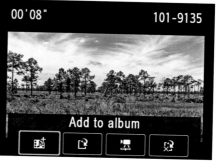

Figure 12-20: Creating a video album.

To return to normal video shooting after creating a video album, follow these steps:

1. Use the cross keys to navigate to the Video Settings 2 tab, use the cross keys to highlight Video Snapshot, and then press the Set button.

The Video Snapshot options display.

2. Use the cross keys to highlight Disable and then press the Set button.

You can now create movies of unlimited length.

After you create an album of video snapshots, you can edit the album to change the position of video clips or delete video clips. To edit a video album

1. Use the cross keys to navigate to the movie you want to edit.

You can press the AE Lock/FE Lock/Index/Reduce button to view four or nine thumbnails. Movies have a filmstrip icon around the border of the thumbnail.

2. Select the video album you want to edit.

Video albums have a distinct icon in the upper-left corner (see the left image in Figure 12-21).

3. Press the Set button.

The playback controls display.

4. **Press the right and up cross keys repeatedly to highlight the Edit icon (that looks like a pair of scissors) and then press the Set button.**

   The screen refreshes, and you see three filmstrip icons with the first frame of each video clip and the editing tools.

5. **Use the cross keys to select the video snapshot you want to edit.**

   The selected video's border is highlighted.

6. **Use the cross keys to select an editing option.**

   You can perform an editing by clicking an icon. The edits the icons perform from left to right are

   - *Move the Selected Snapshot:* Select this icon and use the cross keys to move the snapshot to the desired position. Then press the Set button. The videos trade places.

   - *Delete Snapshot:* After selecting this option (see the right image in Figure 12-21), use the cross keys to select a snapshot, and then press the Set button.

   - *Play a Snapshot:* After selecting this option, use the cross keys to select the desired snapshot and then press the Set button.

     After performing one of the previous options, press the Menu button to return to the main editing screen.

   - *Save:* Select this option after editing your video album and the press the Set button to display the Save dialog box. This saves the edited video album as a new file.

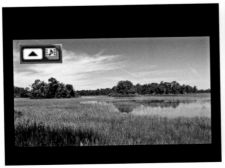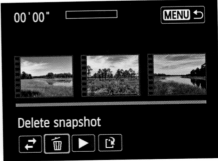

Figure 12-21: Editing a video album.

Rating Images with the Playback Quick Control Menu

Some die hard photographers think an image-editing program is the only way to rate images. I also belong to that group, but realize there are different strokes for different folks. Canon realizes that also, which is why they created a Quick Control menu to use when you're reviewing images. In this section, I show you how to use the Playback Quick Control menu to rate images as follows:

1. **With the image you want to rate selected, press the Quick Control button.**

   The Quick Control Playback menu is displayed.

2. **Use the cross keys to highlight the Rating icon.**

   It's the star on the left side of the menu. Rating is disabled by default (see Figure 12-22).

3. **Use the right cross key to select the desired rating.**

   You can choose a rating from 1 to 5 stars. Typically your 5-star images are the best of the lot.

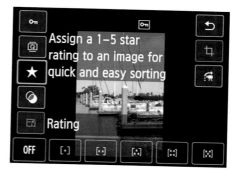

Figure 12-22: Rating an image with the Quick Control Playback Menu.

Index

• T •

• U •

• V •

About the Author

Doug Sahlin is an author and photographer living in Venice, Florida. He's written books on computer applications, such as Adobe Flash and Adobe Acrobat. He's also written books on digital photography and co-authored numerous books on various applications, such as Adobe Photoshop and Photoshop Elements. Recent titles include *Digital Landscape and Nature Photography For Dummies, Digital SLR Shortcuts and Settings For Dummies, Canon EOS 7D For Dummies,* and *Canon EOS 6D For Dummies.* Many of his books have been bestsellers on Amazon.

Doug is president of Doug Plus Rox Photography, a wedding and event photography company. Doug teaches Adobe Acrobat to local businesses and government institutions. He also teaches Adobe Photoshop and Adobe Photoshop Lightroom at local photography stores.

Dedication

Dedicated to my wife Roxanne, the love of my life, and the best and most creative photographer I know.

Author's Acknowledgments

Thanks to Acquisitions Editor Steve Hayes for making this book a possibility. Special thanks to Project Editor Nicole Sholly, and Copy Editor Teresa Artman for making sure my text is squeaky clean with no grammatical errors. Thanks to Technical Editor Dave Hall for making sure the book is technically accurate. Many thanks to the other members of the Wiley team for taking the book from concept to fruition.

Thanks to Margot Hutchison for ironing out the contractual details. Many thanks to Canon for creating some of the greatest cameras on the planet. Special thanks to my friends and family. Kudos to my wife Roxanne for putting up with my late nights and occasional mood swings when I'd written one more page than I should for the day. And thanks to our furry kids, Niki and Micah, for their love, affection, and comic relief.

Publisher's Acknowledgments

Executive Editor: Steve Hayes

Sr. Project Editor: Nicole Sholly

Sr. Copy Editor: Teresa Artman

Technical Editor: David C. Hall

Editorial Assistant: Anne Sullivan

Sr. Editorial Assistant: Cherie Case

Project Coordinator: Katie Crocker

Cover Image: ©iStockphoto.com / Andrew Rich; camera courtesy of Doug Sahlin